ABITUR

Prüfungsaufgaben
mit Lösungen

2012

Englisch

Grund- und Leistungskurs
Gymnasium
Berlin • Brandenburg
2008–2011

STARK

ISBN 978-3-89449-330-1

7. ergänzte Auflage
www.stark-verlag.de

Inhalt

Vorwort
Stichwortverzeichnis

Hinweise und Tipps

Die Anforderungen im Abitur I
1 Ablauf der Prüfung I
2 Inhaltliche Schwerpunkte I
3 Leistungsanforderungen II
4 Anforderungsbereiche und Aufgabenstellungen IV
5 Operatoren V
Hinweise zur Lösung von Abituraufgabenstellungen VII
1 Textzusammenfassung VII
2 Analyse IX
3 Persönliche Stellungnahme/Kommentar und kreatives Schreiben X
Glossary of literary terms XI

Abiturprüfungsaufgaben Brandenburg

Grundkurs 2008
Aufgabe 1: Text A: *My Big Fat Green Wedding* (Artikel) . . . . BB – GK 2008-1
Text B: *Green Weddings* (Webseite) . . . . BB – GK 2008-3
Aufgabe 2: *The Devil Wears Prada* (Roman) . . . . BB – GK 2008-9

Leistungskurs 2008
Aufgabe 1: *On Beauty* (Roman) . . . . BB – LK 2008-1
Aufgabe 2: Text A: *Great "Devil" lesson* (Artikel) . . . . BB – LK 2008-9
Text B: *Corporate Ladders* (Cartoon) . . . . BB – LK 2008-11

Grundkurs 2009
Aufgabe 1: Text A: *Forest protection fund* (Artikel) . . . . BB – GK 2009-1
Text B: *Welcome to Amazonian Forest* (Cartoon) . . . . . BB – GK 2009-2
Aufgabe 2: *American Youth* (Roman) . . . . BB – GK 2009-7

Fortsetzung siehe nächste Seite

Leistungskurs 2009
Aufgabe 1: *Cheerful in the face of Armageddon* (Artikel) .... BB – LK 2009-1
Aufgabe 2: Text A: *The world is still organised to meet the wishes of men* (Artikel) .... BB – LK 2009-8
Text B: *P 45* (Illustration) .... BB – LK 2009-10

Abiturprüfungsaufgaben Berlin

Grundkurs 2008
Aufgabe 1: Text I: *Africa, at the Cineplex* (Artikel) .... B – GK 2008-1
Text II: *Princess Diana* (Foto und Beschriftung) ..... B – GK 2008-2
Aufgabe 2: Text I: *Monolingual Britain* (Artikel) .... B – GK 2008-8
Text II: *Zweite Fremdsprachen an deutschen Schulen* (Artikel) .... B – GK 2008-9

Leistungskurs 2008
Aufgabe 1: *Small Island* (Roman) .... B – LK 2008-1
Aufgabe 2: *India's shrinking families* (Artikel) .... B – LK 2008-9

Grundkurs 2009
Aufgabe 1: Text I: *It's on the Net* (Artikel) .... B – GK 2009-1
Text II: *Abschreiben 2.0* (Artikel) .... B – GK 2009-2
Aufgabe 2: Text I: *Facebook can ruin your life* (Artikel) .... B – GK 2009-9
Text II: *Types of Online Communities* (Grafik) ...... B – GK 2009-10
Social networking growth (Tabelle) .... B – GK 2009-11

Leistungskurs 2009
Aufgabe 1: Text I: *News Blackout* (Blog) .... B – LK 2009-1
Text II: *Letters* (Cartoon) .... B – LK 2009-3
Aufgabe 2: Text I: *A Poor Cousin of the Middle Class* (Artikel) .. B – LK 2009-9
Text II: *Die neue Unterschicht* (Artikel und Grafik) ... B – LK 2009-10

Abiturprüfungsaufgaben Berlin/Brandenburg

Grundkurs 2010
Aufgabe 1: *Teacher Man* (Roman) .... GK 2010-1
Aufgabe 2: Text A: *I squatted my repossessed home* (Artikel) .... GK 2010-9
Text B: *UK House Price Forecast* (Grafik) .... GK 2010-11

Leistungskurs 2010
Aufgabe 1: Text A: *Maximum City: Bombay* (Autobiographie) .... LK 2010-1
Text B: *Globale Wesen* (Artikel) .... LK 2010-2
Aufgabe 2: Text A: *Farm City* (Autobiographie) .... LK 2010-11
Text B: *Homegrown Hunger Relief in Seattle* (Grafik) .... LK 2010-14

Grundkurs 2011
Aufgabe 1: Text A: *Meeting the neighbors* (Artikel) .... GK 2011-1
Text B: *Der Nachbar – das unbekannte Wesen* (Artikel) .... GK 2011-2
Aufgabe 2: *Interpreter of Maladies* (Kurzgeschichte) .... GK 2011-9

Leistungskurs 2011
Aufgabe 1: Text A: *Mixed blessings* (Artikel) .... LK 2011-1
Text B: *Xavier Naidoo* (Interview) .... LK 2011-2
Aufgabe 2: Text A: *Welcome to Lagos* (Artikel) .... LK 2011-11
Text B: *ASAP Africa* (Foto und Motto) .... LK 2011-13

Jeweils im Herbst erscheinen die neuen Ausgaben
der Abiturprüfungsaufgaben mit Lösungen.

Autoren

Cleary, Liam:	Glossary of literary terms
Gärtner, Kerstin:	Lösungen Berlin 2008
Haschke, Heiko / Priesemuth, Sandra:	Lösungen Brandenburg 2008
Husic, Mediha:	Lösungen Berlin / Brandenburg GK 2011 Aufgabe 1, LK 2011 Aufgabe 2
Redaktion:	Lösungen Berlin / Brandenburg GK 2011 Aufgabe 2, LK 2011 Aufgabe 1
Sonntag, Irene:	Lösungen Brandenburg LK 2009, Berlin / Brandenburg LK 2010 Aufgabe 1
Strasbaugh, Gene:	Lösungen Berlin GK 2009, Berlin / Brandenburg GK 2010

Vorwort

Liebe Schülerinnen und Schüler,

der vorliegende Band hat zum Ziel, Sie bei der **Vorbereitung auf die schriftliche Abiturprüfung** im Fach Englisch optimal zu unterstützen, sowohl im Grund- wie im Leistungskurs. Als Grundlage für Ihre effektive Vorbereitung dienen **Abituraufgaben** mit typischen **literarischen Texten und Sachtexten**, die Bezug nehmen auf eine mögliche Themenwahl und Kursabfolge in der Qualifikationsphase.
Zu allen Aufgabenstellungen finden Sie ausformulierte **Lösungsvorschläge**. Sie geben Ihnen Anhaltspunkte, wie eine Lösung aussehen kann.
Damit Sie sich für die Abiturprüfung besser auf die verschiedenen Aufgabentypen einstellen können, haben wir **Bearbeitungshinweise** hinzugefügt. Dadurch wird der Lösungsweg für Sie nachvollziehbar und transparent – die methodischen Schritte können Sie auf die Bearbeitung anderer Texte und Aufgaben übertragen.
Die **ausführlichen Hinweise und Tipps** am Anfang des Buches informieren über die **Anforderungen im Abitur** und geben Ihnen Hilfestellungen zur Lösung von Abiturprüfungsaufgaben.

Wir wünschen Ihnen viel Erfolg bei der Abiturprüfung!

Ihre Autoren

Stichwortverzeichnis

Africa B – GK 08-1 ff.; BB – GK 09-1 ff.; LK 11-11 ff.
ambitions BB – LK 08-1 ff., 9 ff.; BB – GK 08-9 ff.
article B – GK 09-3, 7 f.; B – LK 09-12, 15 f.; GK 11-3, 7 f.; LK 11-14, 18 f.

career choices BB – LK 09-8 ff.
cartoon BB – LK 08-11; BB – GK 09-2; B – LK 09-3
charity B – GK 08-1 ff.; LK 10-11 ff.
charts B – GK 09-10, 12 f.; GK 10-11; LK 10-14
climate BB – LK 09-1 ff.
contrast BB – LK 09-5

developing countries B – LK 08-3; B – GK 08-2; GK 11-11, 15 f.; LK 11-11 ff.
The Devil Wears Prada BB – GK 08-9 ff.
diary BB – GK 09-9

***E**ast is East* B – LK 08-6, 15 f.
education LK 11-13, 15 f.
emotions and drives BB – LK 08-1 ff., 9 ff.; BB – GK 08-1 ff., 9 ff.
employment BB – LK 09-8 ff.
Enoch Powell B – LK 08-6
environment BB – GK 08-1 ff.; BB – GK 09-1 ff.; BB – LK 09-1 ff.
ethnic groups B – LK 08-1 ff.; GK 10-1 ff.; LK 10-1 ff.; GK 11-9 ff.; LK 11-1 ff.
extended families B – LK 08-9 ff.

feminism BB – LK 09-8 ff.
film B – GK 08-3, 10; B – LK 08-3, 15 f.; GK 11-6 f., 14
Fitzgerald, F. Scott, *The Great Gatsby* B – LK 09-14 f.
flyer B – GK 08-3, 10; B – GK 09-15 f.; B – LK 09-7 f.; LK 10-19 ff.
formal letter B – LK 08-11; BB – LK 08-4; GK 10-15 f.; LK 10-9 f.

gender issues BB – LK 08-9 ff.; BB – GK 08-9 ff.
generation gap B – LK 08-9 ff.
globalisation B – LK 08-3, 11; GK 10-9 ff.; LK 10-1 ff.; GK 11-11, 13 f.
Gore, Al, *An Inconvenient Truth* BB – LK 09-6

human relations BB – GK 08-9 ff.; BB – LK 08-1 ff., 9 ff.; GK 10-1 ff.; LK 10-17 f.; GK 11-1 ff.
Huxley, Aldous, *Brave New World* LK 11-17 f.

immigrants GK 10-1 ff.; LK 10-1 ff.; LK 11-1 ff.
India B – LK 08-9 ff.; GK 11-9 ff.
Internet B – GK 09-1 ff., 16
Into the Wild GK 11-6 f.

job B – LK 09-9 ff.
journalism B – LK 09-4 ff.

La Marche, Phil, *American Youth* BB – GK 09-7 ff.
languages B – GK 08-8 ff.
letter to the editor BB – LK 09-3, 6 f.; LK 11-4, 9 f.
Levy, Andrea, *Small Island* B – LK 08-1 ff.

McCourt, Frank, *Teacher Man* GK 10-1 ff.
media B – LK 09-1ff.
mediation B – LK 09-12; B – GK 09-2, 5; LK 10-2, 5 f.; GK 11-2 f., 5; LK 11-2 f., 6
mixed-race relationships LK 11-1 ff.
multicultural society B – LK 08-1 ff.; LK 10-1 ff.; LK 11-1 ff.
My Beautiful Launderette GK 11-14

personal letter BB – GK 08-11
photograph LK 11-13
picture BB – LK 09-10
poverty B – LK 09-9 ff.; LK 10-11 ff.; LK 11-11 ff.
psychological pressure BB – GK 09-7 ff.

racism B – LK 08-1; LK 11-1 ff.

Salinger, J. D., *The Catcher in the Rye* B – GK 09-14
short story GK 11-9
social networking B – GK 09-9 ff.; GK 11-3, 7 f.
Spanglish B – GK 08-13
statistics B – GK 09-10 ff.; GK 10-11 ff.

tourism GK 11-9 ff.
Truman Show B – GK 09-6 f.

urban life LK 10-11 ff.; GK 11-1 ff.; LK 11-1 ff.

weapons BB – GK 09-7 ff.
wedding BB – GK 08-1 ff.
women BB – LK 09-8 ff.
work BB – GK 08-9 ff.; BB – LK 08-9 ff.

xenophobia B – LK 08-1 ff.; LK 11-1 ff.

Hinweise und Tipps

Die Anforderungen im Abitur

Im Folgenden finden Sie alle wichtigen Informationen zur zentralen Abiturprüfung 2012 in Berlin/Brandenburg. Sollten nach Erscheinen dieses Bandes noch entscheidende Änderungen in der Abitur-Prüfung 2012 bekannt gegeben werden, finden Sie aktuelle Informationen dazu im Internet unter:
www.stark-verlag.de/info.asp?zentrale-pruefung-aktuell

1 Ablauf der Prüfung

Zu Beginn der Prüfung werden Ihnen mindestens zwei Aufgabenstellungen vorgelegt. Daraus wählen Sie eine zur Bearbeitung aus. Die Bearbeitungszeit im Leistungskurs beträgt 270 Minuten, im Grundkurs 210 Minuten. Diese Zeiten schließen Ihre individuelle Lese- und Auswahlzeit ein, die Sie auf 30 Minuten beschränken sollten. Sie dürfen bei der Bearbeitung ein einsprachiges Wörterbuch verwenden.

2 Inhaltliche Schwerpunkte

Für die Vorbereitung auf das Abitur im Fach Englisch ist die Kenntnis der Grundlagen der Textauswahl und Aufgabenstellung erforderlich.

Die folgenden Schwerpunkte sind dem Rahmenlehrplan für die gymnasiale Oberstufe sowie den Prüfungsvorgaben und Hinweisen für das Zentralabitur in Englisch in Berlin und Brandenburg entnommen.

- Individuum und Gesellschaft (1. Kurshalbjahr):
  Personal relations in their social context – Zwischenmenschliche Beziehungen
- Nationale und kulturelle Identität (2. Kurshalbjahr):
  Ethnic diversity – Leben in der multikulturellen Gesellschaft
- Eine Welt – globale Fragen (3. Kurshalbjahr):
  The challenge of globalisation – Globalisierung und ihre Auswirkungen
- Herausforderungen der Gegenwart (4. Kurshalbjahr):
  The impact of the media on society – Rolle und Wirkungsweise der Massenmedien

Die Abituraufgabe muss zwei der drei prüfungsrelevanten Halbjahre inhaltlich miteinander verbinden. Es gibt zwei Aufgabenarten:

- Die **Textaufgabe** umfasst einen oder mehrere Texte mit drei bis vier Arbeitsanweisungen. Es kommen literarische Texte, Sachtexte sowie Bilder und Grafiken infrage.
  Der im Leistungskurs vorgelegte Text umfasst zwischen 700 und 900 Wörter, der im Grundkurs zwischen 500 und 700 Wörter. Im Zusammenhang mit Bildern, Grafiken und Statistiken reduziert sich die Länge der Textvorlage auf ca. 500 bis 700 Wörter im Leistungskurs und 300 bis 500 Wörter im Grundkurs. Erst nach dem Lesen der Texte und der Aufgabenstellung beginnt die Ihnen zur Verfügung stehende Arbeitszeit.
- Die **kombinierte Aufgabe** besteht aus zwei Teilen: aus einer verkürzten Textaufgabe (im Leistungskurs zwischen 400 und 600 Wörtern, im Grundkurs zwischen 300 und 400 Wörtern) und aus einem sprachpraktischen Teil zur Sprachmittlung/ Mediation (deren Textlänge im Leistungskurs zwischen 300 und 400 Wörtern, im Grundkurs zwischen 200 und 300 Wörtern liegt). Die Zielsprache ist Englisch. In der kombinierten Aufgabe wird die Textaufgabe im Verhältnis zur sprachpraktischen mit 3:1 gewertet.

3 Leistungsanforderungen

Bei allen Aufgabenarten wird zwischen **inhaltlicher** und **sprachlicher Leistung** unterschieden. Bei der Festlegung der Gesamtnote kommt der sprachlichen Leistung im Vergleich zur inhaltlichen die größere Bedeutung zu. Sie werden im Verhältnis 60 : 40 gewertet.

Bei der Bewertung der **inhaltlichen Leistung** werden folgende Aspekte berücksichtigt:
- Text- und Problemverständnis
- Verfügbarkeit von Kenntnissen und Methoden
- Folgerichtigkeit der Darstellung
- Differenziertheit und Eigenständigkeit der Stellungnahme bzw. Argumentation
- textsortenspezifische Gestaltung

Eine mit 0 Punkten bewertete inhaltliche oder sprachliche Leistung schließt eine Gesamtnote von mehr als drei Punkten einfacher Wertung aus. In der Beurteilung der kombinierten Aufgabe wird diese Regelung für beide Teile getrennt angewendet.

Folgende Punkte gehen in die Bewertung der **sprachlichen Leistung** ein:
- Klarheit der Aussage und Textkohärenz
- Reichhaltigkeit und Differenziertheit des Sach- und Funktionswortschatzes
- Ökonomie und Treffsicherheit des Ausdrucks
- Komplexität und Variation des Satzbaus
- Angemessenheit des Registers
- Flüssigkeit, Eigenständigkeit und Natürlichkeit der Darstellung

Die Beurteilung der Sprachrichtigkeit orientiert sich nicht allein am Verhältnis Fehlerzahl : Wortzahl. Die sprachlichen Verstöße werden vielmehr daraufhin beurteilt, in welchem Maß sie die Kommunikation insgesamt beeinträchtigen.

Exemplarisch im Folgenden die Kriterien für eine „ausreichende" bzw. „gute" Leistung:

Eine „ausreichende" inhaltliche Prüfungsleistung (5 Punkte, Grundkursfach und Leistungskursfach) liegt vor, wenn

- die für die Bearbeitung der Aufgaben erforderlichen Grundkenntnisse nachgewiesen werden, insbesondere Grundkenntnisse der Methoden der Textanalyse (eine analytisch-interpretatorische Bearbeitung wird in Ansätzen erwartet),
- der Vorlage/den Vorlagen die für die Ausführung der Arbeitsanweisungen notwendigen Informationen in Grundzügen entnommen wurden,
- die Arbeit auf den größten Teil der gestellten Aufgabe(n) eingeht und
- Informationen teilweise geordnet zueinander und ggf. zur Textvorlage in Beziehung gesetzt und sprachlich zusammenhängend dargestellt werden.

Eine „gute" inhaltliche Prüfungsleistung (11 Punkte, Grundkursfach und Leistungskurs) liegt vor, wenn

- die für die Bearbeitung der Aufgaben erforderlichen Kenntnisse und Methodenkompetenzen nachgewiesen werden,
- der Vorlage/den Vorlagen die für die Ausführung der Arbeitsanweisungen notwendige Information auch in Details entnommen wurde,
- die Arbeit auf alle Teile der gestellten Aufgabe(n) eingeht und diese analytisch-interpretierend bzw. handlungsorientiert selbstständig bearbeitet werden und
- Informationen in geordneter Weise zueinander und ggf. zur Textvorlage in Beziehung gesetzt und sprachlich zusammenhängend dargestellt werden.

Eine „ausreichende" sprachliche Prüfungsleistung (5 Punkte, Grundkursfach) liegt vor, wenn

- elementare Verknüpfungen zwischen Satzteilen, Sätzen und Satzgruppen in einer der Aufgabenstellung angemessenen Weise eingesetzt werden,
- der Wortschatz ausreicht, um Sachverhalte und Meinungen im Rahmen der Aufgabenstellung weitgehend verständlich auszudrücken,
- die Kenntnis wichtiger Wörter und Wendungen aus den im Rahmen der Aufgabenstellung einschlägigen Sachfeldern zu erkennen ist,
- formalsprachliche Verstöße die Verständlichkeit nicht erheblich beeinträchtigen und
- eine pragmatische Vertrautheit mit elementaren sprachlichen Gesetzmäßigkeiten erkennbar ist.

Eine „gute" sprachliche Prüfungsleistung (11 Punkte, Grundkursfach) liegt vor, wenn

- differenzierte Verknüpfungen zwischen Satzteilen, Sätzen und Satzgruppen in einer der Aufgabenstellung angemessenen Weise eingesetzt werden,
- Sachverhalte und Meinungen differenziert ausgedrückt und wichtige Wörter und Wendungen aus den im Rahmen der Aufgabenstellung einschlägigen Sachfeldern eingebracht werden,
- formalsprachliche Verstöße die Verständlichkeit nicht beeinträchtigen und
- ein differenzierter Umgang mit sprachlichen Gesetzmäßigkeiten erkennbar ist.

Eine „ausreichende“ sprachliche Prüfungsleistung (5 Punkte, Leistungskursfach) liegt vor, wenn

- elementare Verknüpfungen zwischen Satzteilen, Sätzen und Satzgruppen in einer angemessenen Weise eingesetzt werden,
- der Wortschatz ausreicht, um Sachverhalte und Meinungen verständlich auszudrücken,
- die Kenntnis wichtiger Wörter und Wendungen aus den im Rahmen der Aufgabenstellungen einschlägigen Sachfeldern zu erkennen ist,
- formalsprachliche Verstöße die Verständlichkeit nicht erheblich beeinträchtigen und
- Vertrautheit mit relevanten sprachlichen Gesetzmäßigkeiten erkennbar ist.

Eine „gute“ sprachliche Prüfungsleistung (11 Punkte, Leistungskursfach) liegt vor, wenn

- differenzierte Verknüpfungen zwischen Satzteilen, Sätzen und Satzgruppen eingesetzt sind,
- die Arbeit einen reichhaltigen, differenzierten und weitgehend idiomatischen Wortschatz aufweist,
- durch funktions- und themenspezifische Redemittel eine weitgehend differenzierte Kommunikation ermöglicht wird,
- Ökonomie, Treffsicherheit und Selbstständigkeit im Ausdruck erkennbar sind und
- nur geringe formalsprachliche Verstöße vorliegen.

4 Anforderungsbereiche und Aufgabenstellungen

In der Regel werden Ihnen zum Abiturtext drei bis vier Arbeitsaufträge gestellt, die sich im Grundsatz an der Abfolge Zusammenfassung, Analyse und Stellungnahme / Kommentar / kreatives Schreiben orientieren.
Diese Abfolge ergibt sich grob aus den drei Anforderungsbereichen, die vom Lehrplan und den Abiturrichtlinien als Leitgrößen vorgegeben sind:

- Anforderungsbereich I: Textverstehen
- Anforderungsbereich II: Textanalyse
- Anforderungsbereich III: Werten und Gestalten

Der **erste Arbeitsauftrag** bezieht sich in der Regel weitgehend auf den **Anforderungsbereich I (Textverstehen)**. Sie sollen unter Beweis stellen, dass Sie die Textvorlage verstanden haben und in der Lage sind, eine gelenkte Zusammenfassung zu erstellen und sich auf bestimmte Aspekte zu konzentrieren. Dies schließt aber nicht aus, dass eine Textzusammenfassung auch in anderen Aufgaben gestellt werden kann.
Die **zweite Aufgabe** bezieht sich in der Regel schwerpunktmäßig auf den **Anforderungsbereich II (Textanalyse)**. Auf eine traditionelle Stilanalyse wird zugunsten einer Analyse des Informationsgehalts des Textes in Zusammenhang mit der Textgestaltung verzichtet. Bei der Sprachmittlungsaufgabe müssen Sie relevante Informationen situations- und adressatengerecht zusammenfassen.
Im **Anforderungsbereich III (Werten und Gestalten)** geht es um Stellungnahme / Kommentar oder kreatives Schreiben (z. B. aus einer anderen Perspektive) in einer vorgegebenen Textsorte. Hier kann eine situationsgebundene Textart mit dem dazu-

gehörigen Register verlangt werden. Sie müssen sich dabei auf das vorliegende Material und darüber hinausgehende Kenntnisse beziehen. Bezüge zu literarischen Texten und Filmen können in die Analyse einbezogen werden. In diesem Bereich haben Sie meist die Wahlmöglichkeit zwischen zwei bis drei Aufgaben.

5 Operatoren

Operatoren zeigen an, welche Tätigkeit beim Lösen von Prüfungsaufgaben erwartet wird.

Anforderungsbereich I

Reproduktion und Textverstehen

Operatoren	Erläuterungen	Beispiele
Gelenkte Zusammenfassung		
outline	Outline the information required. Give the main features, structure or general principles of a topic in your own words omitting minor details. Do not include your opinion or interpretation.	• Give an outline of the arguments Text A contains against and in favour of … • Outline the information the narrator/author provides on … • Outline the situation of … • Outline what … says about …
give an account of		• Give an account of … (as described in …).
sum up		• Sum up the main ideas on … as presented in the excerpt from …
describe	Give an accurate account of sth. in your own words.	• Describe … as depicted in …
state	Present sth. clearly using your own words.	• State the information the author gives on …
Zusammenfassung		
summarise/ summarize/ sum up	Give a concise account of the main aspects/points in your own words. Write an introductory sentence.	• Summarise the content of the article. • Sum up the content of the excerpt.

Anforderungsbereich II

Reorganisation und Analyse

Operatoren	Erläuterungen	Beispiele
Textanalyse		
analyse/ analyze	Name and explain the meaning of specific aspects and/or features of the text and their effect on the reader/audience.	• State the message of the article (Text A) and analyse how the author tries to make the reader accept and believe what he/she says. • State the message of the text and analyse how the use of imagery serves to convey this message to the reader.

		• Analyse how the relationship between the characters is reflected in their language. • Analyse how the author's use of humour helps to convey his message. • Briefly describe the aim the writer pursues in this excerpt, and analyse how the point of view he/she employs helps to achieve it. • Analyse how the reader's interest in the text is attracted by its content and structure. • Describe the picture/cover … and analyse to what extent it may help to understand … • State the message of … and analyse how the picture, the layout and the use of … convey this message to the reader.
examine		• Examine the problems the protagonist faces …
show (how)	Point out and illustrate.	• State …'s opinion about … and show how the reader is made to share it by analysing relevant literary means. • Show how the boy is characterised in this excerpt.
explain	Describe in detail and give reasons for/refer to causes/effects.	• Explain the protagonist's behaviour in the given conflict … • Explain what is meant by the following statement from the text: "…" (l. …).
describe (the way)	Give an accurate account of sth. in your own words.	• Describe the way the playwright creates an atmosphere of suspense and explain its effect on the reader.
compare/contrast	Point out similarities and differences./Emphasise the differences between two or more things.	• Describe Text B (the picture/two graphics) and compare its information with the information given in the article (Text A). • Describe Text B (the picture/two graphics) and contrast its information with the information given in the article (Text A).
relate	Establish a connection between two things.	• Relate the writer's message as conveyed in Text A to the information given in Text B.

Anforderungsbereich I/II

Reproduktion, Reorganisation und Analyse

Sprachmittlung/Mediation

Operatoren	Erläuterungen	Beispiele
outline/give an account of/sum up	Give the relevant information on the topic. Do not write a letter/an e-mail. Use paraphrases.	• Outline the information from Text B that refers to … Do this in a way that it helps someone write a paper/speech on this issue …

Anforderungsbereich III
Werten und Gestalten

Diskussion / Kommentar

Operatoren	Erläuterungen	Beispiele
discuss	Examine / analyse, give reasons for and against and come to a justified conclusion. Present arguments with supporting evidence and conclude with your personal view.	• Discuss whether the difficulties and chances illustrated in Text A are typical phenomena of globalization. • Discuss if the protagonist has coped with the problem in an adequate way. • Discuss the relevance / chances of …
comment on	Based on arguments express your personal view on a problem / certain behaviour, attitudes or viewpoints.	• Comment on the impact of globalisation on families. • Comment on the author's thesis / view "…" (l. …).
reflect on	Consider / contemplate / think carefully and deeply about a problem / certain behaviour, attitudes or viewpoint.	• Referring to a character from literature or film, reflect on the influence of … on this person's life.
convince	Present arguments so that the addressee will support your view.	• As an exchange student you are attending an American high school for one year. In a formal letter convince the head of your school that the introduction of bilingual classes would be profitable.
justify	Show adequate grounds for decisions or conclusions.	• Justify the protagonist's behaviour in the light of …
verify	Analyse and show that something is true.	• Verify the author's thesis …
assess / evaluate	Decide on the value or the state of something and give reasons for your decision.	• With reference to the quotation, assess the impact of …
interpret	Establish the meaning of something in a wider context and give your own view.	• Interpret the quotation …

Hinweise zur Lösung von Abituraufgabenstellungen

1 Textzusammenfassung

Der erste Arbeitsauftrag der Abituraufgabenstellung zielt in der Regel auf das Textverstehen, d. h., er beinhaltet in gelenkter oder allgemeiner Form die Erstellung einer Zusammenfassung, deren Länge in aller Regel zwischen 25 und 30 % des Ausgangstextes beträgt.

Warum wird eine Zusammenfassung geschrieben?
Die Zusammenfassung hat eine Schlüsselfunktion in der Vorbereitung der Textanalyse und der Interpretation. Zunächst muss man sicher sein, dass auch wirklich erfasst worden ist, worum es in dem Text geht. Erst dann ist es möglich, den Text auf Aufbau, Argumentationsweise, Sprache und Stilmittel, d. h. in Bezug auf seine Gestaltungsmittel hin zu untersuchen. Erst wenn die Textaussage und die Textgestaltung klar erfasst sind, kann man sich der Textauslegung, der Interpretation und der Analyse der Bedeutung des Textes zuwenden, erst dann kann der Text auch in einem größeren inhaltlichen oder stilistischen Zusammenhang betrachtet werden.

Wie wird eine Zusammenfassung vorbereitet?
Jede inhaltliche Zusammenfassung beginnt mit einem *umbrella sentence*, der (soweit bekannt) Angaben zum Autor, zur Textsorte, zum Zeitpunkt des Entstehens und zum thematischen Schwerpunkt des Textes enthält.
Die Gliederung des Textes entwickelt sich bei Sachtexten aus folgenden Leitfragen:
- Um welches Thema/Problem geht es?
- Was will der Autor?
- Wie baut er seine Argumentation auf?
- Welche weitergehende Stellungnahme wird in den Folgeaufgaben verlangt?

Bei literarischen Texten als Klausurvorlage steht nicht der argumentative Charakter im Vordergrund. Es handelt sich in aller Regel um Momentaufnahmen aus einem größeren Zusammenhang, welcher in dieser Situation unbekannt bleibt. Die Gliederung des Textes ergibt sich aus Leitfragen wie z. B.:
- Welche Situation treffen wir an?
- Wer sind die Protagonisten und wie verhalten sie sich?
- Welche Grundstimmung findet man vor?
- Um welches Thema/Problem geht es?
- Wie ist der Text strukturiert?
- Für welche weitergehende Fragestellung wird Information benötigt?

In jedem Falle ist bei diesen Leitfragen immer wieder zu entscheiden:
- Was ist zentral wichtig?
- Was ist rein ornamental, also ausschmückendes Beiwerk?
- Was könnte man erwähnen, muss es aber nicht?

Bei der Entscheidung, was man weglassen kann, helfen Überlegungen wie „Könnte ich den Text verstehen, wenn mir diese Information nicht zur Verfügung gestellt würde?" D. h., es gilt z. B. zu fragen:
- Was ist ein ausschmückender, illustrierender oder konkretisierender Zusatz?
- Was wird wiederholt bzw. ist redundant?

Was ist beim Schreiben zu beachten?
Aus der Beantwortung der Leitfragen ergeben sich Grundbausteine und eine Rohstruktur der Zusammenfassung. Im Einzelfall kann eine detailliertere Gliederung unerlässlich sein.

Grundsätzlich sind nur Äußerungen niederzuschreiben, die sich an der Textvorlage auch tatsächlich überprüfen lassen. Die Argumentationslogik sollte klar, unverschnörkelt und nachvollziehbar sein. Sie wird in den meisten Fällen nicht der Reihenfolge der Argumente im Text folgen. Im Gegenteil: sehr oft wird eine am Schluss der Textvorlage zu findende These/Schlussfolgerung oder überraschende Handlungsvariante den Ausgangspunkt der Zusammenfassung bilden.

Wie wird die Zusammenfassung formal und sprachlich gestaltet?

- **Textlänge:** Der Umfang der Zusammenfassung liegt in der Regel zwischen einem Viertel und einem Drittel der Länge der Textvorlage.
- **Tempus:** Eine Zusammenfassung wird im Präsens verfasst. Im Text vorkommende Vor- bzw. Nachzeitigkeit bleibt erhalten.
- **Bezüge:** Personen-, Zeit- und Ortsbezüge werden wie in der indirekten Rede umgeformt, also wird *I* zu *he* oder *she*; *yesterday* zu *the day before*; *here* zu *there* usw.
- **Tabus:** Die Zusammenfassung enthält keine direkte Rede und keine Zitate. Die Zusammenfassung enthält keine wertende persönliche Stellungnahme.

Sprachlich tendiert die Zusammenfassung zu einem leicht gehobenen Niveau und Abstraktionsgrad. Sie ist eher konzeptionell als berichtend oder ausschmückend; dies und die Textlänge unterscheidet sie von der Nacherzählung. Ein höherer Abstraktionsgrad wird erreicht durch

- **allgemeine Begriffe** (wie z. B. *means of transport* an Stelle von *car, bike and underground*),
- **übergreifend einschätzende Verben** (wie z. B. *to focus on, to claim, to maintain, to criticize, to report, to illustrate)*,
- **generalisierende Verben** (wie z. B. *to be worried about, to be reluctant, to be concerned with*) und
- **Konjunktionen:** temporale *(before, when)*, kausale *(because, as, so)*, konditionale *(if, unless)*, konzessive *(though, although)*, kontrastive *(but, instead of)* und konsekutive *(so that, thus)*.

2 Analyse

Prinzipiell können Aufgaben zur Analyse sich zum einen auf die Textanalyse im engeren Sinne beziehen, zum anderen auf das In-den-Zusammenhang-Stellen mit im Unterricht Erarbeitetem.

- Bei der **Analyse im engeren Sinne** geht es um Facetten der Textstrukturierung/Textgestaltung, die aufzuzeigen sind; es kann zusätzlich gefordert sein, das Verhältnis zwischen den Gestaltungsmitteln und dem Inhalt, der Atmosphäre oder der Textaussage auszuloten, d. h., die Funktion der Gestaltungsmittel zu bestimmen – als Teil der Interpretation (siehe a).
- Eine andere Variante der Textanalyse besteht in der **Verknüpfung des gegebenen Textes mit im Unterricht Gelesenem und Diskutiertem** – in der Regel mit Unterrichtsinhalten, die nicht in dem Halbjahr bearbeitet wurden, auf die sich der Text vornehmlich bezieht (siehe b).

a) Auf der Basis der Zusammenfassung und dem damit gewährleisteten Textüberblick wird das erworbene Wissen um Textkonstitution systematisch auf den Text angewendet. Wenn in der Aufgabenstellung keine die Arbeit lenkenden Vorhinweise gegeben werden, so ist der Text daraufhin zu *scannen,* welche Gestaltungsmittel besonders in den Vordergrund treten. Das *Scannen* kann sich beziehen auf
   - die Wortwahl (Register, Häufigkeiten),
   - den Satzbau (komplex/einfach),
   - Stilmittel (z. B. Kontrast, Parallelität, Repetition/Wiederholung) und
   - Sprachfiguren (z. B. Vergleich, Metapher).

   Mit dem Aufzeigen von Textgestaltungsmerkmalen kann die Aufgabenstellung erfüllt sein, in vielen Fällen allerdings ist sie das Fundament für eine weiter gehende Betrachtung, die über die formale Analyse hinausgeht. Hier stellt sich die Frage nach dem Zusammenwirken zwischen Form und Inhalt, d. h., die Gestaltungsmittel werden auf ihre Funktion oder ihre Wirkung hin überprüft. Inwiefern unterstützen sie die Textaussage oder inwiefern unterlaufen sie diese, z. B. in der Satire oder der Parodie?

b) Bei der Verknüpfung von bereits Gelerntem mit dem neuen Text wird in der Regel die Aufgabenstellung bereits einen Hinweis darauf enthalten, welche Anknüpfungspunkte die weitere Arbeit steuern. Ist die Aufgabenstellung sehr allgemein gehalten, müssen mögliche Anknüpfungspunkte betrachtet und kurz durchdacht werden.
   Sind die Überlegungsaspekte einmal gewählt, so ist dieser Ansatz konsequent und möglichst differenziert weiter zu verfolgen und es ist z. B. zu klären, inwiefern sich Gelerntes und Neues im Widerspruch zueinander oder in Übereinstimmung befinden, bzw. inwiefern die Informationen sich wechselseitig erhellen.

3 Persönliche Stellungnahme/Kommentar und kreatives Schreiben

Traditionellerweise wird in der letzten Aufgabe eine eher persönliche Stellungnahme, ein eher kritischer Kommentar oder eine eher analytisch orientierte Diskussion gefordert. Immer häufiger tritt an die Stelle dieser Anforderung die sogenannte kreative, gestalterische Aufgabenstellung.

In einer **persönlichen Stellungnahme**/einem Kommentar wird von Ihnen erwartet, dass Sie Ihre eigene Meinung zu dem gegebenen Problem äußern. Damit steht es Ihnen frei, das Problem unter Umständen auch sehr emotional und unter Bezug auf Ihre eigenen Erfahrungen und Wertvorstellungen zu beleuchten.
Es wird erwartet, dass Sie einen oder mehrere Hauptaspekte auswählen und diese Auswahl kurz reflektieren und begründen. Diese Aspekte werden systematisch bearbeitet und Thesen aufgestellt. Über eine eng gefasste persönliche Stellungnahme hinaus sollte eine Einbettung der Problemstellung und der Hauptaspekte in einen größeren Kontext vorgenommen werden.

Im Rahmen einer **Diskussion** sollten Sie möglichst viele Facetten eines Problems analytisch durchdringen und eine Bewertung vornehmen. Die Grundlagen dieser Bewertung müssen offengelegt und reflektiert werden. Die Diskussion ist mehr der ana-

lytischen Schärfe verpflichtet und weniger den Bedürfnissen und Emotionen des Einzelnen. Sie können also bei der Diskussion eines Problems zu anderen Ergebnissen kommen als bei einer persönlichen Stellungnahme zu demselben Problem.
Methodisch empfiehlt es sich, vor dem Schreiben eine Stichwortsammlung zu erstellen, zusammengehörige Stichwörter zu bündeln und in eine sinnvolle, für den Leser nachvollziehbare Anordnung zu bringen. Immer mit Blick auf den Adressaten ist beim Schreiben zu entscheiden, an welchen Stellen Beispiele/illustrierende Passagen eingefügt werden.

Bei der Bearbeitung der ***creative writing*-Aufgabe** liegt die besondere Schwierigkeit in der geforderten Textsorte. Fragen Sie sich: Welche Anforderungen stellt die Textsorte, welche Merkmale sind zu beachten? Nach dieser formalen Vorentscheidung über die Textsorte sollten Sie

- Aussage und Ziel Ihres Textes bestimmen,
- inhaltliche Elemente sammeln und gliedern und
- den Argumentationsgang skizzieren.

Für das Schreiben Ihres Textes ist es wichtig, dass Ihre Formulierungen der Textsorte, dem Adressaten und dem Verwendungszusammenhang angemessen sind.

Glossary of literary terms

1. **Allegory:** a poem, play or story in which the characters and events are used to symbolize a **deeper moral or spiritual meaning.**

   Example: Typical allegories would be Bunyan's *Pilgrim's Progress* or George Orwell's *Animal Farm.* In *Animal Farm* the pigs represent a totalitarian regime.

2. **Alliteration:** sometimes referred to as **head rhyme** or **initial rhyme**, alliteration is a term we use to describe the **repetition of the initial sounds**, usually consonants, in a line of poetry or in closely adjacent lines. A good poet uses alliteration not just because it sounds nice but because it reinforces the meaning and purpose of the lines in question. Alliteration therefore is used **to create melody, establish mood, or call attention to important words.** It also highlights similarities or contrasts.

   Example: "Scooping spilt, soft, broken oil with a silver spoon from a flagstone floor." *(M-M-Memory from The Other Country by Carol Ann Duffy)*

3. **Allusion:** when a writer alludes to something in the course of writing a poem, he refers to **information assumed to be known** by the reader. This can be a reference to a person or a well-known occurrence such as a battle or war, a TV character or a well-known literary character.

   Example: "'An old woman who looked like one of the witches from Macbeth' he said. This allusion was lost on Sally. Seeing her puzzlement he went on, 'wrinkled, don't you know, and hideous and so forth' …"
   (The Ruby in the Smoke by Philip Pullman)

4. **Ambiguity:** the state of being **doubtful, unclear or indistinct**. It is a characteristic of writing which makes something capable of being understood in more than one way. A poet will often do this deliberately.

   Example: A simple example of ambiguity is to be found in the sentence "They found me a good worker." This is ambiguous in that it has two meanings, i.e. They found me to be a good worker or They found a good worker for me. The context is necessary for it to be properly understood. A writer making effective use of ambiguity will use language and context to leave something unclear or open to more than one interpretation.

5. **Analogy: agreement or similarity** in some things which are otherwise quite different from one another.

   Example: Sleep and death are not really similar but would be analogous in that both normally involve no movement and often happen when a person is lying down.

6. **Anaphora:** the **repetition** of a word or phrase at the start of a succession of phrases in order to achieve **rhetorical effect.** This is most commonly used in plays or famous speeches.

   Example: "*We shall fight* in France, *we shall fight* on the seas and oceans, *we shall fight* with growing confidence and growing strength in the air, *we shall* defend our island, whatever the cost may be, *we shall fight* on the beaches, *we shall fight* on the landing grounds, *we shall fight* in the fields and in the streets, *we shall fight* in the hills. *We shall* never surrender."
   (Winston Churchill)

7. **Antithesis:** this term refers to the exact **opposite** of something being **highlighted in parallel words or** in the **juxtaposition** of contrasting ideas or phrases.

   Example: BRUTUS "Not that I loved Caesar less, but that I loved Rome more."
   (Julius Caesar by William Shakespeare)

8. **Antonym:** a word which is the **opposite** of something else.

   Example: good – bad / easy – difficult.

9. **Aside:** a **statement uttered** during a play which is intended for the ears of the audience only and is **not heard by the other characters** on stage at the time.

   Example: MACBETH "Thanks for that.
   (Aside) There the grown serpent lies, the worm that's fled."
   (Macbeth by William Shakespeare)

10. **Assonance:** the use of the **same vowel sound with different consonants** in successive words or stressed syllables.

    Example: "time and light"

11. **Blank Verse:** verse which does not rhyme but has a set metrical pattern, mostly of **iambic pentameters** (i. e. an unstressed syllable followed by a stressed syllable in each poetic foot). It is used extensively in **dramatic or narrative verse.**

    Example: "The qua / lity / of mer / cy is / not strain'd /
    It drop / peth as / the gen / tle rain / from heaven / "
    (The Merchant of Venice by William Shakespeare)

12. **Characterisation:** the method an author uses to present his characters to the reader. This may involve **physical description**, an account of **speech and behaviour**, a character's **opinions and reactions**, or finally, what a character **feels or thinks** about something.

    Example: "Frances Lennox was a minor, steady, reliable actress, and had never been asked for anything more. This part was in a brilliant new play, a two-hander, and the male part would be taken by Tony Wilde who until now had seemed so far above her she would never have had the ambition to think of her name and his side by side on a poster …"
    (The Sweetest Dream by Doris Lessing)

13. **Cliché:** words or phrases that have been used so often that they are more or less meaningless.

    Example: "As dead as a doornail." *or* "As cool as a cucumber."

14. **Climax:** a group of sentences or clauses which starts with the weakest and then **builds to a high point** in order to achieve effect. The term can also refer to the high point of a story or play.

    Example: "It is an outrage to bind a Roman citizen; to scourge him is an atrocious crime; to put him to death is almost a parricide; but to crucify him, what shall I call it?" *(Cicero)*

15. **Conflict:** this term is used when talking about a **problem or struggle between two opposing forces** in a story. The main types of conflicts are: person against person, person against self, person against society and person against nature.

    Example: One of the central themes of *How to be Good* by Nick Hornby is the struggle the main character experiences between the person she is and the person she wants to be. This conflict is the main driving force behind her story.

16. **Consonance: repetition of specific consonant sounds** after different vowel sounds.

    Example: Consonance is the similarity between consonants, but not between vowels, as between the *s* and *t* sounds in "sweet silent thought."

17. **Elements of fiction:** certain aspects of a literary work. A criticism or analysis of a book or story might concentrate on any of the following elements: the **action**, the **antagonist** (i. e. the person or force that works against the **protagonist** or hero of the story), the **characters**, the **climax**, the **conflict**, the **dialogue**, the

exposition, (i. e. the part of the story in which the characters first appear, the background is explained and the setting is described), the **falling action** (i. e. the action and dialogue following the climax that lead the reader into the story's end), the **mood**, the **moral**, the **narrator**, the **plot**, the **resolution**, (i. e. how everything turns out), the **rising action** (i. e. the central part of the story during which various problems arise after a conflict is introduced), the **setting**, the **style** and the **theme**.

Example: The theme of the short story collection *Dubliners* by James Joyce is essentially one of life and human nature in Dublin as seen through the eyes of the characters involved.

18. **Ellipsis:** a stylistic device used to achieve poetic effect by **omitting a word or phrase** which is easily known to the reader.

    Example: "And he to England shall along with you." (The word "go" has been omitted between "shall" and "along.")

    (Hamlet by William Shakespeare 3.3.1)

19. **Epigram:** a **witty paradoxical remark**.

    Example: "A poet can survive everything but a misprint." *or* "I can resist everything but temptation."

    (Oscar Wilde)

20. **Euphemism:** a **polite phrase or word** which is used to say something that is considered unpleasant or hurtful in a nice and acceptable manner.

    Example: "China is a country where you often get different accounts of the same thing." *(... where many lies are told) or* "He passed away." *(He died)*

21. **Figurative language** takes in such devices as **simile, hyperbole, personification** and **metaphor**.

    Example: "He clasps the crag with crooked hands
    Close to the sun in lonely lands
    Ringed with the azure world, he stands."

    (The Eagle by Lord Tennyson)

22. **Foreshadowing** happens when the author gives **hints** about things which will later come to pass in the course of a story.
    Example: In *Julius Caesar* by William Shakespeare, Caesar's wife has nightmares in which she foresees his death (Act II Scene II):
    Thunder and lightning. Enter CAESAR, in his night-gown
    "Nor heaven nor earth have been at peace to-night:
    Thrice hath Calphurnia in her sleep cried out,
    'Help, ho! they murder Caesar!' Who's within?"

23. **Flashback:** the opposite of foreshadowing. An interruption in the action of a story or work of non-fiction **to show an episode that happened at an earlier time**. A flashback is usually used to provide background information.

    Example: In *The Snows of Kilimanjaro*, Harry Street, who is dying, becomes preoccupied with incidents in his past. In a flashback Street remembers one of his wartime comrades dying painfully on barbed wire on a battlefield in Spain.

24. **Hyperbole: exaggerated form** of language used to increase effect.

    Example: "I could eat a horse." *or* "All the perfume of Arabia could not sweeten this little hand."
    (Macbeth by William Shakespeare)

25. **Imagery:** those elements in a poem which evoke **mental pictures**; not just visual ones but emotional ones also. Many images are conveyed by figurative language such as **similes, metaphors and personification.**

    Example: "When the evening is spread out against the sky
    Like a patient etherized upon a table."
    (The Love Song of J. Alfred Prufrock – T. S. Eliot)

26. **Irony:** a humorous use of words **to imply the opposite** of what they actually mean. There is a contrast between what seems to be and what actually is. We speak of verbal irony, dramatic irony, irony of situation, irony of tone.

    Example: "Moments after Eileen shot herself, having earlier been told that John, her husband, had been killed in the war, he came walking up the drive with his rucksack over his shoulder."

27. **Literary forms:** various **types of writing**. These include such well-known types as comedy, drama, essay, historical fiction, novel, poetry, science fiction and the short story. Other literary forms include myth, folktale, autobiography, biography, realistic fiction and prose.

    Example: The novel *The Time Machine* by H. G. Wells is a good example of early science fiction writing.

28. **Metaphor:** a figure of speech that **implies comparison** without using "like" or "as". A resemblance is indicated but not expressed directly.

    Example: "All the world's a stage." (Not: … is *like* a stage)
    (As You Like It by William Shakespeare)

29. **Mood:** the overall **emotional effect** created by a piece of literature.

    Example: The mood created in the poem *Originally* (Carol Ann Duffy) is a reflective one, one full of memories and uncertainty. The poet is considering a time when she lived in a different country and is wondering where she actually comes from. The conclusion of the poem reads "And I hesitate", a finish which contributes to, and is typical of, the overall mood of the poem.

30. **Paradox:** a seemingly **absurd or self-contradictory statement** that is or may be true.

Example: "What a pity that youth must be wasted on the young."
(George Bernard Shaw)

31. **Personification:** the **attribution of human qualities** to something which is not human.

Example: "As the wind undressed the trees, fear grabbed at his throat …"
or "The plane began to creak and protest as it fought its way through the storm."

32. **Plot: pattern of action** in a short story, novel or play. In a book with a good plot all the details are important and are arranged so that the outcome depends on each one and the interaction of all the details with one another. The plot may have a **protagonist** who is opposed by an **antagonist**, creating what is known as **conflict**. A plot may include flashback or it may include a subplot which is a mirror image of the main plot.

Example: In Shakespeare's *King Lear,* the relationship between the Earl of Gloucester and his sons mirrors the relationship between Lear and his daughters.

33. **Point of view:** the writer's **choice of narrator** for his story. A writer has three basic choices when it comes to deciding on what point of view will be used in a novel.

Example: Personal or first-person: the narrator "I" is a character in the story who can reveal only his own thoughts and what he sees and is told. *Robinson Crusoe* is told from a first-person point of view.
Third person objective is where the narrator is an outsider who can report only what he sees and hears. An example would be *Hard Times* by Charles Dickens.
An omniscient point of view is where the narrator knows everything and can enter the minds of his characters. He may enter the minds of all the characters or the mind of just one if he wishes to focus on one character. Joyce's *Ulysses* is told in this manner.

34. **Pun: play on words** in which words are used to exploit ambiguities in meaning, usually for humorous effect.

Example: Ben Battle was a soldier bold and used to *war's* alarms
But a cannonball took off his *legs* so he laid down his *arms*.

35. **Repetition:** one of the most frequently used stylistic devices. It simply involves the **frequent use of the same word or phrase** in a piece of writing.

Example: "You cannot sir, take from me anything that I would more willingly part withal, except my life, except my life, except my life."
(Hamlet by William Shakespeare)

36. **Rhetoric:** the effective use of language, particularly in a **speech**, when one is trying to persuade someone or convert them to one's opinion.

Example: "Friends, Romans, countrymen
Lend me your ears
I come …"
(Julius Caesar by William Shakespeare)

37. **Rhetorical question:** a question to which **no answer is required** because the answer is obvious.

    Example: "Who knows?" (The answer "nobody knows" is clear from the question itself.)

38. **Rhyme:** a term we use to describe the **repetition of syllable sounds**. We speak of **end rhyme** and **internal rhyme.** The pattern created by rhyme in a poem is referred to as the rhyming scheme.

    Example: "I'm a lean dog, a keen dog, a wild dog and lone;
    I'm a rough dog, a tough dog, hunting on my own."
    (Irene Rutherford McLeod)

39. **Sarcasm:** particular **type of irony**. Sarcasm is usually intended to be aggressive and is often insulting and aimed at a person.

    Example: "You are a wonderful goalkeeper." (To someone who has just conceded 9 goals in a match …)

40. **Satire:** a literary work which exposes and ridicules human folly and uses **sarcasm, wit** and **irony** to do so. It is usually directed against the injustice of social wrongs e. g. poverty, corruption.

    Example: Famous satirists would include Dryden, Swift, Pope and Orwell. *Animal Farm* (Orwell) and *Gulliver's Travels* (Swift) are among the most famous works of satire ever written.

41. **Setting:** the **time and place** in which the events of a story or novel take place.

    Example: The book *Ulysses*, by Irish writer James Joyce, has perhaps the most well-known setting of any modern novel. It is set in Dublin on one particular day in 1904, a day that has since become known as Bloomsday in honour of a character, Leopold Bloom, who appears in the book.

42. **Simile:** a **comparison** of two completely different objects using "**like**" or "**as**". It is not generally considered as powerful as a metaphor since it does not defy logic.

    Example: "Errors, like straws, upon the surface flow …" *(Nesfield)*

43. **Soliloquy:** a **speech** which is spoken by a character in a play at a time when he or she is unaccompanied on the stage.

    Example: The best-known soliloquy in the English language is Hamlet's speech in which he utters his famous "to be or not to be" statement.

44. **Sonnet: fixed poetic form of fourteen lines in iambic pentameter**. In the Elizabethan or Shakespearean sonnet the lines are divided into three quatrains and a couplet (abab, cdcd, efef, gg) The original Italian form is divided into an octave of two rhyme-sounds following an abba abba pattern and a sestet of two additional rhyme patterns cdc, dcd or cde, cde. Eventually, the ability to write a sonnet became part of a wealthy man's education.

    Example: Shakespeare's *Shall I compare thee to a summer's day?* is one of the most famous sonnets.

45. **Stream of consciousness: narrative technique** developed towards the end of the 19th century used to portray and evoke the psychic life of a character and depict subjective as well as objective reality. Stream of consciousness refers to the **presentation of a character's thoughts, feelings, actions** and so on.

    Example: In his work *The Butcher Boy* the Irish author Patrick McCabe uses the first person stream of consciousness to show his main character's descent into madness.

46. **Symbol:** a word which stands for or is somehow connected to an idea and is therefore a **sign** of something.

    Example: The Union Jack stands for Britain. In Robert Frost's poem *Acquainted with the Night* both the night and darkness are symbols for death or depression.

47. **Tautology:** the **repetition of an idea in different words**, phrases or in a sentence.

    Example: With malice toward none, with charity for all.
    (Second Inaugural Address – A. Lincoln)

48. **Theme: unifying motif** in, or the **main meaning** of, a work; often a general truth about life. A theme can be stated directly or implied.

    Example: One of the main themes of Edna O'Brien's collection of short stories *Lantern Slides* is the confinement provincial life in Ireland places upon those who live there.

49. **Tone:** when a reader refers to the tone of a poem, he or she is usually speaking about the **writer's attitude** to the subject he is writing about. More specifically it can refer to the **moral outlook** of a piece. Tone is sometimes used to describe the overall feeling of a poem and thus is quite related to the mood.

    Example: The tone of the book *Cannery Row* by John Steinbeck is objective, neutral and non-judgemental. The writer does not express disapproval of the actions of Mack and his band.

50. **Tragedy:** a word used primarily at a literary level to refer to a **medieval narrative poem** or a **Renaissance drama** in which the downfall of a great person – be it a king, an emperor or a good person – is the main theme of the work.

Example: *Julius Caesar* and *King Lear* by William Shakespeare both describe the downfall of great individuals and are among the greatest tragedies ever written.

51. **Understatement:** a **comment made in a restrained and somehow less important way** to achieve heightened effect and increase the actual importance of what is being said. This is often done in an ironic way.

    Example: After Macbeth murders his friend Banquo, he goes on to play down the deed by referring to the number of people who have been murdered since the beginning of time, saying, "Blood hath been shed ere now."

Abiturprüfung Brandenburg 2008
Englisch Grundkurs – Aufgabe 1

Text A Making a commitment to the planet:

My Big Fat Green Wedding

The dress came from Oxfam, the food was organic, and the guests had to offset their air-miles. Ian Herbert reports on the couple who tied the knot without harming the environment.

For the prospective bride and groom who dream of flying their entire family to Barbados for a £ 100,000 knees-up, the idea of a green wedding must sound about as welcome as a bad speech from the best man followed by a punch-up over the wedding breakfast.

But a young groom's decision to buy his bride an engagement ring with a conflict-free diamond culminated in their ethical wedding this weekend – the latest in a growing number – with flowers grown in the bride's mother's garden and recycled toilet paper at the reception venue.

It was after Joe Carrick, a 20-year-old youth worker, sought out the ethical white gold ring that his fiancée, Jessica Randall, 24, of Keighley, west Yorkshire, became determined to place sustainability at the heart of their big day. She dug out a £ 70 wedding dress from one of Oxfam's seven UK bridal stores, in Bradford, asked relatives flying in from Australia and Switzerland to offset the carbon emissions of their flights, and a green, 1948 Bentley which had been converted to gas was found to replace the usual gas-guzzling wedding limo. Out went the reams of paper which weddings entail, and in their place was a dedicated "Jessi-caandjoe" website from which guests could order presents and get directions.

More couples are opting for a green, rather than white, wedding because of an awareness of the colossal carbon footprint attached to their big day. The Climate Care group estimates that the average wedding emits 14.5 tonnes of carbon dioxide – a hefty environmental toll; the entire annual carbon footprint of the average Briton stands at 10.92 tonnes of CO_2, the Carbon Trust revealed last month.

"The image often conveyed about green events is that they're going to be a bit hippy," said Ruth Culver, whose Green Weddings organisation is the first dedicated to focusing the happy couple on their carbon footprint. "We like to say it's eco-chic and just as fabulous as any wedding."

Ms Randall had some pre-wedding jitters about her decision to buy a second hand silk dress from Oxfam. "I wasn't sure how people might respond to it, though the reaction was amazing when I told people where it was from," she said. Her full-length veil, also from Oxfam, was £ 4.99 though there was one indulgence – a new, £ 70 tiara. The couple pulled the event off on a £ 3,000 budget – a snip, compared to the £ 20,000 of consumption attached to the average big day, in Britain.

True to their eco-principles, the couple are honeymooning in Dorset, cutting out the biggest environmental cost attached to most weddings – the overseas holiday which follows. Their presents, which have all gone straight to the developing world, via Oxfam unwrapped, include a donkey, an alpaca, three health care workers, 125 planted trees and 25 condom kits. *(469 words)*

Source: Ian Herbert, THE INDEPENDENT, 29 January 2007

	Big Fat Green Wedding: Big Fat Greek Wedding, title of the movie from 2002
	tie the knot: get married
l. 2	knees-up: (infml) a noisy party, with dancing
l. 3	punch-up: (infml) a physical fight
l. 12	Oxfam: (abbr) Oxford Committee for Famine Relief, a large charity that helps poor people all over the world, e. g. by selling second-hand clothes
ll. 13/14	offset the carbon emissions of the flight: make up for the pollution caused by the wedding guests
l. 19	carbon footprint: the impact human activities have on the environment in terms of the amount of CO_2 produced
ll. 30/31	tiara: piece of jewellery like a small crown, worn by a woman on formal occasions
l. 33	Dorset: county in South West England

Text B
The following website was used by the couple to plan their wedding.

Celebrations that don't cost the earth

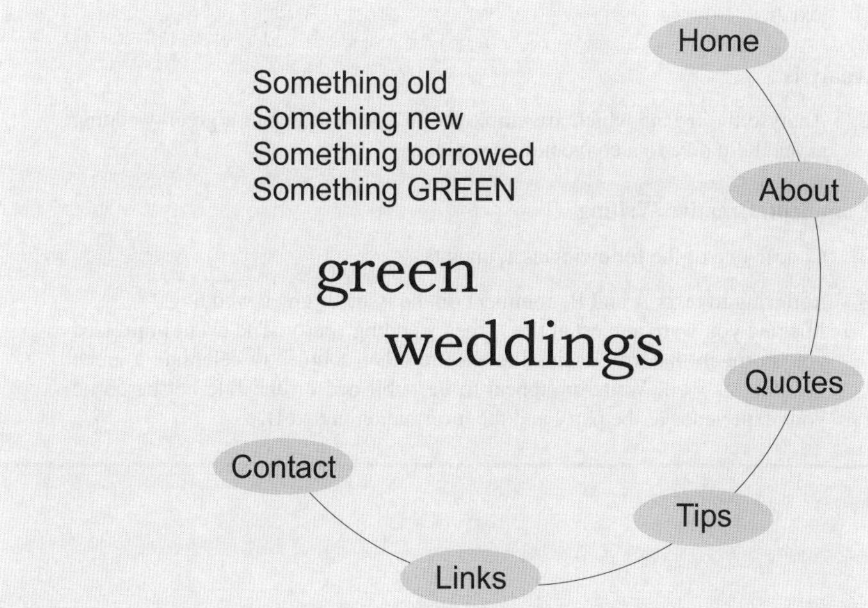

Green Tips

You can, of course, plan your own wedding – many people enjoy the process.
The tips below will help you make it a green one.

However, if you want to save time, effort and headaches, plus have someone on hand with experience of what works, just contact Green Weddings.

- Go local with your food & drink to cut food miles. Request organic and fair trade.
- Source recycled materials for your invitations, or just use e-mail.
- Use biodegradable confetti, or collect petals from flowers a florist was throwing out.
- Do you really need new kitchenware? Consider a charity wedding list or select eco-friendly products.
- Rent outfits or look for vintage – only buy things you'll definitely wear again.
- Have a local stag/hen party – you'll spend less time travelling and more having fun. Or take the train – so much more sociable.
- Honeymoon locally – you'll be so tired you'll be glad you didn't travel far.
- Offset the carbon emissions produced by your wedding (and honeymoon flights) through www.co2balance.com

Assignments

Comprehension

1. Summarise the information given about the green wedding described in text A.

Analysis

2. Analyse the means which are employed in text A to depict a green wedding as an alternative to a conventional wedding.

Comment/Creative Writing

3. Choose <u>one</u> of the following assignments.

3.1 Referring to texts A and B, comment on the issue of green weddings.

3.2 Imagine you were a guest at the "green wedding" party. The event impressed you so much that you decided to inspire other couples to celebrate a green wedding as well. Write an appeal to be published on the Internet based on your experience at the party and the information in text B.

Lösungsvorschläge

Die Aufgabenstellung bezieht sich auf den Prüfungsschwerpunkt One world – global issues *sowie* Emotions and drives. *Sie steht in engem Zusammenhang mit den Aspekten* global economy, environmental destruction and saving the planet.

1. *Sie sollen die für die Bearbeitung der Aufgabe notwendigen Informationen entnehmen und sie geordnet und sprachlich zusammenhängend entsprechend der Konventionen der Textsorte* summary *darstellen. Folgende Aspekte sollten Sie aufführen:*
   - *using second-hand clothes and accessories, recycled paper, an environmentally-friendly car*
   - *spending their honeymoon in Britain and not overseas*
   - *having a limited budget*
   - *creating a website to organise their wedding*
   - *asking guests to make up for the pollution they caused*
   - *sending their presents to the developing world*

   The given article describes the environmentally friendly wedding procedures that Joe Carrick and Jessica Randall chose for themselves. It is outlined in the article to what extent this wedding could be called a green wedding. The idea behind it is to reduce the amount of CO_2 that is produced by a wedding. Thus, the couple opted for second-hand clothes from Oxfam or recycled toilet paper. Moreover, the 1948 Bentley had been converted to gas so as not to harm the environment. Since the couple had a limited budget and a strong belief in protecting the environment they also decided to spend their honeymoon in Dorset/England rather than overseas. To further reduce the use of paper they created a website where all necessary wedding data was published. Moreover, all guests were asked to make up for the pollution they may have caused by using planes etc. Finally, the wedding presents, such as a donkey or condom kits were sent to developing countries via Oxfam, naturally unwrapped.

2. *Bei dieser Aufgabe müssen Sie den Text analytisch interpretieren. Hierbei geht es darum, die Intention und Wirkung herauszuarbeiten. Inhaltlich sollten Sie jene* means *identifizieren, die Ihnen als Leser aufzeigen, dass eine „Grüne Hochzeit" weniger umweltbelastend ist als konventionelle Hochzeiten.*

   The first striking example catching the reader's attention is probably the headline of the text since it is an allusion, a brief reference, to the well-known movie "My Big, Fat Greek Wedding". It is, of course, left to the reader to identify that connection. The real couple Jessica Randall and Joe Carrick serves as an authentic example. This personification allows the reader's identification and surely intensifies the vivid picture one receives throughout the whole text. Thus, factual credibility is created. This is further emphasised by the use of the given facts and figures (l. 2, ll. 10–14, ll. 20–22, ll. 30–32, l. 37 etc.) in the entire text, which strongly stress the importance of eco-friendly weddings in contrast to traditional weddings. Ian Herbert, the author, also introduces metaphorical language ("conflict-free diamond", ll. 5/6; "at the heart of their big day", l. 11 etc.) and irony ("as welcome as a bad speech", ll. 2/3) to both illustrate the issue and to emphasise the positive effects of a green wedding. To further compare the two different wedding procedures, Herbert uses various enumerations (ll. 12–17) to visualise the various activities and opportunities one certainly has got to maybe convince the reader of the overall positive effects of green weddings. Any clichés that might occur on the reader's side are, in advance, nipped in the bud: green weddings are eco-chic and not at all hippy. The author thus counters possible arguments against a green wedding.

3.1 *Sie sollen in einem* comment *Ihre eigene Meinung über eine umweltbewusste Hochzeit darlegen. Dabei müssen Sie auch die Webseite in Text B einbeziehen. Es gilt, einen argumentativen Text zu erstellen, in dem die Elemente* introduction – main part – conclusion *klar erkennbar sein müssen. Es obliegt Ihnen, positive oder negative Effekte zu beschreiben, oder beide kontrastierend zu erläutern.*

The ultimate necessity of becoming environmentally aware seems somehow rather fashionable nowadays. Whereas some decades ago only Hippies seemed to think about the globe, it has become cool to a certain extent in modern times.
Pop- and Rock stars like Jack Johnson have released songs concerning our environmental behaviour. Politicians like Al Gore who proclaim the urgency to reduce pollution have launched a strong appeal all across the planet. The issue includes different facets, from fair trade via better isolated homes to significant changes in our eating habits. Thus, let us consider the recent success of *Bionade*, a soft drink brand in Germany. People have just recently become aware of it due to the prefix "Bio" which stands for healthy organic food. Everything that sounds healthy must be healthy. Does that have something to do with the pure fear of losing our permanent residence, our blue planet? Are green weddings just one of the many examples today that exactly mirror this global development? Green goes global.
In fact, I very much appreciate a greener, a more environmentally-oriented lifestyle. We are familiar with smart homes, the computer industry has found a green motto "Green IT", and so why not have a green wedding? According to my humble opinion there are not any serious reasons against such a procedure, are there? Well, I guess, many of us would not mind a traditional horse wagon? But what about recycled invitations, recycled gold for your wedding rings, green bridal registries, no gifts, limited catering, choosing close to home venues to cut distances for travelling, using locally grown food and flowers or even fair trade flowers? Well, I must admit some of these are surely not to everyone's taste. Not to mention the idea of marrying in a borrowed wedding coat or to seriously make up one's mind about how to save the planet from getting polluted. However, the numbers presented by Herbert spark the need of doing something good; although 14.5 tons seem very little in comparison to the billions of tons worldwide which are blown in the air. That's why ideas like biodegradable confetti or spending your honeymoon locally do not seem that bad at all. Let us recall the wise words of Don Helder Camara, a famous Archbishop of

Recife and Olinda, Brazil, who once said something like, when you dream alone, it's just a dream; but when several people have the same dream, it's already the beginning of reality.

3.2 *Sie müssen einen* appeal *verfassen, in dem Sie die Vorteile eines* green wedding *herausstellen. Dabei sollten Sie versuchen, so überzeugend zu argumentieren, dass andere Paare angeregt werden, dem Beispiel zu folgen. Besonders die bewusste sprachliche Gestaltung wird bei dieser Aufgabe bewertet.*

Your big fat green wedding!

Weddings are usually an extravagant affair. That's why lots of people are even afraid of possibly ruining this happiest day of your entire life.
Hey guys out there, I might have witnessed something completely alien that could be the option for you.
It was last week that I was invited to a friend's wedding in our neighbourhood. First I thought about finding some silly excuse for not going to the wedding, because I do not particularly like such big festive occasions where you only get stuffed. However, in the end I went there and today, gladly enough, I even consider organising the same stylish and sustainable celebration. I proudly and unexpectedly witnessed a green wedding that also had this essence of elegance and sophistication many would expect from an everlastingly important event.
Here it is: a brief what-to-do-list to green your wedding. Gather all your friends and relatives at a nearby organic-run farmhouse for a pre-wedding day environmental expedition. Calculate the mileage your guests might have to travel and offset their carbon dioxide emissions by donating to programmes that preserve environmental hotspots. Use locally grown flowers for your bride's bouquet or the decorations in general. Use recycled paper for your invitations. Use recycled gold for your wedding rings. First precisely calculate and then limit your catering. Design an organic seasonal menu. Donate gifts to charity. That does not sound like a good idea? Well then just think about starting a new period in your life fully connected to your innermost values and beliefs. Would you not like the fact that thought rather than money had gone into your wedding? Reduce yourself to the essentials. Live life longer. You also do not want this precious moment to be at the expense of our environment, do you? Do you care? Then go for the green option and enjoy a special and unforgettable wedding reception that does not cost the earth …

The Devil Wears Prada

By Lauren Weisberger

Note: The following text is an excerpt from the novel "The Devil Wears Prada" by Lauren Weisberger. Andrea (also called Andy) works for Miranda Priestly, the chief editor of "Runway", the most famous fashion magazine in the US. Her boyfriend Alex is visiting her at the apartment she shares with her friend Lily. Alex and Andrea have planned to go to his homecoming in Providence together.

[…]

"Well, it's not normally the way it works. Since it's considered a huge privilege, usually the senior assistant is the only one who gets to go, but since Emily is sick, then, yes, now I will be going. I have to leave next Tuesday, so I can't go to Providence that weekend. I'm really, really sorry." I moved off my chair and went to sit closer to him on the couch, but he immediately stiffened.

"So it's just that simple, right? You know, I already paid for the entire room to guarantee the rate. Never mind the fact that I rearranged my whole schedule to go with you that weekend. I told my mom she had to find a sitter because you wanted to go. Not a big deal, though, right? Just another *Runway* obligation." In all the years we'd spent together, I'd never seen him so angry. Even Lily looked up from her magazine long enough to excuse herself and get the hell out of the room before this turned into an all-out war.

I tried to curl up on his lap, but he crossed his legs and waved his head "Seriously. Andrea –" He called me that only when he was really annoyed. "Is all of this really worth it? Be honest with me for a second. Is it worth it to you?"

"All of what? Is missing a homecoming weekend when there will be dozens more worth it to do something I'm required to do for my job? A job that is going to open doors for me I never thought possible, and sooner than I ever expected? Yes! It's worth it."

His chin dropped to his chest and for a moment I thought he was crying, but when he lifted it again, his face revealed nothing but rage.

"Don't you think I'd rather go with you than go be someone's slave twenty-four-seven for a straight week?" I shouted, forgetting entirely that Lily was somewhere in the apartment. "Can't you stop for one second to think about the fact that I may not want to go either, but I have no choice?"

"No choice? You have nothing but choices! Andy, this job isn't just a job anymore, in case you've failed to notice – it's taken over your entire life!" he yelled back, the redness in his face expanding to his neck and ears. Normally I thought this was very cute, even sexy, but tonight I just wanted to go to sleep.

"Alex, listen, I know –"

"No, you listen! Forget about me for a second, not like that's such a stretch, but forget that we never, ever, see each other any more because of the hours you keep at work, because of your never-ending work emergencies. What about your parents? When was the last time you actually saw them? And your sister? You do realize that she just had her first baby and you haven't even seen your own nephew yet, don't you? Doesn't that mean anything?" He lowered his voice and leaned in closer. I thought he might be getting ready to apologize, but he said, "What about Lily? Have you not noticed that your best friend has turned into a raging alcoholic?" I must have looked absolutely shocked because he barreled on. "You can't even think of saying you didn't realize that, Andy. It's the most obvious thing in the world."

"Yes, of course she drinks. So do you and so do I and so does everyone we know. Lily's a student, and that's what students do, Alex. What's so weird about that?" It sounded even more pathetic when I said it out loud, and he only shook his head. We were both quiet for a few minutes until he spoke.

"You just don't get it, Andy. I'm not exactly sure how it happened, but I feel like I don't know you anymore. I think we need a break." […] *(670 words)*

note	homecoming: an annual event held by high-schools and colleges for visiting graduates/alumni
l. 3	senior assistant: assistant to sb., high in rank or status
l. 9	sitter: *here:* sb. who looks after somebody's house
l. 13	all-out: total
l. 23	go be: go and be/to operate as sth.
ll. 23/24	twenty-four-seven: twenty-four hours a day, seven days a week
l. 24	straight: here; without a break
l. 32	not like that's such a stretch: here: it is not hard to imagine
l. 39	raging: very strong or painful
l. 40	barrel on: *here:* continue to argue

Assignments

Comprehension

1 Summarise the reasons for Alex' anger and concern.

Analysis

2 Analyse the means used to convey a vivid picture of the conflict.

Comment/Creative Writing

3 Choose <u>one</u> of the following assignments.

3.1 A week later, after having considered their arguments and their relationships, Andrea decided to write a letter to Alex. Write this letter.

3.2 Comment on Alex' suggestion "I think we need a break." (cf. l. 47) and the future of Alex and Andrea's relationship.

Lösungsvorschläge

Die Aufgabenstellung bezieht sich auf den Prüfungsschwerpunkt Emotions and drives *und steht in engem Zusammenhang mit den Aspekten* human relations and love.

1. *Sie sollen die für die Bearbeitung der Aufgabe notwendigen Informationen entnehmen und sie geordnet und sprachlich zusammenhängend entsprechend der Konventionen der Textsorte* summary *darstellen. Folgende Aspekte sollten aufgeführt werden:*
   - *he has planned and paid all the necessary arrangements for his homecoming weekend*
   - *he has told his mother he is not available that weekend*
   - *Andrea works all day long*
   - *she does not care about her family*
   - *she never has time to see Alex*
   - *she does not realise that her friend Lily is turning into an alcoholic*

   The given text is an extract from the novel *The Devil Wears Prada* in which a young couple, Alex and Andrea, have an ongoing discussion about fundamental pillar stones of their relationship. To start with, Alex has organised and paid all necessary arrangements for his homecoming weekend in Providence, where both should have been spending the weekend together and been seeing their friends and family. Instead, he is confronted with Andrea's refusal due to her work for the famous fashion magazine "Runway". Alex seems rather disappointed and now confronts Andrea with his thoughts, namely that she works all day long and does not socialise any more. Andrea tries to defend herself which enrages Alex even more. Besides, he accuses Andrea of not caring about her family for she has not even seen her newly born nephew yet. Moreover, Alex blames her for not wanting to see him either whereas Andrea tells him that she has not got any choice, if she wants to climb the career ladder. The final straw for Alex is that Andrea seems totally unaware of the fact that her friend Lily has turned into an alcoholic. Alex tells her off for not even realising the tense situation.

2. *Bei dieser Aufgabe müssen Sie den Text analytisch interpretieren. Arbeiten Sie dabei vor allem Intention und Wirkung heraus. Inhaltlich sollten Sie die Mittel identifizieren, die es dem Leser erlauben, jenes lebendige Bild des Konflikts zwischen Alex und Andrea zu erkennen.*

   A first striking example that catches the reader's attention is Andrea's limited perspective. The reader is thus able to relate to the way Andrea perceives the whole conflict ("I moved off my chair…but he immediately stiffened", ll. 5/6 or "In all the years we'd spent together, I'd never seen him so angry.", ll. 10/11). Due to the chosen form of direct speech we are given the actual words spoken as if we were seeing a theatre play or the film version of the book. This is defined as a scenic mode of presentation, where the actual dialogues are delivered to the reader ("So it's just that simple, right?", l. 7), to allow him/her to realise the increasing tension within the development of the conflict ("... He called me that only when he was really annoyed.", l. 15) and to understand how both contribute to this increase of tension within the conflict ("Is all of this really worth it? Be honest with me for a second. Is it worth it to you?", ll. 15/16). This conveys a lively picture of the conflict. Therein, the conflict situation is enhanced by the figurative language the author has chosen ("...your never-ending work emergencies", l. 34) to illustrate the increasing seriousness of their dilemma. Furthermore, the very choice of dynamic verbs ("I shouted", l. 24; "he yelled back", ll. 28/29; "he barrelled on", l. 40) mirrors the emotionally heated discussion. Depicting opposing views within the argument by formulating contrasts ("but he immediately stiffened", l. 6 etc.) is mainly to further increase the tension. Thus, Lauren Weisberger uses various means to convey a vivid picture to portray an all too familiar situation between arguing couples.

3.1 *Diese Aufgabenstellung verlangt die Ausarbeitung eines Brief aus Andreas Perspektive. Es gilt, einen* personal letter *zu verfassen, in dem Sie den Schreibanlass deutlich machen sollten, um Andreas Sicht auf den Streit erlebbar werden zu lassen. Sie können Ansatzpunkte aus dem Text aufgreifen und weiter entwickeln.*

Dear Alex,

It has been two days now since we last talked to each other. What should I say? What can I do? The way you left me I understand our conflict has reached a point where we both should make clear what we expect from life in general and what we do expect from a possible partner.
Alex, I still love you. My feelings for you have not changed. Maybe my perspective on my job and on my life in general have changed recently. I consider it a great opportunity to prove to Miranda that she can rely on me. You know that I have had bad times with her, where I felt devastated. But you were there for me then. You gave me all your strength and your support. To me everything seemed to be going all right. I have now realised that I might have neglected your point of view and your needs. But can't you see my point? I'd be utterly stupid to stop half way. You made me choose my way and now you seemingly want me to change direction again. But I have come too far now and I feel good about it, too good to return. I feel trusted, needed but most of all respected by Miranda and my colleagues.
Alex, I know that you need me too. But do you really respect my work and above all my feelings for that? Alex, I thoroughly believe in our future. But to do this we'll have to let the other one go at times.

Take care,
Love you, Andrea

3.2 *Es wird erwartet, dass Sie einen Kommentar zu Alex' Aussage* „I think we need a break“ *verfassen und dabei Ihre eigene Meinung zur Zukunft des Paares darlegen. Erstellen Sie einen argumentativen Text zu erstellen, in dem die Elemente* introduction – main part – conclusion *klar erkennbar sein müssen. Sie können positive oder negative Möglichkeiten beschreiben. Die eigene Wertung ist entscheidend.*

There are always reasons to break up, but some are more common than others. In my opinion, it is high time to break up if you are in an abusive relationship. Trust should be an important part in any relationship. Sometimes we find another person we might feel attached to, perhaps a friend or a colleague we are interested in. Sometimes we figure out that there is no future together. Sometimes many couples just lose interest in each other, not only sexually, but also as friends. Simply, if you cannot talk to your partner, it is definitely time to break up. So what about Alex and Andrea? Alex suggested that they needed a break. As I am trying to understand his suggestion, I cannot but ask myself if he really means what he says. His statement actually means that the two of them are standing at a junction going in two different directions. It is about two perspectives on life when he confronts Andrea with his statement. Andrea seemingly wants to climb the career ladder whereas Alex is seemingly interested in having a family. How else could you understand his accusations that she does not care about her family anymore? This is why it is hard for me to believe in *their* future. Alex does not seem to comprehend Andrea's dilemma. Alex has certainly reached a point where he does not want to listen to Andrea's excuses any longer. He simply neglects the fact that his girlfriend has somehow become cosmopolitan due to her job. You see different people; you perceive different problems and maybe all of a sudden you feel important and able to help out. You feel needed. I thoroughly claim that this has happened to Andrea. She has gained more self-confidence, which Alex is not used to. Andrea probably still loves Alex, but does not want to give up a certain amount of independence she has won for herself. Nowadays, a harmonious relationship should be built on love, trust, faith and last but not least on respect for what the other one does. Therefore both partners should be ready for compromises.

On Beauty
By Zadie Smith

Note:
The following text is an extract from the novel "On Beauty" by Zadie Smith, set in Boston. At the centre of the novel is the Belsey family with Howard, a white English-born academic, Kiki, a black woman from Florida, and their three children. Two of them are Jerome (20) and Levi (16). The Belseys are acquainted with the Kippses. The Caribbean-born Mr Kipps and Howard both work at the local college.
One day when cleaning Levi's room, Kiki accidentally discovers a Haitian painting, which has been stolen from Mr Kipps' office. Being shocked, Kiki confronts Levi with the theft.

[…]

"Oh shit:"

They heard the front door open and slam again, Levi looked in that direction hopefully, as if some intervention from upstairs might save him, but Kiki ignored it, yanking him by his sweatshirt to face her. "[…] I *know* no son of mine steals ANYTHING – no child I ever raised took it into his head to steal ANYTHING FROM ANYBODY, Levi, you better open your mouth!"

"We didn't steal it!" managed Levi. "I mean, we took it, but it ain't stealing."

"We?"

"This guy and me, this … guy."

"Levi, give me his name before I break your neck. I am *not* playing with you today, young man. There ain't no games here today."

Levi squirmed. From upstairs came the noise of shouting. "What's …?" he said, but that was never going to work.

"Never *mind* what's going on up there – you better start worrying about what's going on down *here*. Levi, tell me the name of this man *now."*

"Man … it's like … I can't do that. He's a guy … and he's a Haitian guy and –" Levi took a breath and began to speak extremely quickly. "Trust me, you don't even understand, it's like – OK, so, *this painting is stolen anyway.* It don't even *belong* to that guy Kipps, not really – it was like twenty years ago and he just went to Haiti and got all these paintings by lying to poor people and buying them for a few dollars and now they be worth all this money and it ain't *his* money and we're just trying to –"

Kiki pushed Levi hard in the chest. "You *stole* this from Mr Kipps's office because some *guy* told you a lot of *bullshit?* Because some brother spun you a load of conspiracy bullshit? Are you an *idiot?"*

"No! I'm not an idiot – and it's not bullshit! You don't know anything about it!"

"Of *course* it's bullshit – I happen to know this painting, Levi. It belonged to Mrs Kipps. And *she* bought it herself, before she was even married."

This silenced Levi. "Oh, Levi," said Jerome.

"And that isn't even the point, the point is you *stole.* You just *believed* anything these people say. You just gonna believe them all the way to jail. Just want to be cool, show you the big man around a load of *no-good Negroes* who don't even –"

"IT AIN'T LIKE THAT!"

"That's *exactly* what it's like. It's those guys you been spending all your time with – you can't lie to me. I am so angry at you right now. I am so MAD right now! Levi – I'm trying to understand what you think you've achieved by stealing somebody's property. Why would you *do* this?"

"You don't understand anything," said Levi very quietly.

"What was that? *Excuse* me? WHAT WAS THAT?"

"People in Haiti, they got NOTHING, RIGHT? We living off these people, man! We – we – living off them! We sucking their – blood – we're like vampires! *You* OK, married to your white man in the land of plenty – *you* OK. *You* doing fine. You're living off these people, man!"

Kiki stuck a shaky finger in his face. "You crossing a line right now, Levi. I don't know what you're talking about – I don't think you do either. And I *really* don't know what any of this has to do with you becoming a *thief.*"

"Then why don't you *listen* to what I'm talking about. That painting don't belong to him! Or his wife! These people I'm talking about, they remember how things went down, man – and now look how much it's worth. But that money belongs to the Haitian people, not some … some Caucasian *art dealer,*" said Levi, confidently remembering Choo's phrase. "That money needs to be redis – to be shared."

Kiki was briefly too astounded to speak.

"Umm, that's not the way the world works," said Jerome. "I study economics and I can tell you that isn't the way the world works."

"That's exactly the way the world works! I know you all think I'm some kind of a fool – I'm not a fool. And I been reading, I been watching the news – this shit is *real.* With that money from that painting you could go build a hospital in Haiti!"

"Oh, is *that* what you were intending to do with the money?" asked Jerome, "Build a hospital?"

Levi made a face both sheepish and defiant, "No, not zackly. We was going to *redistribute,*" said Levi successfully. "The funds."

"I see. So how exactly were you gonna sell it? Ebay?"

"Choo had people on that."

Kiki found her voice again. "Choo? Choo? WHO IS CHOO?"

Levi covered his face with both hands. "Oh, *shit.*"

"Levi, … I'm trying to understand what you're telling me," said Kiki slowly, making an effort to calm herself. "And I … I understand that you had concerns about these people, but, baby, Jerome's right, this is not the way you go about solving social problems, this is not how you –"

"So how *do* you do it?" demanded Levi. "By paying people four dollars an hour to clean? That's how much you pay Monique, man! Four dollars! If she was American you wouldn't be paying her no four dollars an hour. Would you? Would you?"

Kiki was stunned.

"You know what, Levi?" she said, her voice breaking. She bent down to put her hands to one side of the painting, "I don't want to talk to you any more."

"Cause you ain't got no answer to that!"

[…] *(904 words)*

Source: Smith, Zadie: On Beauty. London: Penguin, 2006; pp. 427–430

l. 32 show you the big man: non-standard: show that you are the big man
l. 51 Choo: one of Levi's friends (immigrant from Haiti)
l. 60 zackly: exactly
l. 71 Monique: the Belseys' housemaid (of Haitian origin)

Assignments

Comprehension

1 Summarise the contents of the excerpt.

Analysis

2 Analyse the means employed by the author to illustrate the development of the argument between Levi and his mother.

Comment/Creative writing

3 Choose <u>one</u> of the following assignments.

3.1 Discuss Kiki's statement "I understand that you had concerns about these people, but, baby, [...], this is not the way you go about solving social problems ..." (ll. 67–69).

3.2 Forced by his mother, Levi has to write a formal letter of apology to Mr Kipps. Write his letter.

Lösungsvorschläge

Die Aufgabenstellung bezieht sich auf den Prüfungsschwerpunkt Emotions and Drives *(13/1) und steht im engen Zusammenhang mit den Aspekten* human relations, aims and ambitions in one's life, human failure. *Über diesen Prüfungsschwerpunkt hinaus ergeben sich Bezüge zu den Themen* Living in a multicultural society *(12/1) und* One world – global issues *(12/2) der verbindlichen curricularen Vorgaben, aber auch in Ansätzen zu* The postcolonial experience.

1. The novel *On Beauty* was written by Zadie Smith and was published in 2006 by London's Penguin Books Industries.
   The extract of the novel is about a 16-year-old boy, Levi, who stole a Haitian painting from the Caribbean-born Mr Kipps who works at the local college with Levi's father. Dominantly the text is about the heated argument between Levi and his black-skinned mother Kiki who has accidentally found the painting while cleaning Levi's room. In an emotional discussion she strongly disapproves of her son's stealing and therefore demands Levi's viewpoint on the issue. Levi claims that the actual theft was committed by Mr Kipps years ago by buying the painting under value from the Haitian people. Kiki informs her son about the real owner – Mrs Kipps, who bought it before her marriage. She insists that it was theft and that he will end up in prison. Levi defends his position accusing Americans including his own family of living at the Haitians' expense. Kiki and her older son Jerome think that stealing is the wrong way to solve social problems. Finally Levi holds the example of their underpaid Haitian housemaid against his mother. The extract finishes with this, leaving a stunned mother who is extremely upset and breaks up the argument with a broken voice.

2. The excerpt of the novel is written in the perspective of a third person narrator which allows access to an unlimited point of view. As a result the presentation of Kiki's and Levi's positions is based on an unbiased and detached angle. The author succeeds in gaining a high degree of objectivity as the readers are observers and are allowed to witness the developing argument. This enables them to form their own opinion. The author chose a scenic mode of presentation to show the development of the argument. He aims at illustrating their contrasting views on the issue. Additionally he underlines their emotional involvement in the argument. As a result the author reveals the reversal of their position in the course of the discussion. When the argument starts Kiki speaks long sentences. The author shows her self-confidence, anger and persistence to take the matter seriously at the beginning (ll. 5–7, 11/12, 15/16). Her unchanged position on the issue in the course of the quarrel is shown in lines 31–33 and 45/46. As the argument reaches its climax Kiki's replies show a clear lack of self-confidence and power. Therefore her disappointment and defeat and thus the end of the clash are presented in lines 66–69 and 73–76. In contrast to Kiki, Levi starts his part of the dialogue in a rather unstructured way, characterized through short and more emotional replies rather than strong and powerful counterarguments. He states his opposing position (ll. 19–22), defends himself (l. 26, l. 33),

gets furious during the argument (ll. 47–51, ll. 55–57), challenges his mother (ll. 70–72) in order to finally celebrate his rhetorical triumph over his mother.
The language used by the protagonists is informal, partly slang "man" (ll. 17, 49, 71), "Oh shit" (ll. 2, 65), "bullshit" (ll. 24, 26, 27), "You OK [...] You doing fine." (l. 42) or "No, not zackly. We was going to distribute ..." (ll. 60/61). By employing the register of non-standard English the author succeeds in illustrating the heated argument, as it is very likely and authentic that arguing people do not think about appropriate language when they are screaming at each other. Also when Kiki is losing her temper and when Levi rebels against his middle-class background the language reflects their behaviour.
Other stylistic means that emphasize both protagonists' determination and anger are repetitions and anaphora such as in "I know no son of mine steals anything – no child I ever raised took it into his head to steal anything From anybody" (ll. 5/6) or in "I know you all think I'm some kind of fool – I'm not a fool." (ll. 55/56). Additionally one can find hyperbolic sentences such as "before I break your neck" (l. 11), "believe them all the way to jail" (l. 31), which express the mother's fury and her awareness of the seriousness of the situation. "We are sucking their – blood – we are like vampires" (l. 41) Levi replies and states his view on the stealing and his rebellion against his father and American background.

3.1 In Zadie Smith's novel *On Beauty* the 16-year-old boy Levi tries to help poor Haitians by stealing a rich man's property and plans to redistribute the money he earns by selling the stolen picture. His mother replies in a heated argument that she understands that Levi has concerns about those people, but that this is not the way to solve social problems. But is she right in her assumption that the small man cannot do anything about social problems?
On the one hand she is right, as it is the wrong way to start changing the world by stealing someone's property. That was maybe accepted in times of Robin Hood, but it is definitely not an appropriate way to right wrongs in today's society. On the other hand he has done it correctly, because he just went outside and with his youthful idealism did something against unequal treatment instead of sitting at home and just talking about it. Despite that it is always important what you believe in and whom you believe in. Levi just followed a friend agreeing to the theft, because he did not question his motives. It is common knowledge that blind obedience is always a bad guide. It is of paramount importance to be critical on the matter and then to agree after thorough consideration. Kiki for sure meant a procedure like that when she criticized Levi's acting. After having discussed the question of how to approach this social issue, there is still the question of responsibility especially the responsibility Levi feels Americans have. He clearly feels a responsibility of the rich nations to support the poor and accuses his parents of doing nothing for those people. He claims that they are even released from that responsibility to such an extent that they can follow their American middle-class lifestyle. Levi does not experience that his parents even think about legal ways of aid. Maybe that's why he chose an illegal one. The excerpt of the novel is only an example of the problems occurring in our

global world. It is undeniable that all rich nations should be concerned about social injustices. It is not far enough to say that developing countries merely profit from globalization. Of course foreign investments stimulate their economy and let them feed their families, but that does not justify ignoring exploitation of any kind.
In conclusion it has to be said that crime is never a solution. However sometimes especially young people feel forced by their youthful carelessness to do something immediately. Mothers like Kiki only doubt the way their children chose and fear the possible influence supposed friends, who pretend to be interested in doing something good but mainly long for money, could have on their kids. I do not think that they question the necessity of encouraging progress in developing countries. Unfortunately or thank goodness adults are not as passionate and spontaneous as teenagers. As a result they are less likely to get actively involved. Consequently they think more about their actions, a necessary step to educate their children.

3.2 *Hier müssen Sie einen formellen Brief verfassen. Achten Sie dabei auf den Bezug zu dem im Text dargestellten Problem. Sie müssen den Anlass Ihres Schreibens deutlich machen und die Entschuldigung angemessen formulieren. Legen Sie auch Levis Beweggründe dar.*

Dear Mr Kipps,

To follow my mother's order I am writing to you today to apologize for stealing "your" Haitian painting. You need to know that I feel really sorry about that, but not because you lost your property – I feel sorry for the way I did that.
I know that my dad is your colleague, and beg you not to blame him for the thoughts and opinion I will reveal to you in my letter. You know that my mother is black and you also know that we have a certain standard of living because my mother married my white American father. Our little world and the way we perceive society is free of injustices. But beyond the fortunate circumstances of our family there are those who still suffer exploitation. The painting me and my friend stole from your office is a Haitian painting. Even if your wife brought it into your marriage, I cannot imagine that any of you paid the price the painting is worth. I heard and saw a lot about how people in Haiti are deceived. They sell the painting they have worked on for months for a few dollars not because they are dumb, but because they have no other chance to earn money. Of course tourists like you and your wife think you are doing them a favour, but in fact you treat them badly. I was especially shocked when I got to know that you as a Caribbean behave in the same exploitive way as other Americans who pay their Haitian housemaid only little money. You live off those people just like vampires who suck blood out of their victims. I thought you had a different attitude. Maybe you ask what a teenager like me knows about these issues, but I really care about others and know what I am talking about.
Let me emphasise again that it was not my intention to harm you and that I regret the way things turned out to be. I still hope that my words give you food for thought.

Best wishes, Levi Belsey

Abiturprüfung Brandenburg 2008
Englisch Leistungskurs – Aufgabe 2

Text A Great "Devil" lesson: Life is too short to work for Miranda Priestly

By Jennifer Hunter

So, I asked my daughter, who always has strong opinions about everything: "How would you like to have a boss like Miranda Priestly (as played by Meryl Streep in the film "The Devil Wears Prada")?"

Her reply: "How would I like to have hemorrhoids?"

Yes, Miranda Priestly, editor of the fictitious Runway fashion magazine, is a witch. She's abusive, she's mercurial, she accepts nothing less than perfection and she never, ever says thank you unless she's absolutely forced to.

But think how much you can learn from a woman who cares so much about her job, who pays so much attention to detail, who demands only the best and won't accept anything less, who pushes and pushes her employees so the magazine they produce is the envy of the industry.

My daughter says you can learn from your boss without being kicked in the butt, and she has a point. And Miranda-style bosses are generally detested by their underlings because they seem to take and take and never give back, and their turnover of minions is legendary. But Miranda is also that cliché about the working woman who has risen to the top by employing every drop of testosterone in her body and outmaneuvering the men surrounding her, which she does in the movie with aplomb. In fact, the movie character is much more true to life than the cardboardish one in the book; occasionally Streep has a little gleam in her eye, hinting that underneath the Brunhilda breastplate lurks a humane soul who's afraid to let anyone know she's a real person.

I once had a boss like Miranda – although I must add I've had some wretched male bosses, too. My Miranda was very good at managing up but bad at managing down. She had oodles of panache and wore miniskirts and spike heels to the office. And since she had terrific legs, her male bosses ogled her every time she walked by. She was highly intelligent and brash about the way she ran our magazine, and readers responded positively.

But she was imperious and ungenerous to her employees and rarely tossed us a word of approval. In fact, she seemed to go out of her way to make our lives more miserable by changing her mind again and again. And, like Miranda Priestly's subordinates, we often tried to second-guess what she would want – which never worked because none of us could ever think like she did.

Once a colleague had to take time off work because his son was in the hospital. When he got back to the office, my boss didn't ask how his son was. Her first words: "So, you've decided to return to work." She really was soulless.

We were afraid to take one minute extra on lunch hour; we sweated as she edited our copy; we talked in hushed tones so we wouldn't disturb her. But we admired her brilliance; she could help us craft a beautiful sentence and use her red marker to slash the superfluous. We recognized that despite the crap she threw at us, we could learn from her about writing, reporting and structuring a magazine story. She was mean but she was gifted.

And despite the Valkyrie-like exterior, she seemed deeply uncomfortable in her skin, as if the persona of the well-put-together, smarter-than-anyone-else-in-the-room gal was a script she herself sometimes found hard to follow.

The Anne Hathaway character in "The Devil Wears Prada" couldn't tolerate Miranda Priestly's depredations and quit; I eventually said adieu to my bulldozer of a boss, too. But at least I could tell my daughter I never developed hemorrhoids.

(621 words)

l. 15	minions: (derog.) employee of low rank
l. 17	aplomb: confidence, esp. in difficult situations
l. 20	Brunhilda: masculine queen in the "Nibelungen Lied"
ll. 23/24	manage up/manage down: here: cooperate with superiors/subordinates
l. 24	oodles: great amounts of sth.
l. 24	panache: manner that has style and confidence
l. 25	ogle: (derog.) to look or stare at sb., esp. a woman
l. 26	brash: (derog.) confident in a rude, noisy or aggressive way
l. 28	imperious: proud and expecting obedience
l. 42	Valkyrie: warrior-maiden
l. 45	Anne Hathaway: actress starring in the movie "The Devil Wears Prada"
l. 46	depredation: damage caused by an attack, accident etc

Text B

Source: Thompson, Robert: www.cartoonstock.com

corporate ladder: here: career ladder

Assignments

Comprehension

1. Summarise what you learn about the boss Jennifer Hunter once had.

Analysis

2. Analyse the means the author employs to create a vivid picture of female high-pressure bosses (Text A).

3. Describe the cartoon and explain its message (Text B).

Comment/Creative writing

4. Choose one of the following assignments.

4.1 Considering texts A and B (cartoon), discuss whether a female employee can only rise to the top "… by employing every drop of testosterone in her body and outmaneuvering the men surrounding her …" (cf. ll. 16/17).

4.2 The year 2007 was the "European Year of Equal Opportunities for All". For this reason the European Union provides a platform for young people to voice their opinion related to equal opportunities on the website: http:/ec.europa.eu.

Against the background of texts A and B, submit your view on women's underrepresentation in high-profile jobs in an online article.

Lösungsvorschläge

Die Aufgabenstellung bezieht sich auf den Prüfungsschwerpunkt Emotions and Drives *(13/1) und steht im engen Zusammenhang mit den Aspekten* human relations, aims and ambitions in one's life, human failure.

1. *Aufgrund der verschiedenen im Text verwendeten Zeitebenen können Sie für Ihre Darstellung sowohl das Präsens als auch das Präteritum verwenden.*

   In her article, published on the 12th of July in 2006 in the Chicago Sunday Times, Jennifer Hunter writes about a mean and horrible female boss she once worked for. Without saying her name, the author describes her as a very clever woman, with an extremely strict nature and states that she is looked at for her female attraction by her male superiors. In her authentic way to run the magazine, she never seemed to make any mistake and is determined to instruct her employees. Her style of running the magazine in a rather presumptuous way demands a lot from her employees in terms of obedience, punctuality and discipline. The author's boss never shows any interest in a harmonic atmosphere at work. She rather puts her employees under pressure, failing to give them any praise. Her insensitive behaviour always caused a tense and frightened mood amongst her employees. Besides she lacks showing any emotions or interest in private matters, caring only about business. Despite that, Hunter points out that the boss is admired for doing her job excellently. It sometimes seems hard for her to live up to her own ideals, so she seems arrogant, but is in fact self-conscious.

2. The author succeeds by employing various means to create a clear picture of women in leading positions. Those means describe all characteristics necessary to instruct employees or to assure respect. Furthermore the chosen means show how hard, demanding and careless female bosses act with others and themselves. Additionally the high level of proficiency those bosses possess is mentioned, which contrasts their utter lack of social competences. In order to develop this picture the author uses various enumerations like "She's abusive, she is mercurial, […]" (l. 6), "… who pushes and pushes her employees […]" (ll. 10 f.) and "But think […] who cares so much about her job, who pays […]" (ll. 8 f.). The author's aim is to emphasize that the two females are brilliant on the one hand and to depict the fear they cause among their employees on the other hand. To give the reader an idea of what it means to work under such demanding bosses and to illustrate their behaviour exaggerations are employed such as "… she never, ever … […] unless she's absolutely forced to." (l. 7), "… and won't accept anything less …" (ll. 9/10), "… employing every drop of testosterone […]" l. 16) and "their turnovers of minions is legendary." (ll. 14/15). To cause a strong impact on the reader's imagination of bosses that act inhumane, brutal, strict and reckless the author uses various adjectives and intensifying adverbs such as "imperious and ungenerous" (l. 28), "rarely tossed us a word of approval" (ll. 28/29), "to make our lives more miserable" (ll. 29/30) and "she really was soul-

less" (l. 35). To point out their tough management and their excellence at their job various contrasts are employed such as in "But think how much you can learn […] who cares so much about her job …" (ll. 8/9), "But we admired her brilliance …" (ll. 37/38) or in "She was mean but she was gifted" (ll. 40/41). Finally two metaphors create a last very strong image of their dreadful behaviour. The author calls them "witch[es] (l. 6), refers to "the Brunhilda breastplate" (l. 20) and "the Valkyrie-like exterior" (l. 42) or calls them derogatively "my bulldozer of a boss" (ll. 46/47).

3. *Bei Ihrer Cartoonbeschreibung sollten Sie zuerst auf die Quelle und das Thema des Cartoons eingehen. Beschreiben Sie dann Elemente und Details. Am Schluss sollten Sie diese erklären. Dabei können Sie folgende Punkte anführen:*
   - *women's chances to get a high-profile job are limited*
   - *women faced with obstacles when wanting to make a career for themselves*
   - *no equality of opportunity*
   - *men advantaged position*
   - *women need more strength, higher motivation and greater effort to climb the career ladder*

The cartoon was drawn by Robert Thomson and published on the Internet (www.cartoonstock.com). The subject of the cartoon can be defined "women and career". A woman is shown on the left, dressed in business-like fashion. Her face exemplifies a harsh and disappointed expression. She is coming around a corner and finds herself standing in front of two differently sized ladders propped against a wall. Two labels clearly identify those two ladders. The short one for women and the longer one for men. In the centre the caption "corporate ladders" is placed.
Women's chances to get a high profile job are limited. It is not doubtful that this is exactly the message the cartoon wants to convey. Most women are faced with obstacles if they want to have a career for themselves. Still there is no equality of opportunity and men enjoy an advantageous position in the world of labour. Much more strength, motivation and a greater effort are necessary for women to climb up the career ladder. Even if a woman meets all these prerequisites her career opportunities may not be as great as those of her male colleagues.

4.1 *Hier müssen Sie einen klar strukturierten, argumentativen Text erstellen, dessen Elemente* main part – introduction – conclusion *deutlich erkennbar sein müssen. Achten Sie dabei auch auf Textbezug, integrieren Sie aber ebenso außertextliche Sachverhalte in Ihre Darstellung. Ihre eigene Wertung muss überzeugend dargestellt werden.*

If you look at the development of society, it is quite obvious, that the role of men and women has changed enormously over the last decades. The lives of many women have altered from traditional, home-centred to flexible ones that are focused on work and a successful career. More and more men do the housework or take care of the children during their maternity leave. The whole development seems to show, that both men and women have an equal state in society that does not depend on their gender. It is good to see that the development is going in this direction. Despite this however I am not convinced that we have already reached a state of total equality. I strongly oppose the quotation whereas female employees can rise to the top … "only by employing every drop of testosterone in her body and outmanoeuvring the men surrounding …". It is far too easy to reduce the current situation to gender issues only. Furthermore there are various reason to be mentioned which complicate a woman's career. It is common knowledge that job positions like politicians, artists and bosses of huge enterprises are strongly dominated by men. It is an undisputable fact that women have to face certain obstacles that make their careers rather difficult. Considering the quotation it is true that most women need to take advantage of their female attractiveness (ll. 24/25) to impress their employers beginning with the job interview, because male superiors don't even consider a female being able to cope with demanding job profiles. But once they have caught their attention, there might be at least a slight chance to compete against male applicants. Employers expect perfection and demand maximum effort (l. 6) from women. In order to keep the job, they have to work very hard. When instructing inferiors they hide their feelings so nobody accuses them of too much emotion and less professionalism. As far as that the quotation might have some truth but the fact that society does not provide women with appropriate means to surmount obstacles additionally complicates the women's situation. Many women do not even get this far. For many it is impossible to work after they have finished their studies successfully and decided to have children. Germany's family minister von der Leyen initiated more kindergarten places to be installed to enable women to return to work a short time after giving birth to their children. So even if women are offered high positions it is demanding and challenging for them to find a balance between job, career and family. The female high-pressure bosses like in J. Hunter's article show terrible examples for women in high positions and it is true that many successful women seem to be a bit brutal – maybe masculine too. In my opinion it seems like women really have to be strict and even more confident to compete with their male colleagues but I do not believe that success directly depends on gender, but rather on a self-confident, ambitious and authentic attitude.

However there is one issue that still concerns me a lot: success does not only mean success in terms of well-paid jobs. A loving family or a vital relationship also seems worth longing for. For some women the management of a little family business includes everything success consists of and for sure in this sector women do not need to employ every drop of testosterone to be successful. Finally it is important for everyone to think about personal prospects and to define clearly which career matches one's attitude most.

4.2 *Legen Sie zuerst Ihre Sichtweise bezüglich der geringen Zahl von Frauen in Spitzenpositionen dar. Beziehen Sie dabei Beispiele aus dem Unterricht oder Ihre eigenen Erfahrungen mit ein. Folgende Ansatzpunkte können Sie aus Text A nehmen:*
- *women in top positions behave like men*
- *they must be determined and have a dog-eat-dog mentality*
- *they assert themselves rather than to cooperate*

Folgende Ansatzpunkte aus Text B können Sie aufgreifen:
- *obstacles prevent women from having careers*
- *women lack equal means to surmount obstacles*

Stand by your (wo)man

Once a survey was carried out in the classrooms of high schools. A teacher wrote the sentence "A woman without her man is nothing" on the blackboard and asked the pupils to set the punctuation. Most of the boys wrote: "A woman, without her man, is nothing" whereas the girls preferred "A woman: without her, man is nothing."
This story is always good for a laugh but there is a deeper wisdom in it that cannot be ignored: After years of emancipation it becomes clear, men and women are still different. What a surprise? But one cannot deny the fact that improvements have been made. In the past women had to pretend to be male to reach credibility and success. Today a woman can be a woman, can't she? Not if we believe the article of J. Hunter. She says that women have to awake their "inner man" if they want to survive in the world of business and career. That would be like a "please-be-heartless-call" to every woman. Hey Eva, forget that you like children. Sell your soul and natural destination for money and success! No wait, you do not have to draw a moustache on your face. Does it really make sense to state that the reason for women's underrepresentation lies in them not being willing to be rough and tough and mean? Why should women deny their emotional and sensitive qualities? These qualities could actually help us be a nice boss everybody likes to work for. So what is the secret of women like Angela Merkel and Hilary Clinton? How did they manage to get to the top? Some weeks ago Angela Merkel wore an extremely feminine dress for an evening in the opera. Every newspaper showed this picture of Germany's number one and her décolleté. It was a huge scream running through the nation: Oh my Goodness she is a woman. Congratulations. You finally got it. I can only advise every woman who reads this article: Do not hide you feminine side! Use it! Your gender does not tell you how far you can get. If a man is allowed to show his muscles then you are allowed to make a statement through your décolleté!
The favourite argument of our masculine colleagues is that we are the only ones who can give birth to children and therefore need to make a decision between job and career. Our generation was brought up differently. We put a lot of effort into our education and the reason why women are underrepresented in high-profile jobs cannot only be seen in our gender, but also in today's society which does not provide equal chances for women to find a balance between a job, children and family. Women need to decide between sneakers and high heels and no longer between children and career. Because we are women and we can have it all.

Abiturprüfung Brandenburg 2009
Englisch Grundkurs – Aufgabe 1

Text A One world – global issues

Forest protection fund targets Congo basin

By Julian Borger

Africans are offered an alternative to logging and subsistence farms

The biggest ever fund set up to battle deforestation has been launched this month, targeting the vast Congo basin rainforest in central Africa. Britain and Norway are providing \$ 216 m and will also supply satellite imaging technology to monitor the area.

The fund is intended to provide African governments and people living in the rainforest with a viable alternative to logging, mining, and felling trees for firewood and subsistence farming.

The Congo basin rainforest is the world's biggest after the Amazon, at about twice the size of France, but is rapidly dwindling. It is being cut down at the rate of 25,000 football pitches a week, accounting for 18 % of annual carbon dioxide emissions.

Projects will be eligible for funds if they can demonstrate that they will curb the destruction of forest by providing alternative sources of income or energy, for example. Their effectiveness will be monitored by high-definition cameras made in the UK due to be mounted on satellites. "We are pledging to work together to secure the future of one of the world's largest remaining ancient forests," Gordon Brown said at the scheme's launch. Britain initiated the fund and is providing \$ 116 m.

Jens Stoltenberg, the Norwegian prime minister, whose government is putting \$ 100 m into the scheme, said the money spent was the most immediate and cost-effective way to combat greenhouse gas emissions. "By doing something about deforestation is \$ 6 per metric tonne of CO_2 compared with \$ 100–200 a tonne for carbon-capture schemes.

British and Norwegian officials acknowledge that the biggest challenge will be ensuring that the money is effectively spent. The Congo rainforest sprawls across Cameroon, the Central African Republic, the Democratic Republic of the Congo, Equatorial Guinea, Gabon and Congo-Brazzaville. Across large swaths, corruption is rife and mining and logging companies are prepared to offer large rewards to communities and regional authorities to open up their forests.

"Everyone knows how not to cut down a tree," Stoltenberg said. "The big challenge is the institutions, the framework, the monitoring and the control, I don't believe that is easy but that cannot prevent us from trying." [...] *(360 words)*

Source: Borger, Julian, THE GUARDIAN WEEKLY, June 27, 2008, p. 5

subsistence farm: farm that produces just enough food for the farmer to live on, but does not produce enough food to sell

l. 5 viable: successful

l. 11 eligible: qualified to be chosen

l. 15 Gordon Brown: British prime minister

l. 20 metric tonne: a unit for measuring weight equal to 1000 kg

l. 20/21 carbon-capture scheme: method to store CO_2 underground e. g. in spent oil fields rather than releasing it into the atmosphere

l. 25 swath: area of land

Text B

Source: Kondenko, Igor, Ukraine: Welcome to Amazonia, www.kenspraguefund.org. Reproduced courtesy of the Ken Sprague Fund

Kettensäge: chainsaw

Assignments

Comprehension

1. Outline the information on the Congo Basin Forest Fund and the challenges it might face. (Text A)

Analysis

2. Analyse the means the author employs to show the importance of the project. (Text A)

3. Describe the cartoon and explain its message. (Text B)

Comment/Creative Writing

4. Choose <u>one</u> of the following assignments.

4.1 Referring to the project introduced in the article (Text A), discuss its relevance to fight climate change. Also consider the message of the cartoon. (Text B)

4.2 Assume the *Guardian Weekly's* publisher intends to illustrate the article (Text A) with a cartoon. Discuss whether the given cartoon (Text B) is a suitable choice.

Lösungsvorschläge

1. *Markieren sie sich im Text die Informationen zum Fond und dessen Herausforderung(en). Es gelten die Regeln der* summary, *d. h. Sie müssen das Wichtigste in einem zusammenhängenden, logisch strukturierten Text zusammenfassen.*

   The Congo Basin Forest Fund is the biggest fund ever founded to combat deforestation. Norway and Britain both provide $216 m and also supply the necessary technology. The fund was set up to give locals and the African government an opportunity to move away from logging and subsistence farming. Alternative sources of income or energy are thus encouraged and financed by this project. To ensure that the fund's money is used effectively, surveillance cameras were mounted. The fund's aim is to provide an opportunity to benefit from alternative sources of income and to fight against greenhouse gas emissions.
   It is however difficult to monitor the process and to guarantee that the money is effectively spent, because corruption is widely spread and mining companies offer huge rewards if forests are opened up for them. To undermine such proceedings will certainly be the fund's greatest challenge.

2. *Hier können Sie auf inhaltliche (detaillierte Beschreibungen, Zerschlagen von Zweifeln und Gegenargumenten, Zitate, Zahlen, positives Zitat am Textende) sowie sprachliche Mittel (Superlative, Vergleiche, Wortwahl) und Stilmittel eingehen und so Ihren Text gliedern. Vergessen Sie dabei nicht, Textbelege zu bringen.*

   The importance of the project is stressed by the article's structure: it contains detailed explanations about the Congo basin and its deforestation and about the project and its effectiveness. Concrete numbers are given to convince the reader: "25,000 football pitches a week" (l. 9) are destroyed, "accounting for 18 % of annual carbon dioxide emissions" (ll. 9/10). Also the cost-effectiveness of the project is stressed in lines 19 to 21. The reader is also assured that the money will not go down the drain, because the "effectiveness will be monitored" (l. 13) and "the money is effectively spent" (l. 23), so any arising doubts are dissipated at once. In the end, the positive quotation that even if it is a big challenge it "cannot prevent us from trying" (l. 30) sets the mood of the text and the reader gets the impression that the project is well-thought-out and bound to be a success.
   Also the author's choice of words reflects the importance of the fund. Superlatives stress the gigantic scope of the project: it is "the biggest ever fund" (l. 1), the Congo basin is "the world's biggest after the Amazon" (l. 7), the money spent is "the most immediate and cost-effective way" (ll. 18/19) and the project is "the biggest challenge" (l. 22). Quotations from "officials" (l. 22) also add to the project's importance. Stoltenberg and Brown assure the readers not only of their determination, but also of the project's effectiveness and necessity. The author also tries to make the scope of the project palpable to his readers by comparing the Congo basin's size (which probably no reader has a clear conception of) to that of France and the di-

mension of the deforestation to the size of football pitches. This stimulates the reader's imagination and emphasizes the urgency to start acting and venture such a huge project.

3. *Der Cartoon enthält wenige Details. Das bedeutet für Sie aber, dass Sie auf alle eingehen sollten (Säge, Umgebung, Skeletthand, Schild und Ufo). Vergessen Sie nicht, nach einer Beschreibung auch auf die Botschaft des Cartoons einzugehen.*

In the cartoon you can see a huge chain saw right in the middle. The hand that once was operating it has now been reduced to bones in the middle of a desert where nothing grows – a very bleak scene indeed. Into the sand someone has planted a sign saying "Welcome to Amazonian Forest", but the thing is, there is no such forest. This is also what the state of the sign suggests: it looks destroyed and has certainly seen better days. A small UFO is just about to leave this sad place, not without commenting that they had visited a "stupid planet". This indicates that they must have known that humans destroyed this Amazonian forest where once huge trees had grown and where life had been prospering. They are of course right about the stupid planet, because by destroying nature man has finally destroyed himself, as the skeleton remains indicate. The message of the cartoon is a simple one: we are about to destroy the basis of our lives, the earth we live on and will eventually eradicate ourselves, which is a very stupid action. The cartoon may thus be seen as a warning that nature will not forgive and that man is totally dependent on her. By gradually destroying his own basis of life, man will finally meet his own death.

4.1 The project mentioned in Text A has been launched to combat deforestation in the Congo Basin in Africa by showing the government and inhabitants alternatives to logging, mining, subsistence farming and felling trees for firewood. More ecological sources of income and energy should be used. Britain and Norway supply the necessary technology and monitor the project's success. In addition to saving costs, the project is also supposed to reduce greenhouse gas emissions.

On the one hand I think it is high time that such projects are put into action, because, as the cartoon's scenario shows, nature will not forgive us the ecological crimes we are committing and sooner or later the consequences will backfire. Especially in Africa, people lack the necessary technology and the financial means to fight against deforestation and the destruction of nature. For many Africans, life is a daily struggle to survive and who cares about nature when his own life is in grave danger? They have a hard time making ends meet for them and their families and any means to earn money is more than welcome. This is, on the other hand, exactly the reason why I am not especially convinced about the project's final success. If mining companies offer more money than the people in charge of the project, deforestation will go on. This is also the main concern referred to in the text: corruption is widely spread in those regions and this could endanger the project immensely. Another question is whether other companies will follow suit and set up comparable projects in other countries. Fighting climate change only makes sense if people all work to-

gether for a common goal and are prepared to make sacrifices. As long as this remains an isolated attempt to fight climate change it will not be successful.
For many people climate change is something theoretical that might not even concern their children in the future, so why care? Raising awareness by showing scenarios that could happen might be the first step. The cartoon already creates such a scenario, but as it is "just" a cartoon, it might seem funny and exaggerated. However there are grains of truth in it, which are not to be underestimated …

4.2 *Wenn Sie sich nicht wirklich entscheiden können oder zu wenige Argumente haben, um in die ein oder andere Richtung zu argumentieren, können Sie auch Argumente dafür und dagegen anbieten. Wichtig ist allerdings, dass Sie am Ende ein Resümee ziehen und sich einer Seite anschließen.*

If I were in charge of illustrating the article, I would certainly consider using the cartoon for two reasons: first, the cartoon depicts a scenario that might happen if deforestation goes on. We are certainly still a long way from destroying humanity by destroying nature, but it might be a possible consequence of our crimes against the environment. As the UFO suggests, we will probably notice too late how stupid we have been. Thus the cartoon emphasizes the urgency of the project mentioned in the text and could therefore be a good choice to accompany the text. Second, the cartoon illustrates the drastic consequences a failure of the project due to corruption might have. It might thus shake up authorities in Africa and make them cooperate with those in charge of the project rather than with illegal companies. The cartoon is quite menacing and points to the end of the world as we know it. This is of course exaggerated and might make people refrain from taking its message seriously. The text however is a very serious one and should therefore be accompanied by photos of the disastrous consequences of deforestation. This is my only concern against using a cartoon instead of a photo with such an article.
To sum it up, if I had the chance to use a colour photo instead of the cartoon, I would definitely go for the photo. If the print had to be in black and white, the cartoon might be more impressive and shocking and thus be the better choice.

Abiturprüfung Brandenburg 2009
Englisch Grundkurs – Aufgabe 2

Text Emotions and drives

American Youth
By Phil LaMarche

The following text is an excerpt from the novel American Youth *by Phil LaMarche.*
In a working-class New Hampshire town, Kevin Dennison and his brother visit teenage Theodore (Ted) LeClare. When his friends start being bored, Ted shows them his father's handgun and loads it. After Ted has left the room, Kevin accidentally shoots his brother. Persuaded by his mother, Ted lies to the police and his father about having loaded the gun himself. In the given excerpt, Ted and his father are having breakfast on the day after the incident.

[…] the father sat at the head of the table, quiet, patient. This was the father's method: silence, silence for some time, and then the question, a question generally rhetorical in nature. It set the boy to floundering every time.

"So what are we going to do now?" the father said.

The boy shrugged.

"I know what you been through. With the law fixing to come down on you, I can't see throwing another log on the pyre."

The boy squirmed in his chair as a knot formed in his throat. This was another of the father's tactics: unexpected kindness. It worked to choke him up and send him reeling further.

The father shook his head and paused, perhaps to regain his composure. "I've heard what the police and your mother had to say. But I still can't figure how two kids got their hands on a gun in my house."

The boy looked down at the table.

"Well?" the father said.

"I showed them."

"Yeah?"

The boy shrugged. "They wanted to see it."

"So you do whatever any fool wants you to? You know what that makes you?"

The boy had trouble breathing. His throat started to close and his face grew tight.

"Who loaded that gun?"

The boy shrugged.

"Don't give me that."

"I don't know." The boy coughed it out.

"You realize that what you're saying makes no sense at all?"

"It must've been one of them," the boy said. "I didn't do it." He couldn't hold it back any longer and he went full-blown. His sniffing and gurgling were the only sounds in the room for some time. He used his shirt to wipe the tears and snot from his face.

"Quit the crybaby act," the father said. "It ain't going to work on me."

The boy shook his head.

"You best not be," the father said. "There is a dead kid out of this mess and a family who's got to live with that. Your mother's got to teach in a school next week where every Tom, Dick, and Harry knows some kid just got himself killed in her dining room. And me, Ted, I'm a salesman. All I got is a reputation."

"I know," the boy nearly shouted. "Jesus, you think I ain't thought of all that?"

The father flinched. "Good," he said. "So this is what we're going to do. We're not going to say a word about it. Someone asks, you just shrug it off. Pretend like you don't know what they're talking about, like nothing ever happened. This rumor mill of a town doesn't need its fire stoked any more than it is. You get me?"

"Yes," the boy said.

"Good," said the father. "We're lucky we can leave. I don't know how we could stay here after something like this." He slid the chair back under the table before he left the kitchen. Shortly after his departure, the mother returned from her seclusion in the living room. She rubbed the boy's back.

"You did good," she whispered.

"Ma. We can't do this."

"Yes, we can."

"They're going to find out."

"It's your word against Kevin's," she said. "They can't prove anything."

He shook his head.

"If you don't play your cards right, they're going to take you away from me," she said. "And if that isn't enough, they've got something called a civil suit. They find us guilty of negligence or recklessness or God knows what else, those Dennisons will sue us and they will win. You want to lose the house?" she asked him. "The cars? Everything?"

"No," he said and shook his head.

"Then you keep saying what you're saying. Understand?"

He didn't answer.

"Theodore," she said. "We can't take the gun out of Kevin's hands and we can't give that boy back to his poor mother. It's not going to happen. All we're doing is keeping out of trouble. You get it?"

He nodded. His arms were folded on the table before him and he put his forehead in the crook of the elbow, hiding his face in the darkness his body created.

[…] *(685 words)*

LaMarche, Phil: American Youth, Hodder & Stoughton Ltd., London, 2007, pp. 43–46

l. 6 you been through: *(coll)* you have been through
l. 7 throw a log on the pyre: *here:* make sth worse than it is
l. 11 composure: self-control, calmness
l. 20 close: *here:* get dry/have difficulty swallowing
l. 27 go full-blown: *here:* start crying noisily and uncontrollably

l. 32 you best not be: better not
l. 38 shrug off: dismiss, ignore
l. 39 rumor mill: gossiping people
l. 40 fire stoked: *here:* more reason to gossip about
l. 53 civil suit: facing a trial in a law court

Assignments

Comprehension

1 Outline what Ted's parents expect him to do and why.

Analysis

2 Analyse the means employed by the author to give a vivid picture of the father's reaction to the incident and the impact it has on his son.

Comment/Creative Writing

3 Choose <u>one</u> of the following assignments.

3.1 Comment on the parent's plan to cover up their son's involvement in the accident considering their motives, responsibilities, and the consequences of their behaviour.

3.2 Troubled by the accident, Ted writes a diary entry in which he reflects on the incident, his parents' reactions to it, and his own fears. Write this diary entry of about 200 words.

Lösungsvorschläge

1. *Hier geht es darum, die Motive der beiden Elternteile genauer zu analysieren. Beide wollen, dass Ted nichts sagt, aber aus völlig unterschiedlichen Gründen. Die Mutter kennt das gesamte Ausmaß der Tragödie, der Vater geht jedoch von der Unschuld seines Sohnes aus. Für den Vater zählt der Ruf der Familie, die Mutter dagegen hat panische Angst und versucht Ted moralisch unter Druck zu setzen.*

   Ted's parents both expect him not to say anything, but for totally different motives. The father is left in the dark about who really loaded the gun and just wants his son not to say anything because rumours spread easily in town and he wants to avoid gossip. This is the father's conclusion after having tried unsuccessfully to convince Ted to tell the truth and own up to having loaded the gun. Even though the father proceeds quite cleverly, he cannot make Ted tell him the truth. He tries to be kind and sympathetic; he tries to admonish his son and then directly asks the question that intrigues him, who loaded the gun. When Ted starts crying, his father reacts with impatience and anger. For fear of having the family's reputation destroyed he finally convinces his son to keep his mouth shut.
   It is Ted's mother who tells Ted to lie to his father and the police in the first place and to never own up to having loaded the gun. Her line of argumentation is that nothing can be proven and that it is better to keep out of trouble, because things cannot be mended anymore. She also tries to intimidate Ted by claiming that they could lose everything and exaggerating the consequences that might haunt the family if Ted says a word. This also conveys the impression that she is full of fear and panic herself.

2. *Beachten Sie die doppelte Fragestellung: es geht um die Reaktion des Vaters, aber auch um deren Auswirkung auf Ted. Suchen Sie dafür Mittel heraus, mit denen der Autor diese Vorfälle lebendig darstellt. Gehen Sie auf die Erzählsituation (Erzählperspektive, Beobachtungsgabe etc.) und die direkte Rede ein und suchen Sie im Text treffende Beispiele, um Ihre Erkenntnisse zu belegen.*

   The reader has the impression of experiencing this conversation first-hand. The author shows what's happening rather than only telling it. The passages in direct speech also show characteristics of spoken language: the American "It ain't going to work on me" (l. 30), the omission of the full verb in "I know what you been through" (l. 6), the use of the saying "throwing another log on the pyre" (l. 7) and the short questions "Well?" (l. 15) and "Yeah?" (l. 17) create authenticity. Also the psychologically comprehensible inner change of the father's mood from patience and pity to fury and then calmness again conveys a vivid picture of the father's reaction. The third person narrator also contributes to the vivacity of the narration: the narrator does not tell us about the father's feelings, but he is very observant: "This was the father's method: silence, silence for some time …" (ll. 1 ff.) or "perhaps to regain his composure" (l. 11). Throughout the narration the reader gets the impression that the narrator gives away more about Ted and also knows his feelings and thoughts: "The boy squirmed in his chair as a knot formed in his throat" (l. 8) and "The boy had trouble breathing. His throat started to close and his face grew tight" (l. 20). This inevitably leads to the reader experiencing the situation more from Ted's point of view and feeling with him. That's why Ted's outburst in line 26 ff. has a huge effect on the reader who can sense the tense situation and feels that Ted is close to owning up to everything. The reader however has a limited, but subjective perspective and this creates the special mood of the text: the mode of presentation makes the tension of the situation palpable even if it is not directly addressed by the narrator.

3.1 *Fassen Sie ganz kurz zu Beginn Ihrer Diskussion die Motive der Eltern noch einmal zusammen und urteilen Sie dann.*

Ted's father does not know the details of his son's involvement in the accident, but wants him not to say anything because he is afraid of people gossiping and the reputation of his family. Besides, things cannot be mended anymore and perhaps he also thinks about the dead boy's family who, given what they have to go through, should not additionally be troubled with "the rumor mill of a town" (ll. 39/40). Ted's mother by contrast knows that her son loaded the gun, but urges him to keep quiet for fear of having her whole life destroyed: one wonders if she thinks about Ted's future or if she herself is haunted by having her house, her car and her son taking away from her. Or is it just a means of putting pressure onto Ted and menacing him?
Taking these different reactions and motives into account, one must condemn both parents' reactions. Ted's father does not know about Ted's real involvement, so why does he fear for his reputation? Just because it happened in his house? He behaves quite egoistically, as his reactions towards his son reveal: he is impatient ("Quit the crybaby act", l. 30) and shows no understanding for his son's inner trouble. Also the question of whether he really sympathizes with the dead boy's family must be denied, otherwise he would not be talking so disrespectfully about "some kid" that got himself killed in [his] dining room (ll. 34/35). Considering all these facts it becomes obvious that all he thinks of is his reputation. The mother's reactions might seem more understandable: in her mind's eye she can see her family breaking apart and desperately tries to mend everything by silencing Ted. Her family is of utmost importance to her; she does not care about the other family. She is right that even with Ted confessing everything the dead boy will not come back to life, but what she completely ignores is the burden Kevin has to live with. And even if Ted is now willing to keep his mouth shut, he suffers immensely and won't be able to cope with such a huge responsibility either. So Kevin and Ted are the victims of Ted's parents behaviour and probably won't ever be able to overcome such an immense psychological burden.

3.2 *Den Tagebucheintrag sollten Sie als „interior monologue" abfassen. Gehen Sie dabei auf die drei erwähnten Punkte ein: den Vorfall, die Reaktion der Eltern und Teds eigene Sorgen. Streuen Sie Gefühle und Fragen in Ihren Tagebucheintrag ein und beachten Sie die Konventionen dieser Textsorte.*

Dear diary,
if all this just had not happened. If I could turn back time. If I just had not pulled out that gun and loaded it. Oh my God, why did I load it? What a stupid idea. The thing is, it is too late and nothing can ever be mended again. I have destroyed a family just because I wanted to show off. But why did Kevin … No, I do not want to blame him. Did I also destroy my own family? My mom says that if I own up to everything, we will be separated and all our belongings will be taken from us. I would have to ask my father if this can really happen. But how can I ask him when I am not allowed to tell the truth? My dad is quite angry with me and I think he might be a bit suspicious. Is he aware that Kevin does not know how to load a gun? But for my father the incident seems settled, because I promised not to say anything in order not to endanger the family's reputation. But will I really be able to lie in court when it is my word against Kevin's? I will have to avoid direct eye contact with Kevin and his mom, otherwise there will be another crybaby act, as my father puts it, and I will sure as hell tell the truth. But what if I did? I am still minor and I don't think the judge can blame my parents. But what if mom is right and I am taken away from them? Or if they lost the house. Then they would blame me for having destroyed their life and reputation. So far I have "only" destroyed the life of another family. So why destroy two lives? This won't bring Kevin's brother back. But can I really live with such a lie? Oh my God, dear diary, please help me before I go totally nuts. There must be a way out of this dilemma … there must …

Abiturprüfung Brandenburg 2009
Englisch Leistungskurs – Aufgabe 1

One world – global issues

Cheerful in the face of Armageddon

By Decca Aitkenhead

James Lovelock expects 80 % of the human race to be wiped out by 2100

[…]

Lovelock, 88, has been predicting from his one-man laboratory in an old mill in Cornwall since the mid-1960s, and his accuracy has made him one of Britain's most respected independent scientists. He invented a device that detected CFCs, which helped track the growing hole in the ozone layer, and introduced the Gaia hypothesis, a theory that the Earth is a self-regulating super-organism. Initially ridiculed, it now forms the basis of almost all climate science.

For decades his advocacy of nuclear power appalled fellow environmentalists, but recently many have come around to his way of thinking. His latest book, *The Revenge of Gaia,* predicts that by 2020 extreme weather will be the norm, causing global devastation; that by 2040 much of Europe will be Saharan; and parts of London will be underwater. The most recent intergovernmental Panel on Climate Change report deploys less dramatic language but its calculations aren't a million miles from this.

He presents his thoughts with a quiet, unshakable conviction that can be unnerving. More alarming even than his climate predictions is his utter certainty that almost everything we're trying to do about it is wrong. On the day we met, the Daily Mail launched a campaign to rid Britain of plastic shopping bags. The initiative sits comfortably within the current canon of eco-ideas premised on the calculation that individual life style adjustments can still save the planet. This is, Lovelock says, a deluded fantasy.

"It's just too late for it. Perhaps if we'd gone along routes like that in 1967, it might have helped. But we don't have time." Recycling is "almost certainly a waste of time and energy", while having a "green lifestyle" amounts to "ostentatious grand gestures". He distrusts ethical consumption. "Because always, in the end, it turns out to be a scam. Or if it wasn't one in the beginning, it becomes one."

Lovelock concedes that the Mail's plastic bag campaign seems "a good thing". He regards it as more rearrangement of Titanic deckchairs, "but I've learnt there's no point in causing a quarrel over everything". He saves his thunder for the emptiest false promise: renewable energy. "You're never going to get enough energy from wind to run a society such as ours," he says. "Windmills! Oh no. No way of doing it. You can cover the whole country with the blasted things, millions of them. Waste of time."

Britain is going to become a lifeboat for refugees from mainland Europe, so we need to start planning how to survive. To Lovelock, the logic is clear. The sustainability brigade are insane to think we can save ourselves by going back to nature; our only chance will come not from less technology, but more.

Nuclear power, he argues, can solve our energy problem. The bigger challenge will be food. "Maybe they'll synthesise food. I don't know. Synthesising food is not some mad visionary idea: you can buy it in Tesco's, in the form of Quorn. It's not that good, but people buy it. You can live on it." He fears we won't invent the necessary technologies in time, and expects "about 80 %" of the world's population to be wiped out by 2100. Prophets have foretold Armageddon for a long time "but this is the real thing".

It seems an unlikely coincidence that Lovelock became convinced of the irreversibility of climate change in 2004, at the very point when the international consensus was coming round to the need for urgent action. Aren't his theories partly driven by a fondness for heresy? "Not a bit! All I want is a quiet life! But I can't help noticing when things happen, when you go out and find something."

Interviewers often remark upon the discrepancy between Lovelock's predictions of doom, and his good humour. "Well, I'm cheerful!" he says, smiling. "I'm an optimist. It's going to happen." Humanity is in a period exactly like 1938–9, when "we all knew something terrible was going to happen, but didn't know what to do about it". But once the second world war was under way, "everyone got excited, they loved the things they could do, it was one long holiday, so when I think of the impending crisis now, I think in those terms. A sense of purpose, that's what people want."

But then, when he talks about the Earth it is in the purest scientific terms. "There have been seven disasters since humans came on the earth, very similar to the one that's just about to happen. I think these events keep separating the wheat from the chaff. And eventually we'll have a human on the planet that really does understand it and can live with it properly." What would Lovelock do now, I ask, if he were me? He smiles and says: "Enjoy life while you can. Because if you're lucky it's going to be 20 years before it hits the fan." *(815 words)*

Source: Aitkenhead, Decca, The Guardian Weekly, March 28, 2008, p. 14

Armageddon: (in the Bible) battle between good and evil at the end of the world / a terrible war that could destroy the world

l. 4 CFC: Chlorofluorocarbon, a gas formerly used in fridges and aerosols

l. 5 Gaia: ancient Greek name for earth

l. 24 ostentatious: acting in a way that is meant to impress people

l. 26 scam: clever and dishonest plan for making money

l. 40 Tesco: British supermarket chain

l. 40 Quorn: substance made from a type of fungus, used in cooking instead of meat

l. 48 heresy: belief or opinion that disagrees strongly with what most people believe

ll. 59/60 separate the wheat from the chaff: distinguish the useful / valuable people / things from the ones that are not useful

l. 63 hit the fan: serious trouble will start

Assignments

Comprehension

1 Outline James Lovelock's views on environmentalism and on future developments of the earth.

Analysis

2 Analyse the means used by the author to present Lovelock's vision of the future.

Comment/Creative writing

3 Choose one of the following assignments.

3.1 "Enjoy life while you can. Because if you're lucky it's going to be 20 years before it hits the fan." (ll. 62/63)
Discuss Lovelock's advice to the author considering the global and moral responsibilities of your generation.

3.2 Write a letter to the editor referring to those of Lovelock's views that provoke your response.

Lösungsvorschläge

1. *Es wird erwartet, dass Sie die wesentlichen Aspekte zusammengefasst darlegen und dabei weitgehend eigene Formulierungen verwenden. Achten Sie darauf, Interpretationen, Wertungen und unnötige Details zu vermeiden. Es ist wichtig, ein deutliches Bild von Lovelocks Sichtweisen über aktuelle Umweltschutzbemühungen und zu erwartende Entwicklungen auf der Erde zu zeichnen.*

The article "Cheerful in the face of Armageddon" by Decca Aitkenhead deals on the one hand with Lovelock's opinion about the way people tackle environmental problems, and on the other hand with the consequences he foresees for our planet.
Lovelock, one of Britain's highly regarded scientists, has been observing climatic changes for a long time and concluded that it will definitely end up with the whole world being devastated in the not too distant future.
Turning to the efforts taken by people to save the environment or at least improve conditions, he claims that almost all these attempts are wrong.
He means that all initiatives taken are deceptive as they could never ever produce sufficient effects to bring about the desired alterations. Even if people decided to change their ways of life completely, it would be too late.

Furthermore, Lovelock assumes that activities based on ethical principles might become part of commercial interests sooner or later.
As far as alternative energies are concerned, he criticizes the insufficient effect of wind parks and favours the use of nuclear power instead. He is convinced that the future of the planet will very much depend on the proper development and application of modern technology.
The same applies to nutrition which should be guaranteed with the help of artificial methods.
Lovelock doubts that people grasp the complete seriousness of the situation in order to react fast enough. However, according to him, times of crises have often appeared as impetus to make people aware and become creative and energetic to find solutions.
Finally, the reader is confronted with Lovelock's view that the earth on the one hand has always found ways to recover, even from the worst catastrophes. But all things considered, it can be said that Lovelock is convinced, no matter what will be done or happen, that the majority of the world's population will stop existing. So people should enjoy life as long as possible.

2. *Bearbeiten Sie den Text analytisch, wobei Sie Intention und Wirkung klar herausstellen und belegen müssen. Sie erkennen, dass die Autorin Lovelocks Ansichten überwiegend kommentarlos darbietet. Sie entwirft das Bild eines Wissenschaftlers, der kontroverse Reaktionen hervorruft, dessen Lebenswerk jedoch die Ernsthaftigkeit seiner Arbeitsergebnisse unterstreicht.*

The author presents Lovelock's vision of the future with the help of various means. She starts right away with a catching headline which also represents an allusion and perfectly well illustrates the scientist's sceptical view concerning the capabilities of humankind.
To reflect her controversial ideas she avoids making any personal comments to a large extent. Instead, she employs indirect speech and quotations such as "It's just too late for it." (l. 22), "Recycling is 'almost certainly a waste of time and energy." (ll. 23/24), "I'm an optimist." (ll. 51/52) to illustrate Lovelock's critical, sometimes controversial view of the measures undertaken so far.
Lovelock's concern is expressed in a metaphorical, almost ironic, way by describing certain efforts as a "rearrangement of Titanic deckchairs" (l. 28), calling "foretold Armageddon" (l. 43) as "but this is the real thing" (ll. 43/44) and finally giving advice to enjoy life "[…] before it hits the fan" (l. 63).
When using words such as "emptiest false promise" (ll. 29/30), "bigger challenge" (l. 38), "in the purest scientific terms" (l. 57) Lovelock underlines that serious consideration should be given to the environmental situation. Furthermore, Lovelock's recognition as a scientist is emphasized by referring to his news with expressions such as "with a quiet, unshakable conviction" (l. 15) and "his utter certainty" (l. 16). By including references to what other experts think of Lovelock's achievements like "one of Britain's most respected independent scientists" (ll. 3/4), "recently many

have come around to his way of thinking" (l. 9) and "its calculations aren't a million miles from his" (ll. 13/14) this impression is further manifested. Thus a balanced image of a trustworthy scientist is created.
In the end, the author employs contrast such as in "discrepancy between Lovelock's predictions of doom, and his good humour" (ll. 50/51) not only to show the seriousness of his predictions but also to point out the ambivalence of his hope for the ability of mankind to prevent the worst.
On the whole it can be said that the author has drawn the picture of a scientist who has caused a lot of controversy, but should be taken seriously regarding his life's work and the results of his research.

3.1 *Erstellen Sie einen logisch strukturierten argumentativen Text, in dem Sie das Zitat erläutern. Stellen Sie auch den entsprechenden Textbezug her und illustrieren Sie Ihre Argumentation durch außertextliche Sachverhalte. Sie sollten klar herausarbeiten, dass Lovelocks Sicht im Widerspruch steht zu bekannten Theorien von Umweltschützern und Wissenschaftlern. Außerdem sollten Ihre Gedanken bezüglich der Verantwortung für künftige Generationen einfließen und zu einer kritischen Auseinandersetzung mit dem Zitat führen.*

Regularly fed with predictions about the end of the world – what is left to do for the individual and how far should he or she care at all?
Regarding Mother Earth as our beautiful "home", including that great variety of species and beautiful landscapes, it is almost unbelievable that all that unique wealth is put at stake by the human inhabitants themselves.
So if we are all definitely faced with extinction, why not follow Lovelock's advice to "Enjoy life while you can. Because if you're lucky, it's going to be 20 years before it hits the fan." (ll. 62/63). By saying so Lovelock presents an almost fatalistic view on the future, implying that, whatever will happen, cannot be prevented anyway.
Consequently, we are supposed to believe that in the near future our planet will fall victim to a global ecological and humanitarian disaster. Lovelock, however, also claims that so far people have always coped with catastrophes and finally survived. Moreover, they were then armed with worthwhile experience and knowledge to pave new ways into the future (cf. ll. 57–59).
Furthermore, environmentalists take a lot of efforts to fight further destruction while scientists are trying hard to come up with discoveries and hopefully innovative solutions to stop that process which might take us closer to the "foretold Armageddon" (l. 43).
I mean we should not forget that we, the human beings, are an undeniable part of the circle of life, of nature. It is common knowledge that our planet can do without the species of man, but we cannot live without what nature provides. I am absolutely convinced that we have to face a moral as well as global responsibility. The most pressing environmental problems such as the climate change, the energy question, food and water supply and transportation need to be solved. But it is only too obvi-

ous that they will not be restricted to one or two countries. Pollution does not stop at any border, and while the process of globalisation is continuing, common endeavour is required. I really wonder how a country like Australia, so closely linked with nature, could refuse to sign the Kyoto protocol. I was once deeply impressed by Al Gore's presentation called "An Inconvenient Truth" which deals with the current issue of global warming. He delivers varied, extremely vivid examples that show what drastic changes have already taken place due to human behaviour based on the lack of knowledge, poverty, disrespect, indifference, greed and zest for profit, only to name some motives. But Gore, in contrast to Lovelock, finishes by saying that everyone can contribute and that we should not deny our obligations for future generations.

Not completely agreeing with Lovelock's view, I would say that it might not be too late in every respect. Every person should start by him- or herself to act with care and not to spoil water or energy. But the problem of disposing this huge amount of waste produced in an affluent society like ours, cannot only be tackled by individuals.

Isn't it strange that there are families that decide to establish financial security and take other precautions for their offspring or close relatives, but do not bother about planet earth as the most important basis of life which deserves to be preserved for future generations? Not only we as individuals, but the society as a whole should wonder what the earth we want to pass on to our children and grandchildren should look like.

3.2 *Hier müssen Sie einen Adressaten gerechten, formalen Brief erstellen, der deutlich Bezug zu den Ansichten im Artikel aufweist. Neben wichtigen Aspekten der Textvorlage sind auch außertextliche Ansätze möglich. Ob Sie der Meinung des Wissenschaftlers zustimmen oder widersprechen, bleibt Ihnen überlassen. In jedem Fall aber ist Ihre Darlegung nachvollziehbar zu begründen.*

The Guardian Weekly

Max Mustermann
Mandelweg 12
12157 Berlin

Cheerful in the face of Armageddon

27 April 2009

Sir or Madam,

With reference to your article of 28 March 2008, "Cheerful in the face of Armageddon" I would like to object to the final statement by Lovelock "Enjoy life while you can. Because if you're lucky it's going to be 20 years before it hits the fan." (ll. 62/63) I agree that drastic changes have taken place in recent years and especially the negative effect of global warming cannot be denied any longer. Personally, I am a big animal lover and so I regret in particular the great extent of species which are faced with extinction or have already died out. However, I do not hesitate to clearly voice my scepticism to give advice as quoted in the article.

I am really surprised that there are still people who obviously do not comprehend that everyone has to take responsibility. If we go on carelessly exploiting all our resources, we might end up destroying the foundation we live on. It reminds me of the saying that "we are sawing off the branch we are sitting on." As far as I am concerned I would claim that there is no other alternative than to balance our activities between give and take.

In a way I understand that Lovelock favours nuclear power as it only requires a small amount of radioactivity to produce a lot of energy. But with respect, shouldn't you have found a way to include that nuclear reactors are quite expensive to run and the disposal of nuclear waste has not been solved satisfactorily. Not to mention accidents that could have a devastating effect on people and the environment.

Although the article on the whole is very interesting to read, especially with regard to Mr Lovelock's outstanding personality, I would appreciate it if you had included some more critical questions in the interview. I also miss a hint to a more sustainable lifestyle. Nowadays everything that's possible should be tried and done to raise people's awareness.

However, Lovelock's views might cause some welcome controversy.

I am looking forward to more articles of that kind.

M. Mustermann, Berlin

Abiturprüfung Brandenburg 2009
Englisch Leistungskurs – Aufgabe 2

Text A Gender issues

The world is still organized to meet the wishes of men

By Rosie Boycott

Thirty-six years ago, as the winter of 1971 turned into spring, Marsha Rowe and I were putting together the first issues of Spare Rib. Our tiny office in Soho hummed with excitement and ideas and, above all, hope. Hope that finally women would move out of the shadows and into a world in which we would have equal rights in education and the workplace. Then, although it is hard now to believe it, a woman couldn't even get a mortgage unless her husband or father signed on the dotted line as guarantor.

Over the next decade, the lives of women in Britain were transformed. Girls and young women started out-performing men across the educational spectrum. We had rights to abortion and, legally at least, to equal pay. Once almost impossible career choices – such as law, the armed forces and high-level politics – opened up. The 1969 Divorce Act had meant that women could leave a marriage, confident that they wouldn't be forced leave their children behind. The establishment of the Equal Opportunities Commission made it illegal to sack a woman for being pregnant and introduced statutory maternity pay.

We didn't think it would be easy; even so, it did feel that we were finally entering a new world. Feminism, I always believed, made sense for both sexes. Wasn't it just as much of a trap for a man to be consigned to go to work every day of his life, earning the money to support his wife and children, as it was for a woman to be relegated to stay at home and look after them? Surely, men would welcome living in a more equal world, where childcare and breadwinning could be shared between parents?

Thirty-six years on, the answer is, sadly – and shockingly – no. Far from wanting to share the childcare, men are still just as happy as my father was to leave the task to their partners. Before the arrival of children, more than four out of five (85 %) working women in Britain are in fulltime employment, working more than 30 hours a week. But once they become mothers, the proportion is much lower: only a third (34 %) of working mothers with pre-school children are employed fulltime, and only 41 % of working mothers with a youngest child of school age.

These findings are at the heart of a survey by Dr Gillian Paull, published in the Economic Journal and reported in yesterday's Guardian, and they make disheartening and grim reading. Instead of sharing childcare, the proportion of men working full-time increases once they have children. And women's talents and skills are wasted as they get shunted sideways into part-time jobs, or no jobs, as they frantically juggle their lives to bring up their kids.

What this survey shows horribly clearly is that real equality between men and women is still a pipe dream. It only exists in the years when men and women are inhabiting the same planet as human beings, unencumbered by children, who have the right to sit at a desk – part of our modern work culture, which insists that you not only do your job but be seen to do it every hour of the day between nine and five. Once children enter the picture, this fragile veneer shatters, exposing the deep, sexist divide that still dominates our culture.

It now seems naïve to remember my own optimism in those early feminist years. The dreams of universal childcare have remained just that, and the reality is a free market in which only the richest can afford the sort of childcare that means a working mother can fulfil herself as both a parent and a worker. The world, in short, is still organized to meet the wishes of men. […]

Labour makes much of its commitment to children, yet in 36 years little has happened that supports working mothers. We might have won the battle for equal education, but that counts for little when that talent is squandered in later years. We tell girls to reach for the stars as they're growing up, only to tell them to reach for the door the moment they reproduce. *(678 words)*

Boycott, Rosie, The Guardian, February 28, 2008, p. 32

- l. 1 Marsha Rowe: co-founding editor of Spare Rib, freelance editorial consultant
- l. 2 Spare Rib: one of the most prominent feminist magazines at the time
- l. 13 be forced leave: be forced to leave
- l. 15 statutory: fixed, controlled by law
- l. 29 Dr Gillian Paull: researcher, author of the article 'Children and Women's Hours of Work'
- l. 37 unencumbered: not burdened
- l. 40 veneer: a thin layer of wood or plastic that covers the surface of a piece of furniture made of cheaper material, to make it look better
- l. 47 Labour: the Labour Party

Text B

Source: Tobias Hickey, The Guardian, February 28, 2008, p. 32
Reproduced courtesy of Guardian News & Media Ltd

P45: form/certificate employees are given when they lose their job

Assignments

Comprehension

1. Outline the achievements and failures in attaining women's equality in Britain in the past four decades as seen by the author. (Text A)

Analysis

2. Analyse the choice of words employed by the author to convey her view of the issue. (Text A)

3. Describe the illustration (Text B) and explain how it supports Rosie Boycott's ideas. (Text A)

Comment/Creative writing

4. Choose one of the following assignments.

4.1 'We tell girls to reach for the stars as they're growing up, only to tell them to reach for the door the moment they reproduce.' (cf. Text A, ll. 49–51) Discuss the general validity of the author's conclusion.

4.2 On March 3, 2008, *The Guardian* published a number of letters to the editor responding to Boycott's article. One of them reads: *"Slipping down the career ladder is only a disadvantage if you consider a career to be more valuable, worthwhile and fulfilling than raising a family. […]"*

Continue this letter.

Lösungsvorschläge

1. The article entitled "The world is still organised to meet the wishes of men" written by Rosie Boycott, published in the Guardian, February 28, 2008 deals with the issue of women and their rights in society, respectively the way their situation has changed, or not, within decades.

   At the beginning of the 70s women started to wish more explicitly to be offered chances of being equally educated and getting fair access to jobs, instead of fully depending on their husbands who could decide for them in many ways.

   Fortunately, the process continued positively, so that finally certain improvements were achieved. Women then showed their excellent intellectual potential in the educational field and were enabled to make their own decisions within the family concerning divorce and the termination of pregnancy. Maternity pay was guaranteed by law. It also became unlawful to discriminate against women in case of them being pregnant and regarding pay. New career options became available for them. But the

situation has obviously not really changed, as most men tend to be inclined to accept the traditional gender roles. Comparing the proportion of working women before children come into play with married mothers, the number of those still employed drops drastically; at the same time more men work fulltime once their children are born. Consequently women's chances are spoilt just because they are forced to devote all their time and energy to raise a family, apart from the few opportunities to accept part-time jobs. Concluding from the facts displayed, the author claims that our culture is still dominated by a sexist gap in society.
Boycott goes on by saying that the idea of general childcare is hard to put into practice as it is still linked with financial requirements which cannot be met by every family.
To conclude, Boycott points out the irony in encouraging girls to strive for success, only to send them back to their homes once they have children.

2. *Sie sollen erkennen, dass die Autorin eine sehr persönliche und emotionale Sicht auf die Entwicklung hat. Weisen Sie nach, dass der Gegensatz zwischen Hoffnung und Realität in der Wortwahl zum Ausdruck kommt.*

The author offers a very personal and emotional view on the development of women's rights in society. At the beginning of her article she does not just inform the reader about the situation in the 70s, she also reveals her at that time optimistic attitude towards a more liberal social position of women. To illustrate her point she uses words with positive connotations like "hummed with excitement and ideas and … hope" (ll. 2/3), employs a contrast "winter … turned into spring" (l. 1) and metaphorical language such as "move out of the shadows" (l. 4) and later on "entering a new world" (ll. 16/17), "dreams" (l. 43) and "reach for the stars" (l. 50).
But in the course of time she was increasingly faced with disillusionment as the first positive changes in women's lives were not manifested in a more complex way which finds expression in the author's vivid description with the help of adjectives like "sadly", "shockingly" (l. 22), "disheartening and grim reading" (ll. 30/31), "frantically" (l. 33) and "horribly clearly" (l. 35). She is disappointed and criticises the way women's chances and talents are neglected. Therefore she again makes use of emotive as well as metaphorical expressions such as "women's skills and talents are wasted" (l. 32), "get shunted sideways" (l. 33), "talent is squandered" (l. 49). With the help of figurative language she illustrates her point that women's possibilities are still restricted by using expressions like "juggle their lives" (ll. 33/34), "pipe dream" (l. 36), "once children enter the picture, this fragile veneer shatters" (ll. 39/40). It becomes only too obvious how far rules, regulations and expectations in the working world correspond with the desires and needs of men: "the deep sexist divide that still dominates" (ll. 40/41).
Her conclusion is pessimistic and somehow bitter when she uses words like "counts for little" (l. 49), "talent is squandered" (l. 49) or employs the contrast "reach for the stars … reach for the door" (ll. 50/51) to emphasise her critical, may be thought-provoking opinion about the lack of future prospects for well-educated mothers.

3. *Nehmen Sie bei Ihren Ausarbeitungen Bezug zum Text A. Sie sollten erfassen, dass mehrere symbolische Elemente die dargestellte Lage berufstätiger Mütter unterstreichen. Arbeiten Sie heraus, dass das von der Autorin gezeichnete Bild durch die Illustration unterstützt wird.*

The subject of the illustration given could be called: career prospects of women and mothers in society. It was created by Tobias Hickey and published in the Guardian, February 28, 2008.
We can see a black and white illustration with a long staircase in the centre running down from the bottom-right-hand corner to the top left-hand one. It clearly symbolises the career ladder. At the top of the stairs there is a woman with a small child. To the left and to the right of the staircase everything is dark. Only the area behind the people at the top of the stairs is bright. Left to it appears a sign (P 45) which represents the document given to employees who are forced to quit their jobs. The mother and her child cast a long shadow down the stairs. This shadow stands in contrast to the glaring light behind their backs. The whole situation painted here reminds of the problem described in the article provided that women succeed to "move out of the shadows" (l. 4) and manage to "enter a new world" (l. 16/17). But it seems to be an illusion that they are encouraged and supported: women with small children are more likely to slide down the career ladder than to move up it. The position of their feet pointing downwards and the dark colours adding up to the gloomy atmosphere underline the impression that women with children are faced with obstacles which are extremely hard to overcome. So it can be said that the symbols used in this picture correspond with the dissatisfying situation of working mothers as displayed by Rosie Boycott in the article.

4.1 The overall tone of the article and this quotation in particular seem to imply that women mostly have to choose between family or career. According to the author this is more obvious the better the girls are educated to be prepared for professional career options – and then fail to take them. But shouldn't we be more careful before making generalisations too fast?
Personally I feel, no matter what gender, people should have a fair chance to decide. Nevertheless, it is not always easy to link theory and practice and to find proper solutions for everybody. I am convinced that children need a lot of devotion and care. Regarding the fact that they are the future, society as a whole has to take responsibility. So why not share what it takes in cooperation with the families? It cannot be denied that social institutions, circumstances and a sound legal basis are required to encourage families and to support them with their offspring. I remember statistics that seem to prove that there is a growing tendency of young fathers who enjoy at least part of parental leave. This clearly reflects a positive trend, but without doubt such positive attitudes widely depend on the young men's upbringing themselves and the career conditions they are involved in.
It is, however, true that it is really hard to return to work if you have stayed away for several years. It is quite understandable that companies hesitate to employ young

mothers or even mothers-to-be when they fear that these might be absent quite frequently because of urgent childcare. As commonly known there are always two sides of a coin so that I would like to emphasise again how important it is to aim at social solution patterns as a whole. A friend of mine recently got a work contract in a Berlin firm that also provides day care facilities for its employees. If more enterprises decided on options like that, could it not be a useful contribution to avoid "the decrease in full-time employment of women once they have children" (cf. ll. 22–28)? Certainly our everyday lives contain more examples to prove the author's pessimistic view. But still I would be careful about generalising because the issue is rather complex and its realisation depends on various components. Probably the situation in Scandinavian countries might differ a great deal from Great Britain. And I have heard of France where the proportion of working mothers is much higher than in other European countries. The question is raised whether the countries mentioned give a different priority to educational and child issues. I would welcome greater improvements in the field of family policy.
Certainly, it cannot be denied that those suggestions are always connected with financial aspects and affect the state budget. Consequently, we need a greater awareness in all spheres of our society to put appropriate emphasis on education and family. Finally, I would agree with Boycott saying "We tell girls to reach for the stars as they're growing up, only to tell them to reach for the door the moment they reproduce." (ll. 49–51)
Equality should not only be laid down and widely discussed, it should be realised for and with the people involved. Otherwise a great deal of social trouble might be caused and valuable potential will be spoilt, not to mention the right of each individual "to reach for the stars" (l. 50). Reaching for the door instead of the stars is a step backwards that, in our modern times, should not have to be taken any more.

4.2 *Gefordert wird ein klar strukturierter argumentativer Text, der den Konventionen eines Leserbriefes entspricht. Beachten Sie, dass der Verfasser/die Verfasserin der Grundaussage des Artikels nicht zustimmt. Stellen Sie einen klaren Textbezug her und begründen Sie Ihre Meinung nachvollziehbar. Verwenden Sie mehrere Ansatzpunkte und beziehen Sie gegebenenfalls auch außertextliche Sachverhalte mit ein.*

The Guardian
…

Marie Musterfrau
Sonnengasse 18
1500 Potsdam
Germany

27 April, 2009

The world is still organised to meet the wishes of men

Dear Sir or Madam,

With reference to your article of February 28, 2008 I would like to express my doubts. Slipping down the career ladder is only a disadvantage if you consider a career to be more valuable, worthwhile and fulfilling than raising a family. Personally,

I regard the family as the smallest and most essential core of society. To maintain such precious institution might also demand sacrifices.
On the one hand Boycott may be right when she says that "women's talents and skills are wasted" (l. 32) but on the other hand women could use these qualities to organise their family life and educate their children. At this point, I do not hesitate to clearly voice my scepticism if care and education should be given into the hands of people outside the core family or even authorised too much by state interference.
Furthermore it is mentioned that mothers "frantically juggle their lives to bring up their kids" (ll. 33/34). This again implies that every mother must be discontent with her situation. I am sorry to say that but it depends very much on the attitude. Provided that you truly love your children and your husband, you will be more than willing to devote the time and energy necessary. Don't you know how nerve-wracking and draining it can be to combine job and family?
Certainly, housewives and mothers want to feel respected and acknowledged and without doubt too many things are taken for granted sometimes. The fact that they deliver refuge and contribute to a stable home makes them want to be appreciated for what they do. They deserve to be awarded. So I welcome every agreement on parental support, morally, materialistically and financially. I am also convinced that the first steps into the right direction have already been taken. Boycott concludes by saying that "The world, in short, is still organised to meet the wishes of men." (ll. 45/46). Well, considering the proportion of men and women in certain branches and especially in leading positions, she seems to be right. No matter what potential women have, it often takes more effort for them to achieve their goals. I also agree that there is still a lot to be discussed as regards equal opportunities for men and women alike. But should we carry out this dispute on the shoulders of our children? We should be more realistic when discussing this issue. Life is not fair in most cases and does not prevent us from making choices now and then.
In conclusion, girls and young women should be provided with a fair chance to choose. But apart from this notion I am convinced that being a mother in first place can also be a very rewarding task.

Marie Musterfrau, Potsdam

Text I: Manohla Dargis: Africa, at the Cineplex
(excerpt from an article)

American children used to learn about their deprived African counterparts mostly when their parents admonished them to eat all the food on their plates. Today, those same children have a dizzying variety of ways of reaching out to the continent and its inhabitants: they can shop at the Gap, mind Bono, listen to Kanye West, read Dave Eggers and watch an Oscar-nominated film or two, like "Blood Diamond" or "The Last King of Scotland," and, while reading their favorite magazine, contemplate the AIDS awareness ad campaign in which celebrities like Richard Gere and Gwyneth Paltrow, faces daubed with paint, declare "I am African."

Well, really, aren't we all? The new African awareness isn't just deeply, appreciably earnest; it's personal, too. Angelina Jolie, the head of the new class of celebrity missionaries, not only adopted an Ethiopian girl, but has also poured money into Namibian maternity wards. The same goes for Oprah Winfrey, the television personality who founded a girls' school in South Africa, and the rapper Jay-Z, who last year traveled the world, including parts of Africa, for "The Diary of Jay-Z: Water for Life," a documentary. The diary was the product of a rather unusual collaboration, as signalled on a Web page for the United Nations: "The United Nations, MTV and Jay-Z team up to raise attention of the world water crisis." If you didn't know about the documentary or the United Nations-initiated Water for Life campaign, you are probably not alone. The humanitarian crises in Africa are overwhelming, but they're also now a familiar media fixture. Yet if the bad news out of Africa never seems to end, neither do the popcultural responses. […]

For the last few years or so, every week seems to bring another documentary, another song, another ad campaign, another press conference, another celebrity sighting.

And why not? As George Clooney explained after embarking on a high-profile effort to bring attention to the Darfur region of Sudan, "If you're going to be famous and have cameras follow you around, you might as well go where the cameras will do some good." But it was a tough sell, even for the Sexiest Man Alive, who at one point also admitted that it was hard to capture people's attention because, as he put it, "We have tragedy fatigue on television." […] Most American films about Africa mean well. […] But what, exactly, are we meant to do with all their images, I wonder? *(410 words)*

Source: http//:www.nytimes.com/2007/02/04/weekinreview/04dargis.html

Annotations

Manohla Dargis: American film critic

l. 1 deprived: poor

l. 1 counterpart: someone who has the same position in a different place
l. 2 to admonish: to tell someone to do sth
l. 3 dizzying: confusing
l. 4 Gap: company founded by Bono and Bobby Shriver; half the profits from the textile products go to helping African women and children affected by HIV/AIDS
l. 4 Bono: popular singer – social critic
Kanye West: rapper – social critic
ll. 4/5 Dave Eggers: writer – social critic
l. 6 to contemplate: to consider
l. 8 faces daubed with paint: *here:* the slogan "I am African" painted on their foreheads or cheeks
ll. 9/10 appreciably: significantly
l. 12 maternity ward: the section in a hospital where women have their babies
l. 20 media fixture: sth that is frequently presented in the media
l. 28 a tough sell: a difficult deal
l. 30 tragedy fatigue: overexposure to tragic events; German: Übersättigung

Text II
Photo and Caption

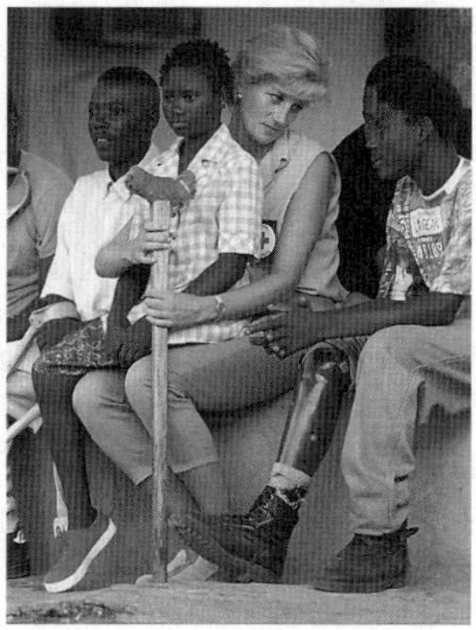

In this photo Princess Diana is talking to amputees on Jan. 14, 1997, at the Neves Bendinha Orthopedic Workshop on the outskirts of Luanda, Angola. The girl in the middle, 13-year-old Sandra Thijica, lost her leg to a landmine while working the land with her mother in Saurimo, eastern Angola, in 1994. Diana was working to rid the world of landmines.

Quelle: ullstein bild – AP

Annotations
l. 1 amputee: someone who has had an arm or a leg amputated/cut off
l. 5 landmine: a bomb hidden in the ground that explodes when someone walks or drives over it

Tasks
Work on a total of three tasks.
Tasks 1 and 2 are compulsory. Choose one task from 3.

1 Briefly outline what Manohla Dargis says about the new publicity given to Africa. Write no more than 150 words. (30 %)

2 Describe Text II (photo and caption) and compare its message to what Manohla Dargis points out in her article. (30 %)

3A Discuss positive and negative aspects of the role that celebrities and/or organizations from industrialized nations play for developing countries. Also comment on possible consequences of their activities for the people in these countries. Refer to Text I and Text II and other material you are familiar with. (40 %)

OR

3B In lines 30–32 the author says: "Most American films about Africa mean well. […] But what, exactly, are we meant to do with all their images, I wonder?"
Take this quotation as a starting point for your discussion as to whether films can contribute to solving the vital problems of humanity. Back up your opinion with reference to at least one film you are familiar with. (40 %)

OR

3C For the project day at your school on a developing country you design a flyer in which you try to create an active interest in and commitment for the country chosen.
Describe the design of this flyer (i. e. layout, illustrations) giving reasons for your choices. Then write its text referring to your knowledge of the country chosen and the facts given in Text I and Text II. (40 %)

You are expected to write at least 500 words in no more than 240 minutes.

Lösungsvorschläge

1. *Die Lösung einer* summary-*Aufgabe sollten Sie mit einem einleitenden Satz beginnen, der Titel, Autor und Thema des Textes nennt. Da Sie sich auf 150 Wörter beschränken müssen, ist es wesentlich, die Hauptaspekte des Texts herauszufiltern und Oberbegriffe zu finden.*

The excerpt from the article "Africa, at the Cineplex", written by Manohla Dargis and published on the Internet, examines the role celebrities from the USA play in solving the problems in Africa. At the beginning, the writer reveals the new African awareness in the media, making the children learn much about this continent in manifold ways. There are not only a lot of films set in Africa, but the public can also watch several documentaries on humanitarian issues there.
Furthermore, a lot of celebrities like Oprah Winfrey and Angelina Jolie act as missionnaries in this part of the world, launch campaigns in order to give aid to the African population and make donations to charity. Throughout the last few years, people can notice a growing presence of humanitarian crises in the media, capturing the audience's attention on the one hand, but causing fatigue amongst the viewers on the other.

2. The photo given shows Princess Diana talking to two young African amputees at an orthopaedic workshop in Luanda, Angola.
In the middle of the picture, you can see the princess sitting there with a crutch in her hands. Her arms are around the teenage girl Sandra, who lost one of her legs in a landmine explosion while working the land with her mother. This is why there is only one shoe visible. Sandra, looking very serious and thoughtful, is sitting on the princess' lap. The girl and the man on her right seem to be watching something which is not visible to us. Princess Diana is looking at the young African on her left, having a friendly conversation with him. This man is wearing an artificial replacement for his right leg, whose lower half can be seen. His leg must have been amputated. The reason for Diana's visit is her commitment to the removal of landmines throughout the world.
Comparing the message of the text with what the photo and the caption express, you can identify a couple of parallels as well as some differences. Both the photo and the text are meant to illustrate a celebrity's personal dedication to finding a solution to essential problems of humankind. Text I mentions stars such as Oprah Winfrey or Angelina Jolie taking action, and the photo presents Princess Diana launching a campaign against landmines. In addition, the photo and the text reveal that famous personalities are becoming increasingly involved in the struggle to increase the public awareness of the difficulties the people in Africa have to face. Another similarity is the growing interest in humanitarian issues conveyed in both texts.
However, there are some contrasting facts to be found, too. The first article includes a critical attitude towards the activities of various celebrities such as Gwyneth Paltrow or Richard Gere, whose faces are "daubed with paint", declaring "I am African" (l. 8), whereas the photo tries to convey only positive feelings through the demonstration of Diana's caring role in Angola. Furthermore, Princess Diana is presented as a positive role model for other people in the picture, while Dargis disapproves of the overexposure of these matters to the media when she enumerates that "every week seems to bring another documentary, another song, another ad campaign, another press conference, another celebrity sighting" (ll. 22 ff.).
This is also demonstrated when she quotes George Clooney, who expresses that "(w)e have tragedy fatigue on television" (l. 30).
In brief, it is very obvious that the photo is connected to the articles as both have several facts in common, like the main topic referring to celebrities and their activities in Africa and the humanitarian issues which are pointed out. But in contrast to the text, only the photo and its accompanying text display the positive aspects, whereas the article also includes criticism.

3A The awareness of global issues like hunger, water problems or the greenhouse effect is urging many individuals and groups in industrialized countries to do something personally.
Celebrities like Oprah Winfrey spending money on African schools, Angelina Jolie adopting an Ethiopian child, or Rapper Jay-Z teaming "up to raise attention of the world water crisis" (l. 17) together with MTV, can be seen as role models who really

show responsible behaviour. They are among many others trying to help poor and oppressed people in developing countries who do not just need food or clean drinking water. Many are really struggling for survival in a very violent environment.
With their campaigns, the famous people attract the attention of the newspapers and TV and focus the people's consciousness on the conflicts the African people have to deal with. Growing support is caused for fair trade, thus increasing the population's awareness of the problems of the developing world. But the well-meant actions of celebrities can also be criticized as a trivialization of serious problems, and some of their activities have been branded as self-promotion. In some cases, the profits from various charity events, such as concerts, might even increase the personal wealth of the people involved. In addition, their initiatives could also be seen as an interference with local cultures and structures, causing ever more dependence on foreign aid and loss of self-esteem.
Furthermore, you cannot deny that financial support from organisations like the World Bank or the IMF may add to a growing feeling that globalization only works for the institutions and multi-national companies of the industrialised world which are exploiting the resources of the Third World. In lessons, we dealt with Mars Inc., a global player, which exploits the workers in Ghana and on the Ivory Coast in order to get cheap cocoa. Traditional structures in producing and trading cocoa were destroyed, mostly for the benefit of the company and some corrupt politicians. The working and living conditions of the labourers became harder, and their dependence on the world market and several organisations like the World Bank grew. Another significant consequence of this situation is that in the industrialised countries, the overexposure of these matters by the media will make people lose interest in the questions raised.
But generally, activities like the late Princess of Wales' initiative against landmines in Angola or the efforts to promote fair trade have more positive than negative effects. They create the images in the media and people's minds which are necessary to activate the public and put pressure on politicians and companies in order to cooperate with developing countries in a fair and responsible way.

3B *Nach einer Analyse des Themas sollten Sie den Bezug zum Text herstellen und Kenntnisse zu mindestens einem Film überzeugend mit dem Thema verbinden. Besonders gut ist es, wenn Sie sowohl ein positives als auch ein negatives Beispiel diskutieren können.*

First of all, I think that the American public has never been very interested in a close look at African affairs and the deeper reasons for the constant crises of this large continent. Africa's misery might be too far away from everyday problems and lifestyles. The two sets of customs and values are obviously too different to be bridged in a simple, or even entertaining way.
From time to time the American public seems to remember the problems in Africa, which often leads to media campaigns and donations. These campaigns, of course, have to compete with all the other topics in the media machine in order to catch the attention of the public.

Dargis' final question holds the age-old question: can art change you? Can films, in particular, teach you positive values as a fundament of ethically correct behaviour? Can these films influence the thinking and behaviour of viewers from the industrialised world in order to solve "the vital problems of humanity", such as war, hunger, and all the other forms of human deprivation?
As Dargis obviously refers to mainstream cinema and not so much to committed independent film productions, the answer, as far as I can see, can only be "only sometimes" or "maybe". Why so pessimistic?
There is not an overwhelmingly large number of film productions with Africa as their setting. Furthermore, the ones I know have one crucial feature in common: the basis of their conflicts is always the encounter of white characters with the African continent. These movies strongly focus on the white, the foreign side. Only there will the viewers find in-depth characters with complex problems. The protagonists can either be well-meaning helpers or representatives of colonialism; whatever the situation, the view of Africa is that of a stranger who has to cope with Africa and the Africans. The latter are often portrayed stereotypically: they are either extremely good and exotic or unbelievably cruel or wise and mysterious. All in all, they are different from us and hard to identify with. Their lack of proficiency in English frequently makes deeper conversations impossible; they often speak a more or less restricted language. So, here the conclusion could be drawn that this one-sided picture of African affairs might at best create a certain positive curiosity in the viewer. But it appears to me that the high demands of "solving the vital problems of humanity" can hardly be achieved so simply.
Let me illustrate this with two examples which were very successful at the American box office, so that one can assume they have reached a large audience.
On the one hand, there is "Out of Africa", telling the tear-jerking story of Danish writer Karen Blixen. Concentrated on the protagonist's life, the film predominantly uses Africa as an exotic stage prop, as another, sometimes hostile obstacle for the heroine. Africans are always more or less inferior; they are servants or other characters who do not participate in the major conflict the courageous Karen Blixen, our white heroine in Africa, has to face. The other, also extremely successful movie is called "Black Hawk Down", which tells the story of a failed American military strike in Mogadishu, Somalia. Like "Out of Africa", the story strictly centres on the "white" side. Africa appears to be in chaos, a country which kills the well-meaning American soldiers who want to arrest Dictator General Aidid. After a short description of the African setting, the usual action scenes set in, and there are two hours of killing, bombing and explosions.
I think it is important to mention that both films perfectly fit the prefabricated categories of Hollywood cinema.
To come to a conclusion, as I already indicated, I have serious doubts about whether American mainstream films on Africa greatly contribute to the viewer's awareness of humanity.
Moreover, I would disagree with the author's opinion that most American films are "well-meaning" concerning Africa, as long as they trivialize or simplify African conflicts and the characters of African people.

Most probably, these highly commercialized films with big production budgets have a different goal: success at the box office. That is why they are made. A "contribution to solving the problems of humanity" under these circumstances appears as a more or less accidental side effect. One should not forget that the tremendous overflow of information devalues the small details and often weakens, even destroys their effect on us. The "vital problems of humanity" are only one topic in the endless pipeline of information and entertainment.

However, I have seen excellent films about Africa made by Egyptian, Somalian, Gambian and other African film-makers. To them Africa was more than just a symbol of something strange that needs help. Suddenly, even African people are not strange at all.

3C The flyer is meant to arouse interest and commitment for a project on Ethiopia.

It will be printed in A4 format so that it can be easily held in one hand.

On its front page you can see a big headline, saying ETHIOPIA IS EVERYWHERE. This should be printed in bold green, yellow and red, the colours of the Ethiopian flag.

Underneath the headline, there are photographs showing former emperor Haile Selassie, Bob Marley, and perhaps a member of the popular Berlin band SEEED, who also looks like a Rastafarian. Famous Ethiopian marathon runners, armed guerrillas and starving children in a deserted landscape are also necessary to give a manifold impression of the relevance of Ethiopia in history, culture and religion as well as the most urgent problems of this country. Photos of Angelina Jolie with her Ethiopian child, people distributing food and doctors curing people must be included as well in order to show what can be done. Underneath these images, one can find the contour of the Ethiopian map with major facts about its capital, form of government, population, size etc. inside and the names of neighbouring countries outside.

This will help to give the reader some orientation. At the bottom of the front page, one can read the name of the project leader and project location at school printed in italics and inside a frame in order to make it very visible. The back page shows a list of the issues the project will deal with. The first one should be the Rastafarian movement, including Reggae music, because this is a good way to arouse interest among students. Other topics should be hunger and diseases, as well as religious conflicts and the country's natural beauty.

All the topics should be similar in form and size, e. g. as questions or keywords underlining their importance. The bottom of the page will show the slogan "The world profits from Ethiopia – how can Ethiopia be helped by the world?" This is meant to make it clear what the main activities during the project day will be about.

Abiturprüfung Berlin 2008
Englisch Grundkurs – Aufgabe 2

Text I: Monolingual Britain/They all speak English

(excerpt from an article)

The image of the Briton abroad, speaking English slowly and loudly in the expectation that eventually the natives will get the idea, is a stereotype with a good deal of truth behind it. According to a survey by the European Commission last year, just 30 % of Britons can converse in a language other than their own (only Hungarians did worse). Bad as these figures are, they are flattered by the one in ten residents of Britain who speak a language other than English at home.

The next generation is unlikely to do even this well. Fewer young people are studying languages in school, a trend that has accelerated since 2004, when the government allowed English schools to make foreign languages optional for students aged 14 and over. Even those who are keen on languages often drop them at this stage now, as schools offer a narrower choice of languages and schedule them against other subjects. Around four in five of all English state schools allow their students to abandon languages at 14 and some private schools are starting to follow suit. In 2006 only half of all students took a foreign-language GCSE exam—the standard test for 16-year-olds. […]

Nearly a quarter of the world's population speaks some English. That includes around 400m who speak it as their mother tongue and about the same number who speak it fluently as their second language. English is the global language of academic research, and perhaps 1,500 masters degrees are taught in English in countries where the language has no official status. It provides the vocabulary for some specialised fields, such as air-traffic control. And it is the working language of a growing number of international companies – a big reason why so many of them choose London for their headquarters. […]

At first sight this means that things are about to get even cushier for native English speakers; they needn't lift a finger to learn other people's subjunctives. But there are two catches. The first is that they will lose the competitive advantage that once came with being among the relatively few to speak the world's most useful language. Competent bilinguals, many of whom have travelled in the course of acquiring English, can offer everything that English monoglots can – as well as an extra language and an international perspective. *(388 words)*

Source: Economist, London, 13 Dec. 2006, p. 33/34.

Annotations

l. 5 to flatter: here: to make sth look more positive than it is
l. 9 optional: voluntary
l. 11 to schedule against: to plan that something will not be on one's timetable
l. 13 to abandon: to stop doing sth
l. 13 to follow suit: to copy somebody else's actions

l. 14 GCSE: General Certificate of Secondary Education – school examination in England and Wales for 15–16-year-olds
l. 17 m: million
l. 24 cushy: comfortable (like a cushion)
l. 26 catch (n.): hidden problem or difficulty
l. 29 monoglot: person who can speak only one language

Text II: Richard Schneider: Zweite Fremdsprachen an deutschen Schulen: Spanisch und Italienisch holen auf. Französisch, Latein und Russisch verlieren

(Auszug aus einem Artikel aus dem Internet)

Folgende Entwicklungen lassen sich beobachten: Die Zahl der Spanisch-Lerner nimmt stark, die der Italienisch-Lerner leicht zu. Französisch, Latein und Russisch werden hingegen von immer weniger Schülern gelernt, […]

„Rund ein Drittel der Abiturienten verlässt die Schule mit Kenntnissen in nur einer lebenden Fremdsprache. Das ist ein Skandal", sagt Professor Franz-Joseph Meißner. Meißner ist Romanist an der Universität Gießen und Vorsitzender der Vereinigung der Französischlehrer in Deutschland. Schüler sollten seiner Ansicht nach nicht mit Englisch, sondern einer anderen lebenden Sprache beginnen.

An Englisch führe ohnehin kein Weg vorbei, so dass es genüge, mit dieser für Deutsche leichtesten Fremdsprache in der schwierigen Lernphase der Pubertät zu beginnen, „Saarländische Schüler, die meist mit Französisch anfangen, können auch nicht schlechter Englisch als andere", so Meißner. Latein kommt für ihn als Alternative nicht in Betracht: „Latein vermittelt keine Strategien für hörendes Verstehen und keine Sprechfähigkeit."

Die Anhänger der Sprachenvielfalt an deutschen Schulen fordern, dass das Erlernen einer zweiten Fremdsprache bis zum Abitur wieder Pflicht wird. Einige Bundesländer wollen deshalb entsprechende Reformen auf den Weg bringen.

(170 words)

Source: Richard Schneider; WAZ 2003_05_02 (online)

Annotations

l. 4 Abiturienten: A-level students
l. 6 Romanist: professor of Romance languages: e. g. Latin, French, Spanish, Italian
ll. 6/7 Vereinigung: Organisation
l. 15 Sprachenvielfalt: multilingualism
l. 16 Pflicht: a compulsory subject

Tasks
Work on a total of three tasks.
Tasks 1, 2 and 3 are compulsory. Choose one task from 4.

1 Briefly outline why most Britons are not able to speak foreign languages and what the consequences of this are according to Text I. Write no more than 150 words. (20 %)

2 Describe the author's (Text I) attitude towards the inability of most Britons to speak foreign languages and analyse the means through which he/she makes this attitude clear to the reader. (20 %)

3 Mediation
Write an account of Richard Schneider's criticism of foreign language teaching, as presented in Text II, for a British friend who admires the role of foreign language courses at German schools. (20 %)

4A "Competent bilinguals, many of whom have travelled in the course of acquiring English, can offer everything that English monoglots can – as well as an extra language and an international perspective." (Text I, ll. 28–30). Referring to the above quotation and to your own learning experiences with foreign languages, discuss which foreign languages and how many of them should be obligatory in your own country. (40 %)

OR

4B Refer to the experiences of a character in literature or film who knows or does not know a foreign language. Comment on the impact it has on the character's life whether or not he/she speaks a foreign language and is familiar with more than one culture. (40 %)

OR

4C The foreign languages department of the high school which you attend during your year in Britain has asked you and your group to design a flyer aimed at convincing students to learn a foreign language. Referring to a specific foreign language, write the text for your flyer and describe and give reasons for the flyer's design (layout, illustrations). Refer to information from Text I as well as to any other relevant information about the foreign language you have chosen. (40 %)

You are expected to write at least 500 words in no more than 240 minutes.

Lösungsvorschläge

1. The excerpt from the newspaper article "Monolingual Britain/They all speak English", published in *The Economist* in London, on 13th December 2006, is a critical review of the Britons' inability to speak foreign languages. As English is the global standard, the Britons do not have to learn another language, a task which they also find very difficult. Furthermore, they can work in all fields of the economy without doing so, and there is a growing number of international corporations based in London. Even the British school system does not promote it, making the learning of foreign languages optional for students above the age of 14, by providing them with a limited choice of languages or offering them at inappropriate times. Nevertheless, this development makes the Britons disadvantaged on the job market as there are a lot of people in the world who are able to speak English well and, apart from speaking a second language, are furnished with a more global point of view.

2. *Bei der Lösung dieser Aufgabe ist es wichtig, zuerst darzustellen, welche Einstellung der Autor des Textes vertritt und anschließend die sprachlichen Mittel zu benennen, die er nutzt, um diesen Effekt zu erzielen. Vergessen Sie nicht, die passenden Textstellen zu zitieren und Ihren Text mit einer passenden Schlussfolgerung zu beenden.*

In the article "Monolingual Britain/They all speak English", the author openly criticises the Britons' inability to speak foreign languages, and he also points out the disadvantageous impact this attitude can have on their lives.

At the beginning of the text, the author employs a few adverbs and nouns with negative connotations, such as "slowly", "loudly" (l. 1) and "stereotype" (l. 2), in order to inveigh against the Britons' way of trying to convey what they want to say to other people, expecting all of them to understand the English language. Such words can also be found in other parts of the text, for instance when he states that "only half" (l. 14) of the students take a foreign-language GCSE exam or voices that the Britons have lost the advantage of belonging to the "relatively few" (l. 27) people in the world to speak English. When mentioning the metaphor that "they needn't lift a finger" (l. 25), the author vividly reveals the British people's lack of interest in acquiring skills in foreign languages. The magnitude of the current trend away from learning languages in Britain described in the article is impressively underlined by statistics and other numerical data, such as "30 % of Britons" (l. 4), "one in ten residents" (l. 5) and "around four in five of all English state schools" (l. 12), making the information more trustworthy and provable. When referring to these figures, the writer even uses the adjective "bad" (l. 5), thus directly presenting his view on the matter and uttering the negative aspects of this phenomenon. Throughout the whole article, the reader is also aware of the author's lack of respect for the Britons not being able to speak any other language, when he calls them "unlikely to do even this well" (l. 7) and expresses that "things are about to get even cushier" (l. 24) for them. Especially the last passage of the text mentions the consequences this development

may have for the monoglots, pointing out that they will be disadvantaged on the job market in the near future.
On the whole, the author of this article places great emphasis on the negative effects of the Britons' incapacity to speak foreign languages, thus revealing that he deeply disapproves of their tendency to be monolingual.

3. The given excerpt from Richard Schneider's article „Zweite Fremdsprachen an deutschen Schulen: Spanisch und Italienisch holen auf. Französisch, Latein und Russisch verlieren", published on the Internet, is about recent developments concerning a second foreign language at German schools.
Current trends show that one third of German A-level students can only speak one modern foreign language, which makes the supporters of multilingualism demand that two languages should be a compulsory part of A-levels in the future. According to recent surveys, Spanish and Italian are growing in popularity, whereas French, Latin and Russian are losing more and more students. Consequently, a professor of Romance languages claims that English should not be the first, but the second language taught at schools because the German students will learn English more easily than other foreign languages anyway. Furthermore, he also states that there is no proof that starting with a different foreign language will impede students' later knowledge of English. However, Latin, which does not help develop the listening and speaking skills of the learners, is not a feasible alternative to him. Trying to solve the problems involved, some German states are already planning reforms to make a second foreign language compulsory for the A-level exams.

4A The fact that a serious paper like *The Economist* discusses the topic of learning foreign languages shows very clearly that it is a controversial issue in Britain.
The article from 13th December 2006 mentions many reasons for the dominance of English, and it also points out that "Competent bilinguals, many of whom have travelled in the course of acquiring English, can offer everything that English monoglots can – as well as an extra language and an international perspective".
From my own point of view, I entirely agree with the article. For Germans, English is relatively easy to learn at the beginning, although it takes hard work in the long run. But as American or English names, pop music and films are quite familiar in our media, this keeps up the attraction of this language. It is normal to see English as the first foreign language to learn, and everyone knows that you cannot do without it, especially if you want to train for a skilled profession or to study academically; it is the lingua franca worldwide. Many business or scientific books or articles are first published in English or only appear in English. If you communicate on the Internet, English is first choice with foreign partners. Travelling in Europe and elsewhere is much easier if you know some English – the only exception being France. And you can help foreign tourists in Berlin much better if you speak English.

Additionally, learning a foreign language such as English not only provides you with an advantage in the economic competition, but also increases your awareness of your own language and offers better access to other countries' cultures and people. Which second foreign language to learn is a more difficult question to answer, however?

The classical choices are either French or Latin. France is our biggest neighbour, but the language is said to be quite difficult to learn. You need Latin in some fields, like law, medicine, or biology and other sciences. Japanese, Russian or Spanish are interesting alternatives depending on your professional orientation. And why not learn a language of growing importance like Chinese or Arabic? But generally speaking, I support the idea that everyone should learn at least one foreign language and people who want to study should do more. Some people say that the more languages you study, the more confused you will get, and, in the end, you do not have perfect command of any language. But this position has been refuted. There are often a lot of similarities between different languages concerning their structures and vocabulary which make the learning process even easier.

I really think that an early beginning helps a lot. The first two years of learning English were the most fun for me and sparked my everlasting interest in it.

4B *Bei der Lösung der Aufgabe ist es sehr wichtig, einen Film zu wählen, der mit dem Thema verbunden werden kann, das heißt, in dem wirklich die Beherrschung oder Nicht-Beherrschung einer Fremdsprache im Mittelpunkt steht. Diesen Film sollten Sie gut kennen, um überzeugend argumentieren zu können. Auch hier dürfen Einleitung und Schluss nicht vergessen werden.*

When discussing the relevance of foreign languages, one might say that this relevance becomes most obvious when people from different cultures meet. This can be seen in real life as well as in literature or films.

A good example to illustrate this is the film *Spanglish* by Albert Brooks.

It deals with a mother and her daughter who emigrate from Mexico to the United States. At the beginning, the mother, Flor, and her daughter Christina are poor and do not speak any real English, so the mother has to take on a badly-paid job at a laundry while her daughter goes to school and starts learning English very quickly. After some time, when Flor gets a job as a maid for a rather well-to-do family, her lack of English becomes very obvious so that she feels isolated and has to struggle hard to meet the needs of her employers. Nevertheless, she manages the situation very well with her open mind and, consequently, she develops a close relationship to the children of the Clasky family, especially to the daughter. This also includes the father, played by Adam Sandler, with whom she even has a kind of romance. But the moment when the importance of foreign languages becomes most obvious is when Christina has to translate English to her mother, even in situations where she hates to translate. These are the funniest scenes of the film. It turns out that before Flor developed her English language skills, she was quite helpless and looked rather stupid. However, taking this obstacle step by step, she gains confidence and respect among the Anglos. Another interesting aspect of the film is that in the course of time her daughter takes on the habits and attitudes of the Clasky family, thus, a conflict between Flor and her daughter develops which may indicate the loss of cultural identity. Christina struggles so hard to look, talk and act like a white American that she does not realize what she is beginning to lose.

The film begins and ends with Christina's letter read from the off, which is basically an application for Princeton University. This shows that her and her mother's efforts have even helped her to go to one of the best universities. And at the same time it makes it clear what successful integration is about – seizing the chances you are offered. In order to reach your goals, you have to meet the demands of the society you live in. One of the basic requirements is a good education, often based on a profound knowledge of the English language.

4C The aim of the flyer is to attract attention and to convince or at least inform the readers about the importance of learning German. Choosing this language is quite obvious for a German exchange student at an English school. Any other choice would look very implausible.

To make it handy, it should be produced in an A4-size vertical format. The slogan on top is "KNOW YOUR GERMAN(S)", printed in black, red and gold, the national colours of Germany. This slogan should catch the reader's attention, as it relates a lot to the slogan "Know your enemy". The subheading could read, "Broaden your horizons". The first paragraph – a quarter of the page – presents a contour of Germany with images of well-known Germans inside, e. g. Angela Merkel, Beethoven, Michael Schumacher, Michael Ballack, Handel – because he composed in Britain too – and the like. This should underline the relevance of Germany in history, culture, sports and politics. And it may also cause some discussion. The second paragraph – half of the page – is headed "Why learn German?" and gives some answers in the form of a list of keywords printed in bold. The first one should be "Spoken by more than 100 million – Give it a try". Among the others there should be "Improved chances of an interesting and well-paid job"; "Easy contacts in Germany, Austria and Switzerland"; "Germany important factor in the EU"; "Overcome splendid isolation" and so on. The phrases showing the reasons for learning the language should be highlighted, e.g. 'job', 'contacts' or 'EU'. The last paragraph should be framed and printed in italics. It should give information about which teacher to ask, about the author or about a meeting or a discussion on the topic which is scheduled.

Abiturprüfung Berlin 2008
Englisch Leistungskurs – Aufgabe 1

Andrea Levy: Small Island
(excerpt from a novel)

In the excerpt Gilbert Joseph, a black Jamaican, remembers a scene taking place in a small village in England shortly after he and his fellow soldiers from the "small island" of Jamaica have arrived in Britain. As they are British citizens, they fight in the British Army in the 1940s during World War II.
All of the English villagers have gathered to look at the Jamaican soldiers.

Staring out from dusty windows, gawping from shop doors, gaping at the edge of the pavement, craning at gates and peering round corners. The villagers kept their distance but held that gaze of curious trepidation firmly on us West Indian RAF volunteers. Under this scrutiny we darkies moved with the awkwardness of thieves caught in a sunbeam.

"Gilbert, ask them what the problem," Hubert told me.

From every point of the compass eyes were on us. "You have a megaphone for me, man?" I said. When I scratched my head the whole village knew. If any one of those people had a stick long enough, I swear they would have poked us with it.

It was some while before the more daring among them took cautious steps toward us, the unfamiliar. A young woman – curling brunette hair, dark eyes, pretty and plump at the hips – finally stood within an arm's distance to ask, "Are you lot American?" She had her mind on feeling some nylon stockings on her graceful leg. Which, as she stood pert and feminine before us, every one of us boys had our mind on too. "No, we are from Jamaica," I told her. "The West Indies," the Trinidadian among us corrected.

Like a chink in a dam, a trickle of villagers approached us. Most merely nodded, as they passed. An old man with a face as cracked as a dry riverbed shook us all hearty by the hand in turn saying, "We're all in this together, lad. We're glad to have you here – glad to have ya."

An elderly couple tapping on James's shoulder asked, "Would you mind, duck – would you mind saying something? Only my husband here says it's not English, you're speaking."

When James replied, "Certainly, madam, but please tell me what you require me to say," her husband shouted, "Bloody hell, Norma, you're right."

As Norma concluded: "There, I told you. They speak it just like us, only funnier. Ta, ducks, sorry to bother ya."

A middle-aged man, not in uniform, kept his hands resolutely in his pockets before addressing me. Eyeing intently the young woman, who was by now getting on very nicely with a lucky Fulton – consorting with him as we had been assured no white woman would – this man, not looking on my face as he spoke, asked me, "Why would you leave a nice sunny place to come here if you didn't have to?"

When I said, "To fight for my country, sir," his eyebrows jumped like two caterpillars in a polka.

"Humph. Your country?" he asked without need of an answer.

He then took the young woman's arm, guiding her, reluctant as she was, away from Fulton and our group.

Let me ask you to imagine this. Living far from you is a beloved relation whom you have never met. Yet this relation is so dear a kin she is known as Mother. Your own mummy talks of Mother all the time. "Oh, Mother. Is a beautiful woman – refined, mannerly and cultured." Your daddy tells you, "Mother thinks of you as her children; like the Lord above she takes care of you from afar." There are many valorous stories told of her, which enthral grown men as well as children. Her photographs are cherished, pinned in your own family album to be admired over and over. Your finest, your best, everything you have that is worthy is sent to Mother as gifts. And on her birthday you sing-song and party.

Then one day you hear Mother calling – she is troubled, she needs your help. Your mummy, your daddy say go. Leave home, leave familiar, leave love. Travel seas with waves that swell about you as substantial as concrete buildings. Shiver, tire, hunger – for no sacrifice is too much to see you at mother's needy side. This surely is adventure. After all you have heard, can you imagine, can you believe, soon, soon you will meet Mother?

The filthy tramp that eventually greets you is she. Ragged, old and dusty as the long dead. Mother has a blackened eye, bad breath and one lone tooth that waves in her head when she speaks. Can this be that fabled relation you heard so much of? This twisted-crooked weary woman. This stinking cantankerous hag. She offers you no comfort after your journey. No smile. No welcome. Yet she looks down on you through lordly eyes and says, "Who the bloody hell are you?"

"Okay, Gilbert, you have gone too far," I can hear you say. You know I am talking of England – you know I am speaking of the Mother Country. But Britain was at war, you might want to tell me, of course she would not be at her best.

Some of the boys shook their heads, sucking their teeth with their first long look at England. Not disappointment – it was the squalid shambles that made them frown so. […] And let me not forget James, perplexed as a newborn, standing with military bearing surrounded by English children – white urchin faces blackened with dirt, dried snot flaking on their mouths – who yelled up at him, "Oi, darkie, show us yer tail."

But for me I had just one question – let me ask the Mother Country just this one simple question: how come England did not know me? *(896 words)*

Source: Andrea Levy, "Small Island". London: Headline, 2004, pp. 137–141

Annotations

The text is partly written in Jamaican English (non-standard English)

l. 3	trepidation: great worry or fear about sth unpleasant that may happen
ll. 3/4	RAF volunteer: soldier who has enlisted voluntarily with the Royal Air Force in the British Army
l. 4	darkie: a very offensive word for a black person
l. 9	to poke: to push a pointed object, your finger, etc. at sth or sb repeatedly with small quick movements
l. 14	pert: (especially of a girl or young woman) showing a lack of respect, especially in a cheerful and amusing way
l. 17	chink in a dam: *German:* Dammbruch
l. 20	ya: (BE, colloquial) you
l. 21	duck: term of endearment showing affection
l. 27	ta: (BE, colloquial) thank you
l. 30	Fulton: first name
l. 30	to consort: to spend time with sb that people do not approve of
l. 39	kin: your family or your relatives
ll. 42/43	valorous stories: *German:* Heldengeschichten
l. 43	to enthral: to make sb very happy
l. 56	cantankerous hag: bad-tempered and always complaining ugly old woman
l. 63	squalid shambles: very dirty and unpleasant place
l. 65	urchin: a young child who is poor and dirty, often one who has no home
l. 66	yer: (BE, colloquial) your
l. 69	how come: why

Tasks

Work on a total of three tasks.
Tasks 1 and 2 are compulsory. Choose one task from 3.

1 Give an account of the encounter between Jamaican RAF soldiers and English villagers as described in the excerpt from "Small Island" in no more than 200 words. (30 %)

2 Show how the reader is made to share Gilbert's opinion about the "Mother Country" by analysing relevant literary means. (30 %)

3A Compare Gilbert's expectations towards Britain and his first experiences there with those of an immigrant to an English-speaking country from literature and/or films you are familiar with.
Comment on Gilbert's and the other character's attitudes and experiences. (40 %)

3B Compare Gilbert's motives for leaving Jamaica to fight for Britain in World War II with those of people who leave developing countries to live in industrialised English-speaking countries today.
Discuss these motives against the background of immigration in our globalised world. (40 %)

3C As an old man Gilbert writes an article for a British immigrants' magazine in order to give advice to new immigrants.
In his article Gilbert evaluates his first experiences and compares them with those of immigrants in today's multicultural Britain.
Write Gilbert's article. Refer to material you are familiar with. (40 %)

You are expected to write at least 700 words in no more than 300 minutes.

Lösungsvorschläge

1. The given excerpt from the novel *Small Island* by Andrea Levy, published in London in 2004, deals with several black Jamaican soldiers meeting some British villagers and having to cope with intolerance and discrimination.
When Gilbert Joseph and the other soldiers get into the village, all the residents have gathered, staring at them from a distance. Eventually, some of the villagers approach them, starting a conversation with the Jamaicans. The British people's reactions range from friendly expressions of gratitude for the Jamaicans' willingness to help the British in the war to complete ignorance, suspicion and blunt racism. Consequently, the soldiers are deeply frustrated and disappointed as they respect and love Britain and are willing to take upon themselves all kinds of hardship in order to help their mother country during World War II. But to their great dismay, they find out that they are regarded as strangers and inferiors, having to face prejudice and insults.

2. This extract from the novel *Small Island* tells the story of the narrator Gilbert Joseph, a young Jamaican, who has enrolled for service in the RAF during World War II.
Arriving in Britain, he realises the enormous difference between his ideas of this country and what it is really like. Throughout the whole excerpt, a very tense and unpleasant atmosphere is created by the author. The enumeration "staring …, gawping …, gaping …, craning … and peering …" (ll. 1/2) right at the beginning makes the reader feel uneasy and outnumbered by all the villagers watching the soldiers. Additionally, the author employs a lot of words with negative connotations, such as "distance" (ll. 2/3), "trepidation" (l. 3) or "scrutiny" (l. 4), which, just like the metaphor "thieves caught in a sunbeam" (ll. 4/5), support this predominantly alarming and worrying atmosphere. Moreover, the soldiers seem to be treated like wild animals that the villagers are curious about, but would "poke …" (l. 9) with a stick if they got too close. This image also underlines their suspicion and fear. A reason for this fear might be the villagers' lack of education, underlined by colloquialisms they use (cf. ll. 12/13, ll. 25 f., ll. 66 f.). On the other hand, one woman even calls them "ducks" (l. 27), a metaphor showing her friendliness, and others approach the Jamaicans "like a chink in a dam" (l. 17), a simile emphasising that once contact is established, the villagers are really eager to speak to the soldiers.

The uncomfortable situation and the fact that the story is told from a first-person point of view make the reader feel close to Gilbert and the soldiers and sympathise with them. Before Gilbert came to England, he had a very positive picture of this country, which is personified by the word "Mother". He sees it as a "beautiful", "refined, mannerly and cultured" (ll. 40 f.) woman, "a beloved relation" (l. 38) keeping an eye on "her children" (ll. 41 f.), making the reader think of a well-educated, caring person. Thus, the reader is able to feel the admiration of Gilbert and all "grown men as well as children" (l. 43). The usage of superlatives such as "your finest, your best" (ll. 44/45) when speaking about the gifts sent to this mother contributes to Britain's status of being worthy and valuable as well. All in all, all phrases describing the mother country in this part of the text have a very positive connotation.
Facing reality, the young men realize that there is a big contrast to their vision. This is shown very vividly by phrases with a negative connotation like the enumeration of adjectives "ragged, old and dusty" (l. 53) and the fact that the mother has "a blackened eye, bad breath and one lone tooth" (l. 54) and is the "filthy tramp that eventually greets you" (l. 53). This very negative description of England leads to the rhetorical question asked by Gilbert: "Can this be that fabled relation you heard so much of?" (l. 55), expressing the Jamaicans' disappointment very clearly. Consequently, the reader also understands that this is a mother who "offers you no comfort after your journey. No smile. No welcome." (ll. 56 f.), a mother who asks: "Who the bloody hell are you?" (l. 58) Reading this enumeration and the rhetorical question, the reader is as shocked as Gilbert and his fellow soldiers, for example James, who is "perplexed as a newborn" (l. 64), and the explanation that "Britain was at war", so "of course she would not be at her best" (ll. 60 f.) cannot provide any comfort in this situation. So it is not surprising that there is only one rhetorical question left to be asked at the end: "How come England did not know me?" (l. 69) This question summarises Gilbert's alienation and shows that his attitude towards his mother country has changed dramatically.

3A *Bei dieser Aufgabe ist es notwendig, zuerst die Gefühle und Erfahrungen der Hauptperson des Textes zu analysieren und diese dann mit den Emotionen und Erfahrungen eines Immigranten zu vergleichen. Dabei muss besonders auf die richtige Struktur der Erörterung geachtet werden – Einleitung, Fakten zu Gilbert Joseph, Fakten zu einem anderen Immigranten, Vergleich und Schlussfolgerung.*

This extract from the novel *Small Island* by Andrea Levy narrates the story of Gilbert Joseph, a young Jamaican, who has enrolled for service in the RAF during World War II. Arriving in Britain, he realises the enormous difference between the image he had of this country and what it is really like. He imagines his mother country to be very wealthy and beautiful and expects a warm welcome by the British inhabitants because of his willingness to fight for Britain. But when he arrives there, the villagers, who do not seem to know much about his home country and do not appreciate his eagerness to take upon himself all kinds of hardship during the war, confront him with ignorance, arrogance and racial prejudice. In addition, Britain is not the prosperous country he has dreamed about, but has severely suffered in the war

and looks poor and devastated. As a result, the main reason for Gilbert's disappointment is the fact that he has expected too much of Britain and its inhabitants without knowing what the reality is really like. An example of immigrants having to come to terms with similar and also different problems is the Khan family, whose situation is illustrated in the film *East is East*. George Khan has come to Britain from Pakistan and married Ella, an English woman. Together they own a fish and chip shop and are able to lead a secure and comfortable life, having seven children who can be provided with a good education and decent jobs. The story is set in the early 70s, during a very racist period in English history. It is the time of Enoch Powell, a xenophobic politician, whose famous "Birmingham Speech" caused a lot of racist outbreaks and stirred up a lot of prejudice in the British population. Consequently, the Khan family also experiences much hostility and antipathy in their neighbourhood, such as the fact that the boy living next door to them is not allowed to talk or play with the Khan children. The other problems the family has to deal with appear as a result of the clash between the two cultures the family lives in. George Khan wants to raise his children according to the Muslim traditions, which often clash with British reality, for example when he arranges marriages for two of his sons who do not seem to appreciate the thought of marrying some Pakistani girls they do not even know.
In conclusion, you can see that the protagonists in both stories experience similar situations on the one hand, as they have to face prejudice and hostility, but, on the other hand they are also confronted with other problems arising because of the clash between the different cultures the Khan family lives in and the fact that Gilbert Joseph's idealistic expectations of Britain cannot be met. It is obvious that living in a different country brings with it a multitude of conflicts, and solving them is often not very easy.

3B *Bei dieser Erörterung liegt das Hauptaugenmerk auf den Gründen, warum Menschen in andere Staaten emigrieren. Nach einer Einleitung sollten Sie die Motive der Hauptperson des Textes untersuchen, danach die Gründe darstellen, warum Menschen heute ihr Land verlassen, Gemeinsamkeiten und Unterschiede herausarbeiten und am Ende zu einer passenden Schlussfolgerung kommen. Das Thema „Globalisierung" sollte dabei eine Rolle spielen.*

Since the beginning of modern, civilized mankind, people have been emigrating to other countries, mostly for one reason: they hope for a better life.
But some of the people emigrating from their home countries, have different motives. One of these people is Gilbert Joseph, the protagonist in the novel *Small Island*. He does not move to Britain for economic reasons, but comes to England as a soldier, volunteering for the Royal Air Force during the Second World War. As Jamaica belonged to the British Empire at that time, some Jamaicans called Britain their "mother", whom they were willing to help when she was in trouble. However, Gilbert's motives seem quite idealistic if we examine the reasons why people from developing countries immigrate to industrialised countries today. These people are often refugees, escaping war, political and religious persecution or humanitarian and natural disasters in their native countries, who are seeking a place to stay which will

provide them with a better future. Fleeing from atrocious living conditions, they hope for a better life because they often do not have any access to essential health care, education and basic needs, such as a sufficient amount of food, clothing, shelter and water. Furthermore, within the process of globalisation, the gap between the rich and poor countries has become even wider, although there are a lot of measures taken to meet the challenge of bridging this gap. "The survival of the fittest" has become the slogan of globalisation, which means that cheap labour is exploited in the developing countries, making even more people immigrate to the industrialised countries. Despite the fact that some countries impose numerous restrictions on immigration which are intended to stop the steady flow of foreigners, immigration is a very common phenomenon today. Nevertheless, these people often face discrimination, resentment and xenophobia, making it hard for them to become integrated into society. Another problem which adds to this is the fact that they often go to countries to which they have no cultural or historical ties. As a result, they frequently form separate communities, sticking to their own traditions and exclusively speaking their mother tongue.

On the whole, immigration has changed a lot in today's globalised world, as only a few people immigrate because of the feeling of being needed in another country. Most of the immigrants come hoping for a better future and a more desirable life. As long as the industrialised countries do not sufficiently support the developing countries in order to overcome the wide disparity between the rich and the poor, the steady flow of immigrants trying to improve their living conditions will not be stopped.

3C **Immigrants now and then**

An article by Gilbert Joseph

When I was about twenty years old, I travelled to Britain for the first time. At that time, my mother country was suffering from the atrocities of the Second World War and certainly needed me, a strong young man, to defend it the way it had always protected me.

I was longing for adventure, and everything I had been told about Britain seemed rather exciting to me. Especially the ideal, modern living conditions I had heard of attracted me most. From today's point of view, I have to admit that I was rather inexperienced in those days. There was no paradise waiting for me. My first experiences were horrible and embarrassing. Dirt and poverty were to be seen everywhere. When we came into a British village, the people only stared at us at the beginning as if they had never seen a dark-skinned foreigner before. When they approached us and started a conversation, we could sense fear and curiosity on the one hand, but also resentment and discrimination on the other. In short, we were not welcome, and our willingness to fight for this country was not appreciated at all. On the contrary, we were even shut out. However, I have never regretted coming here, and immediately after the war, I started to settle down. I got to know a lot of British people who accepted me, and with their help, I successfully integrated into British society. Now I can en-

joy the pleasures of a safe job and comfortable living conditions. All in all, you could say that my standard of living has risen in contrast to the life I had in the Caribbean. Of course, matters have changed a lot since the time I immigrated, but the solutions to the problems arising are still the same. As an immigrant, do not exclude yourself from society. Show your willingness to integrate. This way, you will be accepted by society immediately. One of the most important aspects is that you have to learn your host country's language. This might open doors to you, in your private life as well as on the job market. On the other hand, do not forget about your traditions and customs either because the people around you can also gain a lot from your culture. At the beginning, it might be helpful to try to find people who speak your mother tongue and are confronted with the same problems you have to face. That way you can help each other and talk about your worries and fears. Nevertheless, you can be sure that even if racial hatred and resentment become quite violent and intense in your neighbourhood, there will always be people willing to support you. I know about a friend's family that experienced very violent racist behaviour some years ago. They were often verbally insulted by some xenophobes who did not want to have foreigners in their neighbourhood. This went so far that the family did not even leave their house anymore, being too terrified and upset. But some local residents noticed what was going on, and therefore protected the family and called the police. Shortly after that, the racists were fined, and some weeks later they moved to another town.
On the whole, you can see that the most important aspect of immigrating is your readiness to integrate into society. If this becomes obvious, there will always be people encouraging you and giving you the strength you need in difficult situations.

Raekha Prasad: India's shrinking families

(excerpt from an article)

India is a country where taking your parents in is a deeply ingrained tradition. But India's sons and daughters are fast abandoning the extended family in favour of careers and consumerism. So what becomes of the grandparents?

Gathering up the folds of her sari, Tulsi Devi Saxena shuffles out of Delhi's piercing sun into the dim light of her dormitory. Nailed on the wall outside is a blue board listing the bed number and name of the 13 elderly women living in the state-run home. Inside, the walls are plastered with images of Hindu gods and Sikh gurus, but not a single family photograph.

But Tulsi Devi has a big family, living near to the bluntly named Old Age Home, where the 81-year-old lives. […]

While her children's refusal to care for Tulsi Devi would fail to raise eyebrows in many other parts of the world, in India it represents an unwinding of ancient and deeply ingrained values. The nation's booming economy is changing attitudes, and with them family structures as urban Indians prioritise incomes and career opportunities over traditional family duties. […]

But in a nation without social security, no comprehensive state healthcare, a mere sprinkling of old people's homes and just 4 % of the 80 million Indians aged over 60 receiving a pension, the family continues to be the principal option of support.

Mindful of this, the Indian government is taking the drastic step of introducing a law to imprison and fine those who fail to care for their elderly relatives. It plans to set up a national network of fast-track tribunals where people over 60 can bring a case of neglect against their children. Magistrates would be able to force children to pay maintenance. Those who fail to financially support their elders could be imprisoned for one month, while those who abuse them face up to three years.

According to India's ministry of social justice and empowerment, the time has come to enforce what it calls "the moral obligation" of caring for parents. "I'm sorry I have to do this, it's not a happy situation," sighs the minister responsible for the act, Meira Kumar, sitting in her Delhi office.

Kumar cites urbanisation, which is robbing villages of young people, and materialism as the culprits behind abandoned old people. "There's such a rat race for acquiring new things that we're losing our basic values," she says. "We used to take our elders' blessings in everything we did; we touched their feet to show them respect. But now we're part of the global village. We look to the west. They look to us." […]

At the root of why the Indian extended family is waning is a generation of middle-class women joining the workforce in greater numbers than ever before: from less than 1 % to 15 % in just one decade. What is driving women out of the home is the sudden appeal of two incomes in a country where shiny new malls are filling with consumables unknown to earlier generations.

The extended family relies on clearly defined responsibilities, in which those of carer and cook fall to women. In today's India, a woman's earning power is increasingly seen as a more valuable asset than her culinary skills.

Moreover, extended families are predicated on the idea that when a woman marries, she leaves her own family and joins her husband's. She is seen to now belong to them; she is expected to adapt to their family and fit in with her mother-in-law's vision for the routine and priorities within the home. But for young and educated women, the gap between that vision and her own has become a yawning chasm.

Sitting in her compact, immaculate, two-bedroom flat in a middle-class suburb of east Delhi, 36-year-old Renu Kumat looks nervously towards her husband, Pavan, 43, when asked about her parents-in-law. The couple, who have two boys aged 11 and nine, lived with Pavan's parents for 11 of the 13 years they have been married. But 18 months ago their joint family split apart: her in-laws moved into a rented apartment nearby. "Speak," Pavan says encouragingly. "Say what you feel."

It was Renu who found the dynamics of joint family life unbearable. She tried, she says, to meet her in-laws' demands and needs. "I always felt I failed to come up to their expectations. They said I wasn't doing a good job taking care of the kids; that I didn't make the right food; I was giving too much time to myself and not enough to them," she explains, "My mother-in-law wanted me to run the house just how she had run hers."

But while her mother-in-law was 14 and semi-literate when she had an arranged marriage, Renu was a 22-year-old graduate, working as a teacher, when her marriage to Pavan was arranged. She has worked full-time ever since. "My mother-in-law has never worked and never understood the problem of how women are under pressure at home and at work."

Pavan came in from work one day to find his parents packing. "They said things weren't working out and that they'd like to live apart." He still calls on his parents every day and helps them financially. "Individualism and being self-centred wasn't part of the way I was brought up. I miss my parents."

A five-minute walk away, Pavan's father, Jeet Ram Lohani, an 82-year-old retired army sergeant, sits in his rented flat. He never imagined that he and his wife, Prema Wati, 70, would live apart from Pavan. Prema Wati snaps an irate "no" when asked if Renu met her expectations. "She never used to listen. She never took our advice."

It was to ease their son's stress, Jeet Ram says, that they decided to leave. "There was a generation gap. They have a very busy life. She's employed; they come home late. We had different perceptions from our daughter-in-law." (…) *(979 words)*

Source: Raekha Prasad, "India's shrinking families", The Guardian, London, 14 April 2007 (online edition), excerpt

Annotations

l. 1	to shuffle: to walk very slowly and noisily, without lifting your feet off the ground
l. 6	bluntly: straightforwardly, tactlessly
l. 9	to unwind: *here:* to destroy
l. 10	ingrained: firmly established, deep-seated
l. 17	to fine: to punish somebody by making him/her pay money
l. 20	maintenance: financial support
l. 27	culprit: reason for a particular problem or difficulty
l. 27	rat race: fiercely competitive struggle for success
l. 32	to wane: to decline
l. 39	asset: plus, advantage, attraction
l. 40	to predicate: to base
l. 44	yawning chasm: very big gap
l. 45	immaculate: spotlessly clean
l. 68	irate: angry

Tasks
Work on a total of three tasks.
Tasks 1 and 2 are compulsory. Choose one task from 3.

1 Summarise the article in no more than 200 words. (30 %)

2 State the message of the text and analyse the stylistic devices the writer employs to convey it and to engage the reader's interest in the topic. (30 %)

3A Referring to the article as well as to material you are familiar with comment on the impact of globalisation on families. (40 %)

3B Discuss the pros and cons of extended families and assess the efforts of the Indian government to enforce "'the moral obligation' of caring for parents" (l. 23). Refer to the text and to your knowledge about the situation in another English-speaking country and in Germany. (40 %)

3C Compare the situation of the young Indian women as described in the text with that of other people who are experiencing a change of values and lifestyles as a consequence of being confronted with different cultures. Refer to the text and other material you are familiar with. (40 %)

3D You are working on a project about an ethnic minority in an English-speaking country. Having read the article you decide to write a letter to Renu Kumar. In your letter tell Renu Kumar to what extent you consider her situation to be comparable to that of the ethnic minority you are working on and why you think she should continue sharing her experiences with anyone interested in them. (40 %)
Address the letter to: Ms Renu Kumar
166 Mayur Vihar
New Delhi, 110091, India

You are expected to write at least 700 words in no more than 300 minutes.

Lösungsvorschläge

1. The given excerpt from the newspaper article "India's shrinking families", by Raekha Prasad, published in *The Guardian* on 14th April 2007, deals with the dissolution of the traditional, extended family in India as a result of fast-moving economic and social changes.
   The author presents two different examples illustrating this situation: an elderly woman living in an old people's home, neglected by her family, and a young woman, having both children and a full-time job and therefore not being able to fulfil her husband's parents' expectations. Reasons for this development can be seen in the flourishing economy in India, attractive career opportunities offered to the younger generation, urbanisation, materialism and globalisation. Especially the young, educated, middle-class Indian women are no longer willing to assume their traditional roles of housewives subordinating their wishes to those of their husbands' parents, but rather want to pursue their own careers. As families cannot cope with these changing role expectations, conflicts in the families arise, making parents or children move out. What is more, the Indian state fails to meet the new demands for a more comprehensive social security and healthcare system resulting from this development. As a consequence, the government plans to introduce a law making the neglect of elderly relatives a punishable offence.

2. *Nach einer kurzen Einleitung, in der Sie darstellen, welche Botschaften der Text dem Leser übermittelt, sollten Sie die sprachlichen Mittel, die der Autor nutzt, benennen und analysieren. Vergessen Sie auf keinen Fall, die betreffenden Textstellen zu zitieren und auch herauszuarbeiten, welchen Effekt das sprachliche Mittel auf den Leser hat.*

   In the excerpt from her newspaper article "India's shrinking families", Raekha Prasad criticises the effects globalisation has on deep-rooted Indian traditions, making the Indian extended family dissolve, thus causing numerous problems in modern Indian society.
   Throughout her article, the author makes use of several stylistic means in order to convey her message to the reader. The general tone of the article is predominantly serious and objective, but also consists of emotional sequences. At the beginning, the author describes Tulsi Devi Saxena's home as very unpleasant, employing various words and phrases with negative connotations like "Nailed on the wall …" (l. 2) and "plastered" (l. 4), suggesting that this anonymous 'Old Age Home' with a "board listing the bed number" (ll. 2/3) is not an adequate home for an old lady. By mentioning that "Tulsi Devi has a big family, living near …" (l. 6), she builds up a contrast between this cold and emotionless atmosphere and a pleasant family life. All these details invoke pity and, consequently, arouse the reader's interest. Subsequently, including official figures and statistics such as "4 % of the 80 million Indians" (l. 14) and "from less than 1 % to 15 %" (ll. 33/34), Prasad wants to make it clear that the old woman's desperate situation is no exception, but that there are a lot

of Indian people suffering from this phenomenon. These data enhance the credibility of the message and illustrate the fast changes within Indian society. In the next part, she captures the reader's attention by mentioning the Indian government's plan to introduce a law in order to solve these problems and by directly quoting the minister responsible for this act, who compares these changes to acts of crime, employing words like "robbing" and "culprits" (ll. 26/27). This reference to these drastic government efforts vividly reflects the dramatic situation, making the reader understand the difficulties and feel sympathy with the people suffering from this situation. In the course of her article, Prasad describes the personal circumstances of a couple who are no longer living together with the husband's parents, thus offering another personal example to underline her message. Employing direct speech, the authoress gives a reliable account of the people's perspectives on this difficult matter, creating both authenticity and immediacy and stirring the reader's emotions at the same time (ll. 50–56). Additionally, the repetition used in lines 59/60: "... has never worked and never understood", and the anaphora: "She never used to listen. She never took our advice" (ll. 69/70), stress the problems the two women have to face as neither of them seems to be able to accept the other's opinion due to their different views on life. By comparing the young, educated, working woman with her semi-literate mother-in-law, Prasad also demonstrates one of the reasons for this generation gap. All in all, the author succeeds in presenting the changing social structures in India and the main impact this has on Indian family life as the result of global developments.

3A As we can see in the newspaper article "India's shrinking families", globalisation and its consequences have a tremendous impact on family life.

First of all, I would like to state that there are families who can benefit from this development, whereas there are a lot of people suffering from these changes. On the one hand, people can experience the positive effects of globalisation, such as the global flow of information via the Internet, a growing choice of goods for the consumers whose demands for new and better products are growing, more independence for women who are also able to join the workforce if they are well-educated, and more choices concerning people's lifestyles and cultures. These favourable influences can mostly be felt in industrialised countries. On the other hand, especially in Third World countries, the impact of globalisation on the families is often disturbing because the whole of a society based on age-old traditions has changed so rapidly way that neither society nor the government is able to find adequate ways to solve the problems resulting from this transformation. In India this is even leading to the dissolution of the extended family which has been an ingrained value for a long time. Some of the problems which might arise are poverty among the older generation and a psychological gap between the generations. Two examples of these circumstances described in the article are Tulsi Devi Saxena, an old Indian woman living in an old people's home under depressing circumstances, and Renu Kumar, a 36-year-old woman having both a full-time job and children and not being able to meet her parents-in-law's expectations, who, therefore, have moved away from them.

Nevertheless, there are numerous negative consequences which people in the industrialised countries also have to cope with. As the demands of the labour market require flexibility, mobility and readiness to adapt to the changing situations, families are pulled apart, and partners, children and other relatives are neglected due to a lack of support. There is a rising age at which people marry, or they do not marry at all and live their own lives without the burden of a family. On the whole, in my opinion, globalisation has a decisive impact on everyone's lives, bringing about benefits, but a lot of negative consequences as well. If the majority of the population of a country has to suffer from the circumstances, the government will have to step in to mitigate its disadvantageous effects and make sure that this is of benefit to all the people.

3B In the newspaper article "India's shrinking families" by Raekha Prasad, we learn that it is a deep-rooted Indian tradition to have extended families, which means that several generations live together under one roof, sharing the care for their children and older family members. As these traditional structures are now threatened by different factors, such as globalisation and India's booming economy, the Indian government plans to introduce a law enforcing "the moral obligation" of caring for parents. Thus, people who neglect their elderly relatives can be imprisoned and forced to pay fines. In my opinion, the extended family is a phenomenon which will slowly disappear within the next few years, as there is a growing need for adaptable workers who are open to change. On the one hand, it is beyond doubt that everyone should contribute to the preservation of ingrained values, such as living in extended families, which should be passed on from one generation to the next. This way, you also create a favourable environment for your offspring and you are able to share a lot of experiences, for example the knowledge about how to raise children. Additionally, extended families also provide considerable support for the working members of the family because there is always someone to care for the children and do the routine work in the household. Moreover, in countries where there is a very weak social security and healthcare system or none at all, like in India, elderly people have to be supported by their families in order to make their lives comfortable and worth living. If they are abandoned, they might have to live in old people's homes under very depressing circumstances, like Tulsi Devi Saxena, whose situation is very bleak and miserable. On the other hand, in our fast-changing, globalised world, people have to be more flexible in the labour market. As a result, moving away from your family to another place is often an economic necessity if you do not want to lose your job. Furthermore, there is a growing importance of individualism today, which means that children leave their parents in order to lead their own lives.
Currently, gender roles are changing as well. There are a lot of women nowadays who no longer want to assume their traditional roles of housewives, but want to pursue their own careers. A good example of this is 36-year-old Renu Kumar, who has both children and a full-time job as a teacher, thus not meeting her parents-in-law's expectations, who have moved out and now live in a rented flat. As we can see from this case, another very important aspect to be considered is the fact that several gen-

erations living together in one house or flat do not always get along with each other well because of their different interests and beliefs and the existing generation gap. Examining the situation in other English-speaking countries and in Germany, you will soon find out that in industrialised countries there is not the same deep-rooted tradition of extended families. Although you might meet families in which several generations live together and share all the chores, in most cases the children move out whenever they are old enough to have a job and support a family and lead their own lives, pursuing their careers and staying in loose contact with their relatives.
Concerning the efforts the Indian government plans to make, I think that although the state has to act when elderly people are neglected, their approach is rather questionable and unfeasible, as forcing the Indian young people to look after their relatives will not really change the situation in general. Besides, in my opinion, the government should not interfere with people's lives, thus violating their privacy. I also hold the view that there will probably not be many parents who bring public litigation against their own children because this would point the blame back at themselves for having raised their children this way. In conclusion, we see that although having an extended family can be rather comfortable and advantageous to the young people, today's situation in the industrialised countries and India as well shows that individualism and careers have become more important in our globalised world, and a state will not be able to stop this development by law. In order to support the older generation, every state should create an effective social security and healthcare system, involving the families in an appropriate way.

3C *Nach einer geeigneten Einleitung sollten Sie bei dieser Aufgabe die Situation der Inderin aus dem Text kurz beschreiben und diese mit der Situation einer anderen Figur aus einem passenden Film oder literarischen Werk vergleichen. Vergessen sie am Ende Ihre Schlussfolgerung nicht, die sich auf beide Charaktere beziehen soll.*

Within the process of globalisation, an increasing number of immigrants are moving to other countries and have to cope with a change of values and lifestyles as a consequence of being confronted with different cultures. This development is also perceptible in the social structure of a country itself. As we have seen in the newspaper article, it is difficult for the young Indian woman Renu Kumar to meet her parents-in-law's expectations of a 'proper' daughter-in-law, join her husband's family and submit herself to the rules of her mother-in-law, and make her dreams of working and leading her own life come true. Consequently, she feels pressure at work and at home as she is caught between the demands of modern society and Indian tradition, which makes conflicts in the family inevitable.
A similar clash between different cultures and expectations is also shown very vividly in the film *East is East*. George, having immigrated to Britain from Pakistan, is married to Ella, an English woman. Together they have raised seven children, who are supposed to fulfil their father's expectations of living in the traditional Muslim way and experiencing the opportunities of modern British society as well. Within the family, the views differ a lot: Maneer, one of the sons, has chosen to live the traditional Muslim way of life, whereas Nazir, who is homosexual, flees from his arrang-

ed marriage and moves out in order to live with his boyfriend. Ella, their mother, is thus caught between her love for George and her wanting the best for her children. The only one who really supports her is her friend Annie, an English woman living in their neighbourhood. At the point when George arranges marriages for his next two sons, the situation escalates because the boys do not want to marry any girl they don't know, and George cannot understand why they do not follow the traditional Muslim rules, not realising that new living conditions also mean a new lifestyle and a change in cultures.
As in the newspaper article, these conflicts not only arise because of the clash between various cultures and the different ethnic backgrounds, but also because of the generation gap. The older generation, like George in the film *East is East* and Renu Kumar's parents-in-law, always have their children's interests at heart, but do not accept it if they do not stick to their deep-rooted traditions and standards. On the whole, globalisation and immigration cause a lot of changes in values and lifestyles, and it is important to be open to these new developments and show a lot of understanding for other cultures and generations, integrating them into your view of the world in order to strengthen the connection between different people and not to stress what separates them.

3D Helen Cannon,
35 Charles Street, Mayfair,
London,
W1J5EB
helencannon@webmail.uk

Ms Renu Kumar,
166 Mayur Vihar,
New Delhi, 110091, India

25th April 2008

Dear Ms Kumar,

I came across the newspaper article "India's shrinking families" by Raekha Prasad the other day, and I must say that I am very interested in your situation.
At the moment, I am working on a project about the Pakistani minority in London, trying to find out how they manage to adapt to the British way of life and still stick to their traditions as well. Most of the people I have interviewed so far have to face a lot of problems similar to yours because of the clash between the British and the Pakistani cultures. While the older generation tends to stick to conventions, the younger ones prefer the modern lifestyle, which they can experience all around them in their daily lives. Some young Pakistanis even refuse to have arranged marriages, which, of course, results in endless discussions with their parents, who cannot understand this behaviour. In the article, I read that you have also experienced the conflict between traditional values and modern life, and that you and your family have found an acceptable way to deal with your problems. Of course, the solution of your pa-

rents-in-law moving out does not satisfy everybody, as they are discontented with the new situation, which may cause hard feelings and frustration. But at least your husband stands by you, though still supporting his parents financially, and maybe one day they will understand your difficulty in meeting their demands and living your way of life at the same time. In my project I heard of a similar case: for three years, a Pakistani woman who was married to an English man had also lived together with the woman's Pakistani parents, who could not understand their daughter's decision to choose her husband on her own. While the woman was suffering from the circumstances, her British husband did not care much about the conflicts and frictions and did not support his wife. Of course, this ended in a big argument, resulting in the woman's decision to leave her husband and move away with her parents. I am sure you can completely understand these immigrants' hopes and worries and can serve as an example from which they might profit by learning more about your experiences, concerns and dreams. That is why I would like to stay in touch with you, and I would be very grateful if you agreed to stay in contact with me.

Yours sincerely,
Helen Cannon

Text I: Anick Jesdanun: It's on the Net – so it must be true, right?
(excerpt from an online article)

Go to Google, search and scroll results, click and copy.

When students do research online these days, many educators worry, those are often about the only steps they take. If they can avoid a trip to the library at all, many students gladly will. […]

Georgia Tech professor Amy Bruckman tried to force students to leave their computers by requiring at least one book for a September class project.

She wasn't prepared for the response: "Someone raised their hand and asked, 'Excuse me, where would I get a book?'"

While the question might just have been a smart aleck's bid for laughs, Bruckman and other educators grapple daily with the challenge of ensuring their students have good skills for discerning the truth. Professors and librarians say many come to college without any such skills, and quite a few leave without having acquired them.

Alex Halavais, professor of informatics at the University of Buffalo, said students are so accustomed to instant information that "the idea of spending an hour or two to find that good source is foreign to them."

In a study on research habits, Wellesley College researchers Panagiotis Metaxas and Leah Graham found that fewer than 2 percent of students in one Wellesley computer science class bothered to use non-Internet sources to answer all six test questions.

And many students failed to check out multiple sources. For instance, 63 percent of students asked to list Microsoft Corp.'s top innovations only visited the company's Web site in search of the answer.

It's a paradox to some that so many young Americans can be so accepting of online information whose origin is unclear.

"Scepticism … is part of their lives, yet they tend to believe things fairly readily because it appears on the Internet," said Roger Casey, who studies youth and pop culture at Rollins College in Winter Park, Fla.

One concern is commercial influence online; some search engines run ads and accept payments to include sites in their indexes, with varying degrees of disclosure.

"If I'm going to go to the library, chances are somebody hasn't paid a librarian 100 bucks to point me to a particular book," said Beau Brendler, director of the Consumer Reports WebWatch.

Another potential minefield is the growing phenomenon of collaborative information assembly. The credentials of the people authoring grass-roots Web journals and a committee-written encyclopedia called Wikipedia are often unclear. Nevertheless, some Internet users believe that such resources can collectively portray events more accurately than any single gatekeeper.

In many ways, the greater diversity of information is healthy.

Paul Duguid, co-author of "The Social Life of Information," points out that no longer, in most of the United States, can school textbooks get away with one-sided views.

Even South Texas College of Law professor Tracy McGaugh finds her curriculum challenged as students can quickly discover how other professors teach the same material. *(499 words)*

Source: Jesdanum, Anick. "It's on the Net – so it must be true, right?" Arizona Daily Star – Online Edition. *http://www.azstarnet.com/sn/specialreports/51578.php. [27 Aug. 2008]*

Annotations

l. 5 Georgia Tech: Georgia Institute of Technology
l. 9 smart aleck: a know-it-all (German: Schlauberger)
l. 10 to grapple: to fight with something or someone
l. 11 to discern: to notice something
l. 29 disclosure: *here:* information on payments to someone
l. 33 collaborative: involving people or groups working together to produce something
l. 34 credentials: personal qualities, achievements, or experiences that make someone suitable for something
l. 37 gatekeeper: someone who makes decisions about which people can use something or see someone

Text II: Julia Bonstein: Abschreiben 2.0 (Auszug aus einem Artikel)

Bei aller Technikbegeisterung der Jugendlichen steht nämlich fest: Der kompetente Umgang mit dem Medium Internet muss erst erlernt werden. […] Lesefähigkeiten, die in der Schule vermittelt werden, befähigen dabei besonders zu einer intelligenten Nutzung des Internet. „Das Lesen ist weiterhin eine wichtige Voraussetzung, um die neuen Medien nutzen zu können", sagt der Medienforscher Stefan Aufenanger. Kinder, die gern und gut läsen, interessierten sich im Internet auch für Texte, schlechte Leser dagegen eher für multimediale Inhalte. „Ich bin ja schon froh, wenn die Schüler im Internet überhaupt nach Hausaufgaben suchen", sagt Studienrat Hofheinz aus Köln. Die meisten Schüler seien geübter darin, im Netz Bildchen und Videos zu finden als korrekte Reaktionsgleichungen für den Chemieunterricht.

„Das Problem besteht eher darin, dass Kinder und Jugendliche das Internet vor allem als Unterhaltungsmedium nutzen", sagt Christine Feil vom Deutschen Jugendinstitut in München. Online-Netzwerke und Videoportale sind dabei besonders beliebt: Knapp zwei Drittel der 14- bis 19-Jährigen tummeln sich mittlerweile auf Seiten wie SchülerVZ, MySpace oder YouTube. Nach schulischen oder beruflichen Belangen suchen im Netz nur 36 Prozent der 12- bis 19-Jährigen regelmäßig. *(177 words)*

Quelle: Bonstein, Julia: Abschreiben 2.0. In: Der Spiegel *33 (2008), S. 86–87.*

Annotations

l. 8 Studienrat: high-school/grammar-school teacher
ll. 9/10 Reaktionsgleichungen: (chemical) reaction equation

Tasks
Work on a total of four tasks.
Tasks 1, 2 and 3 are compulsory. Choose one task from 4.

1 Briefly outline how the Internet is used by young people and what this implies for students' research according to Text I. Write no more than 150 words (20 %)

2 State the message of Text I and analyze the most effective devices used to convey it to the reader. (20 %)

3 Mediation
An American friend of yours has asked for help with a presentation on the use of the Internet by German students. Outline the information from Text II that is relevant to this topic. (20 %)

In all of the following tasks you are expected to refer to Text I and Text II as well as to further relevant material/information.

4A "Someone raised their hand and asked, 'Excuse me, where would I get a book?'" (Text I, ll. 7/8)
With reference to the quotation discuss if the Internet can replace reading books for young people. (40 %)

OR

4B Compare the impact of the Internet on young people as shown in Text I and Text II to the influence of the Internet or other media on a character from literature or film. (40 %)

OR

4C The school you are attending during your year in an English-speaking country has asked you to write an article for the school magazine about the role of the Internet for young people.
Write the article with reference to Text I and Text II as well as your knowledge about the topic. (40 %)

You are expected to write at least 500 words in no more than 240 minutes.

Lösungsvorschläge

1. *Bei diesem Text müssen Sie noch stärker als sonst alle Besonderheiten unerwähnt lassen, sonst wird Ihr* summary *zu lang. Denn der Text enthält eine Vielzahl von Belegen und Beispielen, die unmöglich alle angeführt werden können. Suchen Sie nach Gemeinsamkeiten in den Beispielen und beschreiben Sie nur diese, nicht die Beispiele selbst.*

In a newspaper article, "It's on the Net – so it must be true, right?", printed in the Arizona Daily Star in August 2008, the author Anick Jasdanum demonstrates that

modern students have become accustomed to having unlimited access to unlimited information via the Internet. Professors confirm that students are content with a quick, uncritical search on the Internet to obtain the information they need. In fact, many students do not have the skills to make adequate use of other sources, e. g. real books in libraries. Moreover, Internet users often rely on a first cursory source, without questioning its validity.
It is paradoxical that students brought up to be skeptical nevertheless blindly accept information they find online. This may make them prey to exploitation, e. g. by companies who pay search engines to have their products and information found more easily.
Furthermore, students often do not question the expertise of authors on popular Internet sites such as Wikipedia.
On the positive side, the instant availability of diverse sources provides opportunities to evaluate possibly biased textbooks, and even educators.

2. *Am Anfang Ihrer Textproduktion sollte eine kurze, stringente Zusammenfassung der übergeordneten Botschaft des Textes stehen. Danach untersucht man – am besten chronologisch – die angeführten Argumente und Beispiele mit Blick auf die Art und Weise, wie diese eingesetzt werden.*

The intention of the text is to highlight certain widespread tendencies among today's youth regarding their uncritical acceptance of the Internet as the sole source of information for research work. This attitude has already led to a considerable decrease in academic reading skills among students.
The heading of the text consists of a short eye-catcher which hints that a quick four-step procedure (search and scroll, click and copy) is all one needs to produce reliable research results. The sentence is short and swift, the formula consists of typical computer-speak words and alliteration makes it sound snappy and modern.
The main body begins with the clarification of the author's standpoint regarding students' research habits (ll. 5–15). It then continues with some statistical examples (ll.17–22) which support this standpoint, followed by a gradual broadening of the subject matter to include sociological questions (ll. 23–27), possible commercial influence (ll. 28–32) and the credibility of popular Internet content (ll. 33–35).
Starting in line 36, the conclusion of the text excerpt does not simply repeat arguments given in the main body. Instead, the author quotes other experts who see ways in which the Internet can have a positive effect on high school and college education.
Throughout the text, the author quotes a number of education specialists from various parts of the US. This demonstrates how universal the problem is and how desperate educators are to find a remedy. A number of direct quotations enhance the authenticity of the text and support its validity.
Thus the general text structure proceeds from a brief outlining of the problem (ll. 1–4) to a number of specific examples (ll. 5–15), followed by a broader discussion of

various facets of the problem (ll. 16–35) and a conclusion with a somewhat sweeter aftertaste and a ray of hope.

3. *Zur Erinnerung: eine* mediation *ist keine genaue Übersetzung, denn letztere führt oft zu sperrigen Satzkonstruktionen im Englischen. Sorgen Sie für einen flüssigen, idiomatischen Text, der die wichtigsten Inhalte des Originals treffend wiedergibt.*

Mere enthusiasm for new technologies is not sufficient to provide a solid basis for using the Internet competently.
Reading skills taught at school are an important prerequisite for making intelligent use of the new media. Children who both enjoy reading and read well are interested in what the Internet texts have to say, whereas poor readers show more interest in multimedia contents.
Most children seem to be more experienced in searching the Internet for videos and pictures than in looking for detailed information for school, e. g. chemical equations.
The problem is that children and teenagers mainly see the Internet as an entertainment medium. Online networks and video portals are especially popular. About two-thirds of teenagers in the age group from 14 to 19 years make frequent use of websites such as SchülerVZ, MySpace or YouTube.
Just over a third of teens in the same age group surf the Internet on a regular basis looking for information relevant to school or their job.

4A *Hier wird erwartet, dass Sie einen freien Text schreiben. Sie können Ihre eigene Gewichtung vornehmen, dürfen aber nicht am Thema vorbeischreiben. Als Ausgangspunkt müssen Sie auf das kurze Zitat eingehen, im weiteren Verlauf sollten Sie sich an den wichtigsten Positionen der beiden Texte entlang arbeiten.*

The student's aphorism ("Where could I get a book?") was certainly intended to get some laughs, but it does point to a certain chasm between middle-aged educators, who learned to research along more traditional lines, and younger generations, who grew up with full access to the Internet and who are attuned to accommodating ever new technological possibilities into their lifestyle.
The citations in Text I are, however, very convincing, in that they show how new technologies have led many, perhaps even most, students to take the easy road when performing everyday homework assignments. Let's face it: There is an unbelievable amount of information out there on the Internet, far more than even the teacher can know, and it is all there ready to be reaped with a few clicks and a printer. And in spite of good intentions on the part of the students, the Internet does encourage skim reading off the monitor, which can be rather tedious after a while, so that the average student will hardly continue to search and search for just the right source he needs and will soon settle for a mediocre article. And as mentioned in Text I (ll. 28–35), the quality of the texts most easily found on the Internet can vary greatly, but it is very difficult for students with little experience in research to recognize the true quality of such sources.

Nonetheless, "practice makes perfect," and so it would seem wise for both educators and students to begin making more prudent use of the Internet as both a teaching and a learning medium. Students need reading skills that are applicable to both books and online sources. They need guidelines and exercises for determining the quality and accuracy of information provided on the Web. They need to view the Internet as a starting point, and not as the final solution.

There will always be highly specialized sources that are only available in book form, where the student will have to leave his chair and actually travel to a library to ponder over them. However, these sources are gradually becoming rare. At almost breath-taking speed, literature of all fields of knowledge is being digitized and made available on the Internet. Even though access is sometimes limited to those who pay a fee, the money is often well invested, considering the time and effort it saves. In fact, many scholarly articles, dissertations etc. are now first "published" on the Internet and may or may not subsequently be published in a book with paper and ink.

In summary, there is indeed a problem among students in general regarding their superficial use of the Internet. But the Web is such a powerful medium that its potential should not be disregarded. Through careful guidance along lines that have yet to be developed by educators, today's students can become proficient researchers in tomorrow's professional fields, and they can do this by making use of both, the Internet and more traditional print media.

4B *Die Aufgabe ist klar strukturiert: zuerst sind die tragenden Gedanken der beiden Texte mit dem Stichwort „impact of the Internet on young people" zu verknüpfen, um danach einige dieser Aussagen mit Erkenntnissen aus Ihren Literaturstudien zu vergleichen. Interessant ist die Formulierung „and other media", denn die behandelte Figur muss nicht unbedingt mit dem Internet zu tun haben.*

In the following text, I will first discuss the impact the Internet has on today's youth and then compare that to the role television plays in the lives of viewers as portrayed in the film "The Truman Show."

There can be no doubt that today's younger generation is totally hooked on the Internet and everything connected with it. But what exactly do youth do on the Internet and how does this affect their daily habits, their approach to learning and even their outlook on life?

Well, there isn't much that teens *don't* do on the Net. To begin with, the Internet is used for just about anything that can be done in one's indoor leisure time, whether it be watching TV or a movie (yes, on the Web), playing all sorts of games (harmless and perhaps not so harmless) with friends or total strangers, or catching up on the latest gossip about any of hundreds of famous stars and starlets. (I wonder what Paris Hilton did yesterday …)

As far as school is concerned, one should distinguish between behavior at school and at home. When a teacher takes a class to the computer lab, he usually has an eye on what's going on, how the students approach the assignment, etc., so of course everyone does just what he is supposed to, and little more. At home, however, it is common to look for shortcuts to finishing term papers, filling in worksheets etc. with the aid of solutions that have been posted by other students, with little regard to their quality. Unfortunately, the attitude seems widespread that it is often of little importance exactly what information someone has found and printed out, as long as he has something in front of him when the teacher comes around to check homework. Only more ambitious, more meticulous students go the extra mile to check out the accuracy of the information they retrieve from the Internet and actually make use of multiple sources – including "old-fashioned" books – to increase their knowledge and lay the foundation for their professional lives. In fact, there is evidence that those young people are often the same ones who acquired adequate reading skills at an early age and continue to apply and improve such skills using the material they find on the Internet.

In reference to "The Truman Show", it is actually not the protagonist we need to take a closer look at, but instead the viewers and cast members of the show, who knowingly take advantage first of the baby Truman, then of the adolescent and finally the adult Truman Burbank to satisfy their daily needs for amusement and diversion. Indeed, they are so captivated by the artificial world created especially for this one individual that people around the world become addicted to a daily portion of substitute excitement at Truman's cost to counteract the dullness of their own lives, and they remain a faithful, uncritical audience for almost thirty years. They demonstrate unceasing empathy with a total stranger in this unusual form of soap opera, and even actors in the series are seen to respond to and comment on Truman's actions in a generally supportive fashion.

At the end of the film, Truman discovers a door that leads him from his former artificial world and life out into the possibly dangerous, but certainly unknown world that he is really not prepared for. The all but unanimous response of the worldwide audience appears to be quite encouraging; the same people who watch and thrive on the plight of their victim day in and day out thrill at the prospect that Truman can thus grow to be a full-fledged member of "reality." How can this paradox be explained? One reason is that the daily spectators thus seem to achieve atonement for their selfish behavior in the past, in which they have knowingly allowed Truman to be exploited. Truman's freedom, his introduction to true knowledge upon leaving the modern-day "Garden of Eden" is the redemption from their sins of selfishness and passivity.

This scenario can be compared to the attitude of many teenagers regarding their fixation on the Internet. Even as Truman's most faithful fans during his virtual imprisonment are relieved when he sees real daylight, most youths eventually grow up to make more efficient and prudent use of the powerful media at their disposal.

4C *Diese Aufgabe zielt auf* creative writing *und erfordert Kenntnisse über Form und Inhalt von Zeitungsartikeln mit Jugendlichen als Zielgruppe. Bei aller Freiheit, die die Aufgabe auszeichnet, sollte man ein angemessenes sprachliches Niveau wahren: SMS-Sprache und Jugendslang sollten hier vermieden werden. Vergessen Sie zudem nicht, auf Argumente der beiden Texte Bezug zu nehmen.*

Reflections on the role of the Internet in the everyday lives of teenagers

The article you are reading now is somewhat of a curiosity. Until recently, I could hardly make myself understood in your language, and now I have been asked to write about a subject that is likely just as dear to all of you as it is to me: the Internet. What would life be like today without the Internet? (As for that, how did the cavemen ever survive without it?) The Internet, and everything connected with it, is such a part of our everyday lives that we would likely begin to show withdrawal symptoms if we had to go a whole week without checking our online mailbox. Seriously though, being connected is simply trendy and a question of personal lifestyle. I mean, sure, not everyone wants to display his inner soul, gossip etc. on MySpace, but for lots of people that is a matter of personal expression, while the rest of us may want to upload our latest guitar session to YouTube or download the latest hip-hop hits to our MP3 player. As for me, I have an ongoing photo album at SmugMug.com, so that all my friends and relatives back home can share my exchange experience with me.

Even at school, the Internet and other computer-related technologies play a major role in our daily schedule. Here at your *(our)* school, every student has his or her own school email address, and there are wireless LAN hot spots all over the building. In this and many other ways, your school is far more modern than the average German school. (But the Germans are making strong efforts to catch up!) The relationship between teachers and students seems so relaxed when you get your homework assignment by email. And when you send in your solutions as return mail, it's so cool to find that the teacher really corrected your work on the computer and sent you the results back at one o'clock in the morning!

As much fun as the Internet is, though, we should still be wary of the drawbacks. Who doesn't have friends who are in danger of being totally addicted to their computer, or who resort to Facebook and Internet Messenger for pseudo-"conversations" with complete strangers, when they could be talking to us, their real friends, in person. Nothing against the Internet, but let's help them to get back down to earth.

Now for a serious word on schoolwork. I don't know about you, but I'm beginning to see what my history teacher has been telling me all along that I shouldn't be content with the first (or second, or third) source that Google points out to me. I have begun to realize that some of the "information" which I have hastily copied off the Web for my homework has either been really superficial or sometimes even outright wrong. But how can you tell the difference? This is something we have never been taught to cope with. And that's why I'm looking forward to taking the course Ms Smith is offering next trimester; it's designed to help us devise guidelines to discern which sources offer valid data and which are biased.

So, it's about time to round this article up now. If you want to comment on it (positively, of course), link into the magazine's blog and let us know what you think. By the way, if you're reading this article in the paper version of the school magazine, lay it aside and hop online to check out the linked version. Or you can click on my avatar there and send me a personal message.

Your German friend Markus

Text I: David Randall and Victoria Richards: Facebook can ruin your life. And so can MySpace, Bebo …
(excerpt from an online article)

Note: *People will post just about anything on social networking sites. And the information can be used against them.*

Saucy pictures and intimate confessions on social networking sites can be taken down and used in evidence against you in ways never dreamed of. […]

Just ask the 27 workers at the Automobile Club of Southern California fired for messages about colleagues on their MySpace sites; the Florida sheriff's deputy whose MySpace page revealed his heavy drinking and fascination with female breasts – and swiftly found himself handing in his badge; the Argos worker in Wokingham fired for saying on Facebook that working at the firm was "shit"; the Las Vegas teacher at a Catholic school fired after he declared himself gay on his MySpace page; the staff of an Ottawa grocery chain fired for their "negative comments" on Facebook; the 19 Northampton police officers investigated for Facebook comments; and Kevin Colvin, an intern at Anglo Irish Bank, who told his employers he had a family emergency, but whose Facebook page revealed he had, in reality, been cavorting in drag at a Hallowe'en's party. What these and other cases show is that employers and authorities are now monitoring what people imagined were private websites – and using the contents against them. […]

At Cambridge, at least one don has admitted "discreetly" scanning applicants' pages – a practice now widespread in job recruitment. A survey released by Viadeo said that 62 per cent of British employers now check the Facebook, MySpace or Bebo pages of some applicants, and that a quarter had rejected candidates as a result. Reasons given by employers included concerns about "excess alcohol abuse", ethics and job "disrespect".

Viadeo's UK country manager, Peter Cunningham, said the results should act as a wake-up call to anyone who has ever posted personal information online. "Millions of people are leaving personal information online, much of which is cached and remains available via search engines even after the author has removed the web page," he said. […]

The first Facebook or Bebo divorce case cannot be far away. Divorce specialist Elizabeth Allen, head of family law at Stephens and Scown, Exeter, said: "Social networking has much more scope for trouble because of the public element. It's got the potential to be more explosive. It's just like airing your dirty laundry. We've had divorces that have been due to Friends Reunited in the past and that will be replaced by Facebook with the next generation. Now most people who would never have written a love letter to someone are writing it all down and sending it because they somehow think it's different." *(433 words)*

Source: Randall, David and Richards, Victoria. "Facebook can ruin your life. And so can MySpace, bebo ..." The Independent *10 Feb. 2008. http://www.independent.co.uk/news/science/facebook-can-ruin-your-life-and-so-can-myspace-bebo-780521.html. [10 March 2008]*

Annotations

subheading	social networking sites: sites like Facebook where people meet online to share information
l. 1	saucy: *here:* sexy
ll. 12/13	to cavort in drag: *here:* to jump or dance around in a playful or sexual way wearing women's clothes
l. 16	don: university professor
l. 17/22	Viadeo: online business social network for finding clients, business partners and key business information
l. 24	to cache: to store information in a computer's memory for a short time
l. 25	search engine: computer program that helps you find information on the Internet
l. 29	scope: potential, opportunity to develop something
l. 30	to air dirty laundry: *here:* to discuss something embarrassing about yourself where everyone can see, know or hear it
l. 31	Friends Reunited: site aiming to reunite people who have common backgrounds/interests

Text II: Chart and Table

Types of Online Communities of which US Internet Users Are Members, 2005 & 2007 (% of respondents)

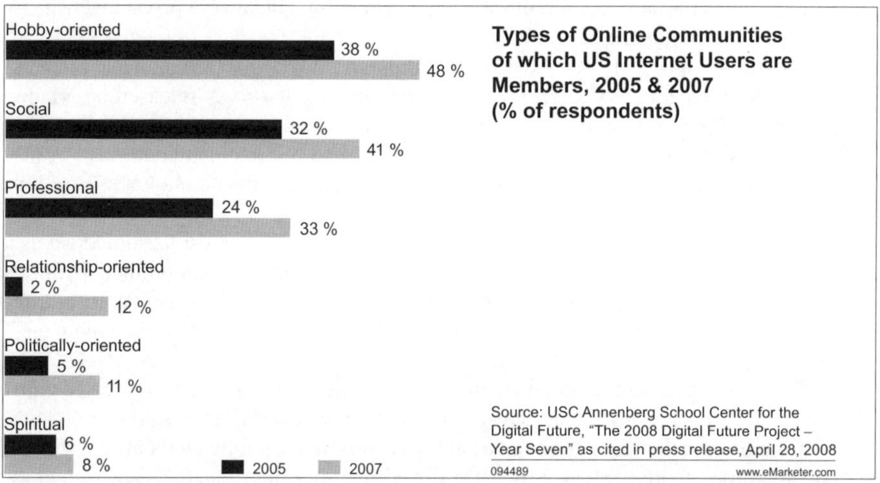

Source: USC Annenberg School Center for the Digital Future. "The 2008 Digital Future Project-Year Seven." Press release 28 April 2008. http://blogs.praized.com/seb/files/2008/05/types-of-online-communities.gif. [10 Sept. 2008]

Social networking growth by worldwide region in June 2008

	Jun-07	Jun-08	Growth
worldwide	464,437	580,510	25 %
Asia Pacific	162,738	200,555	23 %
Europe	122,527	165,256	35 %
North America	120,848	131,255	9 %
Latin America	40,098	53,248	33 %
Middle East – Africa	18,226	30,197	66 %

(Figures are given in millions, e. g. 464,437 = 464,437,000.)

Source: comScore. 2 Sept. 2008. http://www.itfacts.biz/social-networking-growth-by-worldwide-region-in-june-2008/11330. [1 Oct. 2008]

Tasks
Work on a total of three tasks.
Tasks 1 and 2 are compulsory. Choose one task from 3.

1 Outline the impact of social networking sites on their users as described in the article. Do not write more than 120 words. (25 %)

2 Describe the contents of both the chart and the table (Text II) and compare their messages to the information given in Text I. (35 %)

In all the following tasks you are expected to refer to Text I and Text II as well as to further relevant material/information about English-speaking countries.

3A "[E]mployers and authorities are now monitoring what people imagined were private websites – and using the contents against them." (Text I, ll. 13–15) Explain the quote and comment on the role the Internet and other media play in exposing the private lives of people in public. (40 %)

OR

3B Using Text I as a starting point, discuss how a character from literature or film who finds it difficult to express emotions in direct communication deals with his/her feelings. (40 %)

OR

3C You want to design a flyer in which you inform your fellow students about positive and negative aspects of using online social networking sites. Write its text and describe its layout giving reasons for your decisions. (40 %)

You are expected to write at least 500 words in no more than 240 minutes.

Lösungsvorschläge

1. *Aus den vielen Beispielen in diesem Text muss das Verbindende, das Allgemeine extrahiert werden. Achten Sie vor allem auch auf eine logische Verbindung der Gedanken.*

   The article by David Randall und Victoria Richards begins with several examples in which individuals' self-representations on social networking sites led to problems in their real lives, usually the loss of their jobs. This happens because many people speak out more freely there than they would in person. This web content is particularly precarious, in that it remains retrievable by search engines even after the author has withdrawn his web page. Such information is often sought out by employers who question their employees' loyalty or conduct, but also by universities, checking up on their applicants. Also, partners frequently turn to the supposedly private and impersonal websites to air thoughts they would have never stated publicly.

2. *Im Vordergrund der Bearbeitung stehen die beiden Teile von Text 2, aber zum Schluss darf der Vergleich mit Text 1 nicht fehlen. Achten Sie auf Fachbegriffe im Bezug auf „charts" sowie gängige Formulierungen zum Vergleich von Statistiken.*

   The first part of Text II, a horizontal bar chart, shows the relative frequency with which Internet users from the United States are involved in various types of online communities. A gray and a black bar assigned to each type of community allow a comparison of the frequency for each type of community in the years 2005 and 2007.
   The chart covers six different types of communities, which together comprise a broad array of fields, from those of "professional" interest and "politically-oriented" groups to those with "social" and "hobby-oriented" interests. Finally, there are two other groups of a more personal nature, one being "relationship-oriented" and the other built around "spiritual" interests. It should be noted that in *all* types of communities, the numbers of members increased between 2005 and 2007. The relative strength of the first three positions remained intact, the most popular type being the "hobby-oriented" communities, followed by "social" and "professional" communities. The type which showed the greatest increase (1,000 %) was made up of "relationship-oriented" communities. In both years, the type which showed the least activity was the "spiritual" group. The second part of Text II consists of a table which displays the growth of social networking as a whole in various regions of the world between June 2007 and June 2008. Like the chart, the table, too, shows that there has plainly been a significant worldwide increase in the spread of social networking. Perhaps the least expected rate of increase was that in North America (9 %), which was substantially lower than those of all other regions examined, from the Asia Pacific region (23 %) to the top "winner": Middle East – East Africa (66 %).
   Text I and Text II correlate in the fact that the use of social networking sites has grown considerably, most predominantly in fields of personal interest. Text I goes

beyond this conclusion and demonstrates that social networking can have dangerous consequences under certain circumstances.

3A *Diese Aufgabe beinhaltet eine ausführlichere Interpretation der Informationen aus den beiden Texten. Hier sind das Gewichten, Ordnen von Gedanken und das schlüssige Argumentieren wichtig, der Raum für zusätzliche, eigene Gedanken dagegen eher begrenzt.*

The quotation refers to a growing phenomenon: People and organizations who have an interest in knowing about how others conduct themselves both in public and in private life increasingly search out private homepages and personal profile pages in Facebook and other social networking portals for information. The motivation of employers, universities, teachers etc. to search for such information is not harmless curiosity, but rather it is intended to test the loyalty of employees, the propriety of off-hours behavior and many other questions that a company or organization might deem relevant.

The underlying reason for this new development is that numerous people have been found to be more open and explicit when they felt they were participating in a trendy, but basically anonymous, carefree and fun medium. Of course, such an assumption is very naive, and thus any number of people have already lost their jobs or had to bear other adverse effects. And there are other scenarios that can be just as tragic. Someone simply browsing a social networking site looking for people with similar hobbies might come across a juicy tidbit of information that could quickly be spread to print media one day and broadcast throughout the world the next day. Or just imagine what a political opponent might do with a nasty detail about his opponent's sex life or financial status. And even a seemingly unimportant detail can have undesired consequences, such as when a love-stricken stalker or an unrelenting paparazzo chances upon the address or telephone number of a celebrity.

One possible reaction for social networkers can be a loss of trust in their employers and other superiors if they feel they are being spied on, especially if they have done nothing to deserve such treatment. Such incidents lead to the call for stricter data protection and regulation of information collection and dissemination. There are important lessons to be learned from these developments. First and foremost, those who are active in social networking (and their number is on the increase) should be careful about how much and what kinds of information about themselves and about others they make available to the broader Internet world. If someone wants to communicate details about his private life, he should be aware of his personal motivation for doing so and of the potential dangers involved. And as far as remarks about friends and foes are concerned, much of what is posted shows poor taste at the very least, and is often illegal slander.

On the other hand, some of the activities of employers who check up on employees, students and others are morally questionable as well, and the time may not be far off when legislative measures may become necessary to protect unsuspecting, honest people who frequent social networking portals.

3B *Nach der Entscheidung für eine passende Figur aus Literatur oder Film, sollten Sie noch einmal Kerngedanken aus Text I aufgreifen. Erst danach sollte die Besprechung und Deutung der Figur erfolgen, jeweils mit sorgfältig eingestreuten Rückgriffen auf Aussagen aus dem Text. Inhaltlich stehen Fragen der persönlichen Interaktion und der Gefühlsäußerung im Vordergrund.*

Text I vividly demonstrates the urge many people seem to have to take part in social networking as an outlet for thoughts and feelings they are unable to express in more appropriate ways. The text further exemplifies the tragic consequences this has often had for people who mistakenly presume that their unguarded utterances of spite und grudge will go unnoticed. Such persons are often shy and dread personal confrontation with peers, colleagues and employers, perhaps because they have an inferiority complex. But in the illusive anonymity of the Internet, they develop verbal courage they would hardly have face to face with anyone.

In many cases, such behavior bears similarities to that of Holden Caulfield, the sixteen-year-old protagonist in J. D. Salinger's novel, *The Catcher in the Rye*. In the first-person narrative, Holden is full of contradictions, which is probably what makes him seem like an alter ego to many youths going through the throes of puberty. The story opens just when he gets kicked out of boarding school, and thus begins an odyssey that takes him through a brief, but turbulent sequence of events which leave him no alternative but to seek professional help to find ways to communicate with the outside world.

Holden is often self-effacing, but also insulting to others. From the outset, everything and everyone around him appears "lousy", and he is helpless to grasp his own part in various predicaments, such as the fact that his fencing team has to forfeit a match because Holden forgets the foils on the subway. He can hardly defend himself, verbally or physically, and yet he often gets involved in arguments for no apparent reason. Holden abhors "phonies", or people whose shallowness he easily sees through, and yet he often seems to be just as phony as they are.

There is a special place in Holden's heart for his younger sister Phoebe. Is he her guardian? Is she the personification of what he would like to be like? She is perhaps the only person in the book who does not give him advice, but simply accepts him for what he is. In her simple frankness, she – or the thought of her – helps him get back on his feet.

Late in the story, Holden experiences a symbolic second birth by passing through a giant womb in a museum, of all places. Soon after, he realizes his need for a new basis for communication with himself and those around him. If only Holden had access to social networking on the Internet as a means of expression for his thoughts and whims, perhaps his life would be easier …

3C *Hier werden sowohl gestalterisches Geschick als auch* creative writing *verlangt. Wichtige Entscheidungen, z. B. für eine bestimmte Form von Flyer, dessen Aussehen, grafische Zusätze u. ä. sollen kurz begründet werden. Die neutral gehaltenen Textteile sind für „fellow students“ abzufassen, die Inhalte orientieren sich an den beiden Texten.*

General character of flyer: The flyer is intended to be informative (in contrast to an advertising leaflet, a notification or an invitation), and so it contains a considerable amount of text. The language is not sensational, but straightforward and basically formal, and it does not address the reader personally.

Paper size and general format: In spite of the amount of necessary information, the customary DIN A4 size should be adequate. The paper is to be printed in portrait format and only on one side of the paper. The flyer is not to be folded.
If available, the flyer should be printed on colored paper that is beige or light blue. More striking colors, particularly reddish or darker tones, would not fit in with the neutral atmosphere of this particular flyer.

Layout: The entire heading area is rather large, at least 5 cm in height. The actual heading is centered. It is flanked right and left by two similar drawings. Each shows a laptop tuned into MySpace and a figure using the laptop. The person at the left laptop is an attractive girl doing something like talking or singing a song. The other person is recognizable as a young man, but he has no face and seems passive, but attentive.
The remainder of the flyer consists of text in two columns. The left column contains short key words in bold typeface somewhat larger than that in the right column. The right column contains the main text.

Heading: Knock knock – Are you sure you want to know who's there?

Subheading: Are MyFace & Co the ultimate kick or a kick in the face?

Text:

Attraction of online social networking	In an unbelievably short time, social networking has become one of the favorite pastimes of millions of people throughout the world. While the new medium is frequented by all generations, it is especially attractive to people in their late teens and twenties, who are in tune with the Internet and other trendy gadgets, and with … themselves.
Personal motivation	The personal motivation of those who take part in MyFace and similar portals varies considerably. One of the chief reasons is simply to be in on an alternative form of socializing, in addition to (or replacing?) social activities with friends, relatives, colleagues etc. And some undoubtedly hope for Mr or Miss Right to respond. At a more serious level, social networking is excellent for exchanging hobby tips and experiences, finding out more about interesting people from interesting cultures, checking out potential vacation sites and dozens more topics which can have practical value and be fun at the same time.
Drawbacks	Unfortunately, it has also become popular to use social networking sites to spread slanderous gossip, assorted forms of bullying and mobbing, and all sorts of personal insults towards "friends", teachers, parents, etc. Many of these excesses are illegal, and all of them are unethical. You may not realize it, but more and more users of social networking sites are persons, companies and organizations who simply want to check up on the general behavior of people they deal with professionally. These people have good reason to protect themselves and others from slanderous remarks and other forms of questionable conduct.
Do's and don'ts	Netiquette is important in social networking. Anonymity is no excuse to be abusive of anyone. Likewise, "four-letter words" are entirely unnecessary, and many of your readers might take offence at your carelessness. Also be wary of being too open about private matters with the rest of the world. A secret is a secret and is nobody else's business, and there really are people out there who would love to take advantage of you in many different ways.

Abiturprüfung Berlin 2009
Englisch Leistungskurs – Aufgabe 1

Text I: Jon Williams: News Blackout
(excerpt from a BBC [British Broadcasting Corporation] blog)

Note: *Jon Williams is the BBC's World News editor.*

Welcome to The Editors, a site where we, editors from across BBC News, will share our dilemmas and issues.

At its simplest, journalism is about telling people things they don't know. So when the Ministry of Defence approached the BBC – along with other parts of the UK media – to ask us not to tell our audiences about a possible deployment of Prince Harry to Afghanistan, it was something we thought long and hard about.

A news blackout is unusual, but not unique. An agreement exists between the police and the media over the reporting of kidnaps – the police have the right to request that media organisations don't report an abduction while negotiations are under way, in case it makes the release of the hostage more difficult; in return, they accept the responsibility to update the media regularly and reveal the full story, on camera, once the situation has been resolved. When lives are at risk, it's not always helpful to have things played out in the glare of publicity.

Last summer – on the day my colleague Alan Johnston was released in Gaza – the Chief of the General Staff, Sir Richard Dannatt, met editors to make the case for a voluntary agreement. He was very candid; Harry wanted a career in the Army and he needed to be able to be deployed to do what he'd been trained to do, even if it was just for a day.

After five months of discussions, using the kidnap agreement as our model, the MoD and the UK media reached an understanding; we wouldn't speculate or report on the prince's deployments to minimise the danger to him and to others. In return, we'd get access to him before, during and after his time in Afghanistan. It was a voluntary agreement – any of the organisations could have decided to leave at any time. We – and the other UK broadcasters and newspapers – were clear that we would not report his deployment.

So, for the past ten weeks, the BBC, ITV and Sky News have been filming with Prince Harry – the first time we've been up close and personal with him. We interviewed him at Clarence House in mid-December, just before he was sent to Afghanistan, we spent some time with him at the start of January when he was settling in at a remote base in Southern Helmand Province, and most recently, we filmed with him last week at a new location in Helmand Province.

In truth, the surprise is that the agreement lasted so long. We – and the other UK broadcasters – were clear that we would not report his deployment. But nor would we deceive our audiences.

On Christmas Day, when neither Prince William nor Prince Harry attended the regular service with other members of the Royal Family at Sandringham, we agreed with the Ministry of Defence that they would say that both princes were spending Christmas with their regiments – William volunteered for Christmas duty to help out his brother! It prompted some inquiries from one US TV network who had to be briefed on the story. […]

Then yesterday, the Drudge Report – the online US website famous for breaking the story of Bill Clinton's relationship with Monica Lewinsky – put the story on its front page. The game was up. We, and the other broadcasters, agreed with the Ministry of Defence that the story was out and it would be wrong not to tell our audiences what had been going on.

We don't do this stuff lightly – there are no other "voluntary agreements" in place at the moment, there's nothing else we're not telling you. Until yesterday, only a handful of people in the BBC knew about the story – trust me, keeping secrets from other journalists is hard work! Our job normally is to make these things public, not keep them from you. But this was never just about Prince Harry's safety, it was also about the security of the soldiers serving with him. No editor wants to be responsible for increasing the risk they already face from the Taliban. Nor do I think our audiences would have thanked us for doing so. *(688 words)*

Source: Williams, Jon. "News Blackout." Weblog entry. BBC News, The Editors, 1 April 2008. http://www.bbc.co.uk/blogs/theeditors/2008/02/news_blackout.html [3 April 2008]

Annotations

	blog: personal internet page containing specific information
l. 1	site: website
l. 5	deployment: moving soldiers or military equipment
l. 9	abduction: kidnapping, taking someone away by force
l. 9	negotiation: discussion between the representatives of opposing groups
l. 13	glare: the full attention of
l. 16	candid: honest, frank
l. 20	MoD: Ministry of Defence
l. 28	Clarence House: official residence of Prince Charles and his sons
l. 30	remote: far away
l. 30	Helmand Province: province in Afghanistan
l. 34	to deceive: to make sb believe sth that is not true
l. 36	Sandringham: village in Norfolk (England) where the Royal family owns a country house
ll. 39/40	to brief sb on sth: to give sb all the information about a situation that is needed

Text II: Cartoon

Source: http://www.cpj.org/toons/toons.htm?photo=1. [19 Feb. 2009]

Tasks
Work on a total of three tasks.
Tasks 1 and 2 are compulsory. Choose one task from 3.

1 Outline the dilemmas and issues reported in "News Blackout" (Text I). Do not write more than 150 words. (30 %)

2 Briefly state the message of Text I and describe the cartoon (Text II). Find a suitable caption for the cartoon and give reasons for your choice with reference to the message of Text I. (30 %)

In all of the following tasks you are expected to refer to Text I and Text II as well as to further relevant material/information.

3A "At its simplest, journalism is about telling people things they don't know. So when the Ministry of Defence approached the BBC – along with other parts of the UK media – to ask us not to tell our audiences about a possible deployment of Prince Harry to Afghanistan, it was something we thought long and hard about."
Referring to this quote from Text I (ll. 3–6) and to the function of journalism in a democratic society, point out the positive and negative implications of the BBC's decision not to report on Prince Harry's deployment to Afghanistan. (40 %)

OR

3B Considering the information from the blog (Text I) and other information you are familiar with, discuss how websites in which bloggers exchange political information are able to influence our globalized world. (40 %)

OR

3C You have been asked to organize a discussion on how students at your school perceive and use the media in their everyday lives. Invite a student from your school, an editor from the BBC as well as two other guest speakers.
Give reasons for choosing these speakers and suggest what contributions you expect all four of them to make to a meaningful discussion. (40 %)

You are expected to write at least 700 words in no more than 300 minutes.

Lösungsvorschläge

1. Jon Williams argues that the main purpose of journalism is to inform readers or viewers about what is going on in the world. There is however the delicate subject of news blackouts, which, at first glance, may be contrary to the core function of journalism. News blackouts can be agreed on voluntarily, as was the case with Prince Harry's deployment to Afghanistan to save not only the heir to the throne's life, but also that of his fellow soldiers. Another case are kidnappings that are not to be reported on before the police has solved them in order not to block negotiations. This does not mean that the journalists are not allowed to film or process the information they get, but there is no publishing or broadcasting. During this time they may also have to keep information from their colleagues, which provides another challenge.

2. *Die Ihnen vorliegende Aufgabe enthält 4 Punkte, die Sie bearbeiten müssen: fassen Sie kurz die zentrale Aussage von Text I zusammen, beschreiben Sie den Cartoon, finden Sie eine (evtl. mehrere) passende Titel für den Cartoon und begründen Sie Ihre Wahl, indem Sie auf Text I Bezug nehmen. Wenn Sie sich bei der Interpretation des Cartoons unsicher sind, versuchen Sie mehrere plausible Erklärungsansätze, die Sie allerdings immer gut begründen und am Cartoon festmachen sollten.*

   Text I is a weblog entry written by a BBC journalist to justify and explain the reasons for news blackouts in special cases. Even if informing readers and viewers is the key task of journalism, it might be sensible to block news instead of increasing the risk for those involved, especially when it comes to crime or military operations. The cartoon underlines this message visually. We can see a prison cell, with a guard standing outside to keep the prisoners – letters in this case – under surveillance. The letters A to D are chained to the prison wall, whereas the letters H and F are chained to the floor. There are in fact two messages the cartoon wants to get across. It refers, on the one hand, to the information that is kept secret from those who want, and have the right, to be informed. This suggests that the imprisonment is only a temporary one. On the other hand, the cartoon undoubtedly refers to the precarious job of a journalist. They are permanently exposed to moral conflicts and the consequences their reports can have are huge burdens that, to put it bluntly, are comparable to a prison sentence. This is exactly the dilemma described in Text I. That is why the two following captions would be very suitable to link the text and the cartoon: "New blackout – imprisoning information" or "Being a journalist – between moral integrity and prison".

3A *Auch diese Aufgabe enthält 4 zu bearbeitende Punkte, die Ihnen aber im Prinzip schon eine mögliche Gliederung vorgeben: Gehen Sie in Ihrer Einleitung auf das Zitat ein, indem Sie kurz dessen Grundproblematik zusammenfassen und nennen Sie Aufgaben des Journalismus in einer demokratischen Gesellschaft. Ihren Hauptteil gliedern Sie nach positiven und negativen Auswirkungen der BBC Entscheidung für eine Nachrichtensperre. Am Schluss sollten Sie Ihre Ausführungen noch einmal in einer zentralen Aussage zusammenfassen ohne zu wiederholen.*

"At its simplest, journalism is about telling people things they don't know." The question is whether people have to know everything or whether a bit of ignorance can be an advantage rather than a detriment. Another question is whether this is compatible with the principles of our democratic society. A free press is a central cornerstone of a democratic society and an essential tool of education as long as the information provided is accurate and reliable.
So what about the implications of news blackouts, especially the one concerning Prince Harry's deployment in Afghanistan?
The BBC, in a kind of gentlemen's agreement with the Ministry of Defence, agreed on a news blackout in order not to endanger Harry's and the other soldiers' lives. In my opinion, this was the right decision, as the coverage would have been mere sensationalism. There are scarcely any reports on other soldiers doing this highly dangerous job and sacrificing their lives for their country, so why should Harry get special treatment? Is the job he does any different from what the other soldiers do? Does his family fear more for his life than any other family does for their son's? The answer to both questions is "no", which proves that entertainment and the satisfaction of curiosity would have been the driving forces behind this news item.
Another argument for a news blockage in this case is the journalistic commitment to society. There is undoubtedly a certain responsibility involved in selecting stories for publishing or broadcasting. That is why journalists have to assess the consequences of their work. In this case the detriment would have been bigger than the benefit and thus it was the right decision to agree on the news blackout.
The only negative implication borders on the delicate subject of censorship. In our society there is freedom of expression and the citizens have the right to be informed of all that's going on and might affect their lives. If official bodies, in this case the Ministry of Defence, can decide on what is published and what is not, we are not far from a totalitarian influence that endangers the basic principles of our democratic society. In the case in question, the behaviour can be justified with the buzzword of moral integrity. So should there be an official body for moral issues which decides on news blackouts in such cases? Then the question arising is that of a generally-accepted definition of morality.
I think, as in this case, that journalists should not allow their work to be restricted by official bodies, but should assess the benefits and detriments of their reports and be aware that their job is a very responsible one and that not every news item may be a blessing for society.

3B *Wie in der folgenden Lösung können Sie zuerst auf die Beziehung von Blogs und Medien eingehen und danach die Auswirkungen politischer Blogs anhand eines Beispiels, in diesem Fall Chinas Tibet-Politik und deren Auswirkung auf die Internetzensur, erklären.*

Statistics reveal that there are about 150,000 new weblogs created every day in our global blogosphere. More and more people are starting to participate in a global rather than a local culture. And thus it is not surprising that blogs also influence mainstream media, as the BBC weblog shows. Opinions, concerns, advice, articles, statements and questions are posted on the internet in order to get global feedback. This might also have been the reason behind the BBC weblog. News blackouts are an international subject and some countries are more affected by this means than others. Thus it is interesting to get statements on this issue from all over the world. Intercultural learning plays an important part here and the more we blog, the closer we get to each other. Our world will finally change into a global village where everyone is connected and geographical differences do not play that important a role anymore. Local issues become global and vice versa.

Exchanging political opinion via blogs is an efficient tool of education and information. But this also means that, at least in theory, everyone has access to all items of information. And this can of course be a danger to some regimes which do not want their people to be too well informed. During the 2008 Olympic Games China restricted access to unlimited information on the net by blocking sites that contained information that could have been detrimental to China in the context of the Tibet issue. As blogs are a great source for sharing thoughts they might, from a political point of view, be a danger to political freedom in countries where people are not used to having that many rights and could kindle protests and uprisings. "At its simplest, journalism [and blogs] is about telling people things they don't know" and this is exactly the crux of the matter: a huge opportunity for a growing worldwide interconnectedness, but also a potentially dangerous tool laying bare deplorable political and social circumstances.

3C *Bei dieser Aufgabe ist Ihnen im Prinzip kein Format vorgegeben. Sie können einfach ein Erklärungsstatement abgeben oder einen Flyer schreiben, mit dem Sie die entsprechenden Personen anwerben (siehe folgendes Lösungsbeispiel). Geben Sie zuerst kurz an, wen Sie einladen möchten (dabei kommt es vor allem darauf an, dass Sie präzisieren, wer die beiden Gastredner sein sollen) und begründen Sie Ihre Wahl. Dann müssen Sie darauf eingehen, welche Beiträge Sie von den jeweiligen Sprechern im genannten Kontext erwarten.*

Speakers wanted!!

I am in the process of organizing a discussion on how students perceive and use media in their everyday lives and I need you to make this discussion work!

To get as many perspectives as possible I want to invite you if you are:

- a student from the Lemke Gymnasium here in Berlin
  At our school we are very fortunate to be well equipped with modern media and we also have access to various newspapers and magazines. So I would like to know how this affects how you use the media in your spare time. How do you perceive the presence of the media in your everyday life? Is there a difference in the use of media when it comes to information, entertainment or communica-

tion? To get an answer to all these questions, you are the right person to participate in this discussion.

- an editor from the BBC
  This discussion is not just about opinions. The audience should get some background knowledge on a journalist's everyday activities and the influence of modern media, such as blogging and the web. I am convinced that you, as an expert, will not only inform the audience on these questions but will also discuss how journalists react to the changing media usage of young people in their everyday lives.
- a parent of a student from the Lemke Gymnasium Berlin
  I have always wanted to know how parents support their children when it comes to growing up with (modern) media. Do the media play an important role in your household? How do you use media yourself? How can parents lay the foundation for dealing with media information sensibly? These are only a few questions I would like to ask you, so your participation is crucial to the success of my discussion.
- an expert from the Faculty for Media and Information Studies at the University of Berlin
  We are curious to know which trends can be observed in young people's dealings with the media and how you assess future developments. Will there be a return to more traditional forms of media? I am sure that my fellow students await your visit eagerly …

I have tried to trace the contributions I expect to make it easier for you to prepare for this discussion.

It goes without saying that besides substantial arguments flexibility will add zest to our discussion and I am sure that we will have a great, informative evening.

I am looking forward to meeting you. Please contact …

Abiturprüfung Berlin 2009
Englisch Leistungskurs – Aufgabe 2

Text I: David K. Shipler: A Poor Cousin of the Middle Class
(excerpt from an article)

She is the invisible American, unnoticed because she blends in. Like millions at the bottom of the labor force who contribute to the country's prosperity, Caroline's diligence is a camouflage. At the convenience store where she works, customers do not see that she struggles against destitution. [...]

She was out of sight, part of the hidden America. Always in search of something better somewhere else. Caroline has moved from job to job, from place to place, from New England to Florida and back – and now to Indiana – without anchoring herself solidly in a community that can offer support.

Just over a year after arriving in Muncie, where she lives in a small apartment in a public housing project, she remains unconnected. "I don't know many people here still," she told me recently. "I just get out to work and do errands." [...]

Futility has nagged at Caroline for a long time. Four years ago, at the dawn of the new millennium, she sat at her kitchen table in Claremont, N.H., and added up her life. It was the height of the economic boom. The nation wallowed in luxury, burst with microchips, consumed with abandon, swaggered globally. Everything grew larger: homes, vehicles, stock portfolios, life expectancy. Never before in the sweep of human history had so many people been so utterly comfortable.

Caroline was not one of them. She had achieved two of her three goals. She had earned a college diploma (a two-year associate's degree), and she had gone from a homeless shelter into her own house (owned mostly by a bank). The third objective, "a good paying job," as she put it, still eluded her. Back in the mid-'70's, she earned $6 an hour in a Vermont factory that made plastic cigarette lighters and cases for Gillette razors. A quarter century later, she earned $6.60 an hour stocking shelves and working cash registers at a vast Wal-Mart superstore. "And that's sad," she declared. "I'm only making 80 cents more than I did more than 20 years ago." Or less, taking into account the rise in the cost of living.

She was not the victim of racial discrimination; she was white. She was not lazy; she was caustic about colleagues who were. She was punctual, rarely out sick, willing to do night shifts and assiduous in her work habits. The Wal-Mart manager, Mark Brown, called her "a nice lady" with lots of enthusiasm. "She's self-driven," he observed. "She's always willing to learn and better herself. She's got potential. She can definitely move up." But she did not move up. She had never moved up. And that ceased to amaze her; it had been going on for so long, in job after job after job. She was astonished only by Mark Brown's praise. "I'm surprised," she remarked when I told her what he said. She was stacking blank videotapes on a shelf. "I didn't think they liked me here. People don't usually says nice things about me."

Somewhere along this track that leads nowhere, a good many Americans give up on the dream. They sink back onto welfare, or they stop imagining themselves as foremen or managers. Caroline was then 50, with so many years of disappointment that her bouts of depression, for which she was occasionally treated, seemed unsurprising.

Still, she kept striving. She called herself "luckylady" in her e-mail address. She said, "Have a wonderful day," on her answering machine. She did not have big thoughts about corporate profits or dark judgments about society's unfairness. She just tried for basic financial security. Her persistence played like a dissonant melody against the monotone of job stagnation. Again and again, she applied to manage one sales department or another at Wal-Mart, and again and again and again she was passed over in favor of men – or, she observed wryly, women who were younger and slimmer. *(647 words)*

Source: Shipler, David K. "A Poor Cousin of the Middle Class." The New York Times *19 January 2004.*

Annotations

ll. 2/3	diligence (formal): steady effort, hard work
l. 3	camouflage: *here:* pretense
l. 4	destitution: extreme poverty
l. 12	futility: pointlessness, uselessness
l. 13	N.H.: New Hampshire
l. 14	to wallow in something: to enjoy something that causes you pleasure (often disapprovingly)
l. 15	to swagger: to walk in an extremely proud and confident way (often disapprovingly)
l. 19	two-year associate's degree: lowest academic grade
l. 21	to elude: if something eludes you, you are not able to achieve it/it remains out of your grasp
l. 29	assiduous (formal): working very hard and taking care that everything is done as well as it can be
l. 30	self-driven: trying hard to achieve something in order to be successful
l. 33	to cease (formal): to stop
l. 40	bout of (illness): an attack or period of illness
l. 45	dissonant: not in harmony
l. 48	wryly: in an ironically humorous way

Text II: Article
Wolfgang Uchatius: Die neue Unterschicht
(Auszug aus einem Artikel)

Robin Trott ist Wachmann bei einem Berliner Sicherheitsunternehmen. Vor einer Woche saß er in der Pförtnerloge einer Krankenversicherung, danach in einem Bürogebäude in der Friedrichstraße. Heute bewacht er das Parkhaus der Rathaus-Passagen, acht Stockwerke hoch. Platz für 700 Autos. Außen hängt ein großes Plakat: „Parken Sie schon oder suchen Sie noch?"

Trott erfährt oft erst ein oder zwei Tage im Voraus, wo und wann er arbeiten muss, ob Früh-, Spät- oder Nachtschicht. Private Verabredungen sind kaum möglich. Er verdient 865 € netto im Monat, bei 42 Stunden Arbeit pro Woche macht das 5,15 Euro die Stunde. Knapp 400 Euro gehen weg für Miete, Strom und Heizung für seine

Wohnung in sanierter Platte in Berlin-Lichtenberg. Bleiben 465 Euro zum Leben. […]

Er ist 40 Jahre alt, auf dem Konto liegen 750 Euro, das ist sein Vermögen. Was er verdient, braucht er zum Leben.

Es gibt einen Satz, der in den vergangenen Jahren in Deutschland stark an Beliebtheit gewonnen hat. FDP-Chef Guido Westerwelle hat ihn zitiert, der SPD-Politiker Sigmar Gabriel, die Union hat ihn gar zum Wahlkampfslogan gemacht: „Sozial ist, was Arbeit schafft." Natürlich ist es fast allen Leuten lieber, einen Job zu haben, als arbeitslos zu sein. Doch der Satz übergeht, dass Arbeit und Armut in Deutschland längst kein Widerspruch mehr sind und dass es womöglich auch Jobs gibt, die zu schaffen nicht besonders sozial ist.

Nach einer in dieser Woche veröffentlichten Studie des deutschen Instituts für Wirtschaftsforschung in Berlin leben inzwischen drei Millionen Erwerbstätige unterhalb der Armutsgrenze, fast anderthalb mal so viel wie vor zwölf Jahren. Unter ihnen sind Friseurinnen, Verkäufer, Hilfs- und Leiharbeiter, Floristinnen, Reinigungskräfte, kleine Selbstständige. Und Wachleute wie Robin Trott.

Kürzlich haben sich die Sicherheitsunternehmen mit der Gewerkschaft auf einen neuen, niedrigeren Tariflohn geeinigt. Robin Trotts Firma fängt gerade an, die Angestellten einzubestellen und ihnen neue Arbeitsverträge vorzulegen. Trott käme dann netto wohl nicht einmal mehr auf 700 Euro pro Monat. Er sagt, er werde sich das nicht bieten lassen. Aber was bleibt ihm übrig? Eine Bekannte arbeitet bei der Arbeitsagentur in Lichtenberg. Die hat ihm gesagt: „Robin, wir verwalten das blanke Nichts, wir haben nicht mal Reinigungsjobs." *(351 words)*

Quelle: Uchatius, Wolfgang: Die neue Unterschicht. In: DIE ZEIT *(10. März 2005). Nr. 11. http://www.zeit.de/2005/11/Unterschicht. [15. Mai 2008]*

Text II: Bar Chart

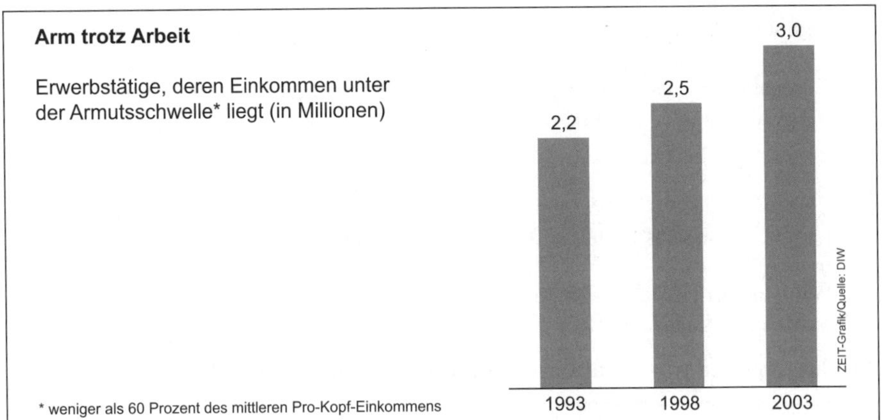

Quelle: http://www.zeit.de/2005/11/Unterschicht. [15. Mai 2008]

Annotations

ll. 8/29	netto: net wage / wage after tax and other reductions
l. 10	sanierte Platte: renovated apartment block made of prefabricated slabs
l. 27	Tariflohn: negotiated/standard wage
chart	Pro-Kopf Einkommen: per-capita income
	DIW: Deutsches Institut für Wirtschaftsforschung

Tasks

Work on a total of four tasks.
Tasks 1, 2 and 3 are compulsory. Choose one task from 4.

1 Give a brief outline of Caroline's life as depicted in Shipler's article. Do not write more than 120 words. (20 %)

2 Point out the writer's aim in presenting Caroline and analyze relevant stylistic and structural means he employs to achieve it. (25 %)

3 Mediation
An American friend of yours has asked for help with a paper that examines the impact of global economic trends on the labor market in Germany.
Outline the information from Text II (article and bar chart) that is relevant to this topic. (25 %)

In all of the following tasks you are expected to refer to Text I and Text II as well as to further relevant material/information.

4A "She is the invisible American." (l. 1)
Explain the meaning of the quote and discuss to what extent Caroline's case is also a typical example of a worldwide socio-economic phenomenon. (30 %)

OR

4B "Somewhere along the track that leads to nowhere a good many Americans give up on the dream." (ll. 37–38)
Compare Caroline's fate with that of a film or literature character for whom his or her personal dream did or did not come true. (30 %)

OR

4C Caroline's niece is in her senior year at an American high school. In one of her classes she has been asked to write an article on mobility and flexibility in today's world.
Write her article. Reflect upon general problems and opportunities as well as on Caroline's case. (30 %)

You are expected to write at least 700 words in no more than 300 minutes.

Lösungsvorschläge

1. Caroline is an ambitious lady and part of the large American labor force. She works at a convenience store, but, despite her efforts, she has to struggle against poverty. She has never managed to settle in a community and has moved to many different places, trying various jobs. Even if her supervisors have always been convinced that she could move up, she has never been considered for promotion. In her life she has been able to fulfil two of the three goals she had set herself: she earned a college diploma and has her own apartment, which, however, is largely financed by the bank. Her third goal has never been in reach and will never be: a well-paid job that would grant her financial security.

2. *Bei dieser Aufgabe sollten Sie die Stil- und Strukturmittel nicht nur aufzählen, sondern auch auf deren konkreten Effekt im Text eingehen.*

   David K. Shipler's article is a critical answer to the American Dream, which for many people will always remain an illusion despite hard work. The writer thus wants to make people aware of the fate of those who belong to America's labor force and cannot enjoy any privileges. The article is well written and figurative; abstract parts are intertwined with concrete, personalized passages that describe Caroline's case. Personalization is an effective means with which the author makes the reader feel with Caroline, and adds credibility and authenticity to his article. Also the more abstract parts also set the reader thinking with the metaphoric language having a great effect: "Her persistence played like a dissonant melody against the monotone of job stagnation" (ll. 45/46) or "this track that leads nowhere" (l. 37) to emphasize Caroline's hopeless situation. The hopeless situation and the fact that a single person does not stand a chance against adverse circumstances is also shown by the use of contrasts in the article: on the one hand there is Caroline and on the other hand we have the "invisible America" (l. 1) and Caroline's "camouflage" (l. 3). This dramatically depicts a person's decline into the anonymity of the labor force and her struggle for a better life: "bouts of depression" (l. 40) are contrasted with the "luckylady" (l. 42). The article's focus is clearly on Caroline, as the parallel constructions and anaphoras show: "She was not the victim" (l. 27), "She was not lazy" (l. 27), "She was punctual" (l. 28). But Caroline does not stand a chance against the system and all her efforts are in vain: "Again and again, she applied … and again and again she was passed over …" (ll. 46–48).

3. *Bei dieser Aufgabe geht es nicht darum, Wort für Wort zu übersetzen, sondern das wesentliche des Textes im Bezug auf die Fragestellung zusammenzufassen. Robin Trotts Schicksal ist nur ein Beispiel und muss daher allgemein formuliert werden (unregelmäßiger Arbeitseinsatz, keine Sparmöglichkeiten, nicht genug Geld zum Leben). Die Aussage der Grafik kommt im Prinzip bereits im Text vor, Sie müssen aber dennoch zeigen, dass Sie auch die Grafik einbinden.*

"Creating jobs is social" is a common political slogan in Germany, but what it does not say is that many jobs are not social at all: having a job does not exclude living below the poverty line. Almost three million people are affected and there has been a dramatic rise in the last ten years: whereas in 1993 2.2 million Germans could not make ends meet despite hard work, it was as many as 3 million in 2003. Newly negotiated wages with trade unions have only aggravated the situation. Mostly it concerns hairdressers, security staff, cleaners or contract workers. For these people this means that saving for retirement is impossible, that they have to live from hand to mouth and must cope with irregular working hours.

4A *Erklären Sie das Zitat und fassen Sie ganz kurz die wesentlichen Punkte von Carolines Fall zusammen. Weiten Sie diesen Fall auf weltweite sozialwirtschaftliche Erscheinungen aus, wie bspw. die Globalisierung und deren Auswirkungen auf den Arbeitsmarkt (z. B. Dumpingpreise, große Konkurrenz bei unqualifizierten Arbeitern, die Auswirkungen des Trends immer billiger einzukaufen etc.).*

She is one among many, she is "the invisible American", because she is an anonymous member of the large bulk of unqualified American workers. Nobody cares what is behind the facade as long as she blends in. Camouflaging one's individuality, and being inconspicuous describes best what the quotation is all about.
Caroline's case is typical of the changes going on in today's socio-economic situation. The fate of the individual does not count; what is important is to fit into modern economic patterns and contribute to a nation's economic prosperity. The lack of appreciation for individual achievements or input and the sole focus on economic output has led to a new materialistic society and widened the gap between rich and poor. Globalization has led to dumping prices and a flood of unqualified workers onto the job markets. It is therefore not surprising that the supply is greater than the demand and that the number of unemployed is on the rise. Moreover there is a social trend towards buying cheap, which also affects wages and social spending. This means tougher conditions for unqualified workers such as Caroline and leads to the fact that there is no payment according to merit. Caroline has too many competitors in the unqualified job sector and thus no chance of a "good paying job" (l. 21). Work and poverty are not exclusive any more. That is why her struggle against the "monotone of job stagnation" (l. 46) is a hopeless fight she will not be able to win.

4B *Folgende Werke bieten sich für die Bearbeitung der Aufgabe A:* The Great Gatsby *von F. Scott Fitzgerald,* Of Mice and Men *von John Steinbeck oder, aus dem Filmbereich,* Forrest Gump, Rocky *oder* Slumdog Millionaire. *Einen guten Eindruck macht es, wenn Sie am Ende Ihrer Ausführungen Parallelen oder Unterschiede zwischen Caroline und dem Hauptcharakter in dem von Ihnen gewählten Werk aufzeigen können.*

The article suggests that Caroline is fighting a battle she can only lose. Despite working hard she struggles against destitution and has no chance of climbing the social and economic ladder. Her track leads nowhere and that is why it would not be surprising if she gave up, but she is a determined person and keeps on struggling to get a "good paying job" (l. 21) one day. So her long and arduous journey to live the American Dream goes on …

In literature also there are many characters struggling to achieve their American Dream and many of them are bound to fail. The most popular example has to be the *Great Gatsby*, who has achieved his American Dream financially, some begrudgingly say by dubious means. But for Gatsby this is not the end of the road; his wealth is only a temporary success, the cornerstone for his actual goal: convincing the love of his life to stay with him instead of sacrificing her life for her snobbish, rowdy husband. For Daisy wealth is crucial and so Gatsby hopes to conquer her heart by displaying all he has accumulated during years of hard work. Gatsby's intentions are honest, but Daisy is too cowardly to make the decision to leave her husband for Gatsby, even though she truly loves him. Her lack of determination as well as a horrible incident shatter Gatsby's dream: he accepts the blame for a crime Daisy committed, which, in the end, costs him his life.

Caroline and Gatsby do not belong to those people who give up on their dreams. They pursue them till the very end, even if they know that their tracks lead nowhere and their dreams will finally be bound to fail. Another parallel between the two characters is that financial wealth is only a means to achieve a greater goal: the pursuit of happiness.

4C *Beachten Sie bei dieser Aufgabe die Form des Artikels (wählen Sie eine passende Überschrift!) und gehen Sie darin auf allgemeine Probleme und Chancen der Globalisierung ein. Ihre allgemeine Ausführung müssen Sie aber mit Carolines Schicksal verbinden. Dabei können Sie sich natürlich an Text I orientieren.*

Flexibility and mobility on the labor market – a blessing or a curse?

Today's labor market demands a high level of flexibility and mobility. This is often connected with managers having to be geographically flexible to meet the requirements of globalisation. Such flexibility is often rewarded with a huge salary package and other perks. Worldwide connections, international marketability and intercultural learning are only a few of the many opportunities globalisation offers. This increases the "global village" effect and leads to a more cosmopolitan attitude.

But there is also a dark side. Consumption is seen as a path to prosperity and a more materialistic lifestyle may be the consequence. Material possessions are gaining increasing importance and there are many people who fall by the wayside.

My cousin Dara[1] is such an example. She is part of the huge American labor force that struggles each day to make ends meet. Despite all her efforts to settle on the job market she is forced to move from job to job and place to place. However her flexibility is not rewarded at all. On the contrary, if she wasn't flexible, she would have to live far below the poverty line. For her, international mobility is a curse rather than a blessing: there is a stream of unqualified workers from poorer countries, who are willing to work for dumping wages. Employers benefit from these cheap work-

ers, but, in the long run, these economy measures destroy our job market and its wages. The problem is of course increased by customers who only want to buy cheap. To be able to offer dumping prices employers have to save on quality and social spending, which endangers the existence of workers such as my cousin.
It is important to honour efforts on the labor market and provide a fair opportunity to climb the economic ladder to all those who contribute so much to our nation's welfare. It is unacceptable that people who work hard are in constant danger of falling below the poverty line and can hardly make ends meet, let alone put money aside for hard times.
Doesn't it strike you as strange that hard work and poverty are not exclusive anymore?

1 name changed for reasons of anonymity

Abiturprüfung Berlin/Brandenburg 2010
Englisch Grundkurs – Aufgabe 1

Themenschwerpunkte: *Ethnic diversity; Personal relations in their social context; Urban, suburban and rural lifestyles*

Text (excerpt from a novel)

Teacher Man

Note: *The following text is an excerpt from Frank McCourt's novel 'Teacher Man'. Frank McCourt (1930–2009) was born in Brooklyn, New York, to Irish immigrant parents, grew up in Ireland, and returned to America in 1949. He taught at several New York City high schools. In his novel he writes about his experiences as a teacher and introduces some of his students and their problems to the reader.*

[…] Sal Battaglia smiled every morning, and said, Hi, teach. Sal sat with his girlfriend, Louise, and looked happy. When they held hands across thc aisle everyone walked around them because it was understood this was the real thing. Someday Sal and Louise would be married and that was sacred.

Sal's Italian family and Louise's Irish didn't approve, but at least the wedding would be Catholic and that was OK. Sal joked to the class his family worried he might starve to death with an Irish wife on account of how the Irish can't cook. He said his mother wondered how the Irish survived at all. Louise spoke up, said they could say what they liked, but the Irish had the most beautiful babies in the world. Sal blushed. Cool Italian, nearly eighteen, with the mass of black curly hair, actually blushed. Louise laughed and we all laughed when she reached across the aisle to touch the redness of his face with her delicate white hand.

The class went quiet when Sal took her hand and kept it against his face. You could see his eyes glistening with tears. What came over him? I stood with my back to the blackboard, not knowing what to say or do, not wanting to break the spell. At a time like this how could I go on with our discussion of *The Scarlet Letter*?

I went behind my desk, pretended to be busy, silently took the attendance again, filled out a form, waited for the bell to ring in ten minutes, watched Sal and Louise leave, hand in hand, and envied them the way everything was laid out. After graduation there would be an engagement. Sal would become a master plumber, Louise a legal stenographer, the highest you can go in the secretarial world unless you got the crazy notion to become a lawyer. I told Louise she was bright enough to be everything, but she said no no, what would her family say? She had to earn a living, get ready for her life with Sal. She'd learn Italian cooking so she wouldn't be beholden all the time to Sal's mother. A year after the wedding a baby would appear, a little round well-fed Italian-Irish-American baby and that would bring two families together forever and who cared what countries their parents came from.

None of that happened because of an Irish kid who went after Sal in a Prospect Park gang rumble and clobbered him with a two-by-four. Sal didn't even belong to a gang. He was just passing through delivering an order from the restaurant where he worked nights and weekends. He and Louise knew these gang wars were stupid, especially with the Irish and Italians, who were all Catholic and white. So why? What was it all about? Something called turf, territory, even worse, girls. Hey, get your Guinea hands off my girl. Get your fat Mick ass out of our neighborhood. Sal and Louise could understand rumbling with the Puerto Ricans or the Negroes, but not one another, for Christ's sake.

Sal returned wearing a bandage to cover his stitches. He swung over to the right side of the room, well away from Louise. He ignored the class and no one looked at him or spoke to him. Louise took her old seat, tried to catch his eye. She turned toward me as if I had answers or could fix things. I felt inadequate and indecisive. Should I go to Sal, apologize for the Irish race, tell him you can't judge a whole people by the actions of one lout in Prospect Park, remind him Louise was still lovely, still loved him? […] *(620 words)*

Source: McCourt, Frank. Teacher Man. New York 2005, 111–113

Annotations

l. 2 aisle: passage between rows of seats
l. 16 *The Scarlet Letter*: novel by American 19th century author Nathaniel Hawthorne
l. 24 to be beholden to sb.: to feel you should do sth for sb because they have done sth for you
l. 29 rumble: *informal:* fight against another gang
l. 29 to clobber: *informal:* to hit sb very hard
l. 29 two-by-four: *German:* Kantholz
l. 33 turf: *here:* gang territory
l. 34 Guinea: *(taboo, slang)* an offensive word for a person from Italy
l. 34 Mick: *(taboo, slang)* an offensive word for a person from Ireland

Tasks

1. Sum up what the reader learns about Louise and her relationship with Sal. (30 %)

2. Examine Sal's character giving evidence from the text. (30 %)

3. Choose <u>one</u> of the following tasks:

3.1 "A year after the wedding a baby would appear, a little round well-fed Italian-Irish-American baby and that would bring two families together forever and who cared what countries their parents came from." (ll. 25–27)
Comment on the statement referring to Sal's and Louise's experiences and your knowledge about young immigrants today. (40 %)

OR

3.2 Compare Sal and Louise's situation with that of another couple from literature or film who also each belong to a different ethnic group. Assess the way the protagonists cope. (40 %)

OR

3.3 The teacher wonders whether he should tell Sal, "you can't judge a whole people by the actions of one lout in Prospect Park" (ll. 41/42). Finally he decides to write a letter to Sal in which he comments on the conflict and reflects on ways to deal with it. Write this letter. (40 %)

Lösungsvorschläge

1. *Die erste Aufgabe einer Aufgabenstellung im Abitur hat in aller Regel die Funktion, nachzuweisen, dass man den Text verstanden hat. Vielleicht haben Sie im Unterricht vor allem das Erstellen von* summaries *geübt, bei dem der wichtigste Inhalt des Textes auf eine Länge von ca. einem Drittel des Ausgangstextes komprimiert wird. Die vorliegende Aufgabe verlangt etwas andere Fähigkeiten. Es handelt sich um eine gelenkte Zusammenfassung, eine Art* summary *mit speziellem Bezug auf ausgewählte Teilinhalte.*

   Louise is a teenage student of Irish origin. Her precise age is not mentioned, but she is in the same class as her boyfriend Sal, who is almost 18, and they will be graduating soon. She is unpretentious and natural, but self-confident. Her teacher implies that she is intelligent enough to do well at college, but she has more modest goals in life, aspiring to be nothing more than a secretary. She has inwardly accepted a role for her future life laid out for her by her Catholic family, tradition and her love and admiration for Sal. The tender relationship of the young couple earns the respect of both their classmates and their teacher.
   After the blind attack on Sal, Louise is at a loss for words as to how to respond to the situation. Unable to comprehend the sudden change in his demeanor, she turns to the teacher, her respected senior, for help and remedy.

2. *Auf den ersten Blick könnte man verleitet sein, auch in dieser Aufgabe eine gelenkte Zusammenfassung zu verfassen, dieses Mal eben in Bezug auf Sal. Lesen Sie die Aufgabenformulierung noch einmal. Der Operator* examine *zielt auf eine genauere Analyse des Textes, und zwar im Hinblick auf Charaktereigenschaften von Sal.*

   Sal's character is unveiled to the reader mainly in an indirect fashion through observations made by the first-person narrator, the teacher, and sometimes the narrator slips into Sal's mind to reveal his thoughts, or he asks questions to make the reader ponder for a second.
   For the major part of the text, Sal is presented as a very likeable chap. He seems cheerful and nonchalant (l. 1, "smiled every morning"; l. 2, "looked happy"), and is known for his sense of humor, as is described by the teacher (l. 6, "Sal joked to the class …"). But Sal is not a show-off. He is revealed as a sensitive and tender person, even in the presence of others. The repetition of the word "blush" serves to strengthen this impression (ll. 10/11). He is not afraid to cry in the presence of other teenagers (l. 14, "his eyes glistening with tears"), and the reader is drawn into the scene by the rhetorical question, "What came over him?" (l. 14).
   Sal is a hard-working young man with clear goals for his future. He earns money by working at a restaurant at night and on the weekends (ll. 30/31). He plans to become a master plumber (l. 20), which indicates that he is willing to invest more than the minimum effort required to become a regular plumber.

Sal apparently has an independent spirit. He seems to make up his own mind about things, as is demonstrated by the opinion he shares with Louise that "gang wars were stupid" (l. 31). Their dismay over such bouts is indicated by the narrator's switch to open questions (ll. 32/33, "So why? What was it all about?"). At this point, Sal's perceptions of cultural and racial relations still seem somewhat immature, as he "could understand rumbling with the Puerto Ricans or the Negroes" (l. 35), but not between Italians and Irish.
Sal is perplexed about what happens to him in the park, indicated by the way he evades all contact with Louise and the rest of the class (ll. 37–39). The encounter with the Irish juveniles wounds his pride and Sal returns to the classroom a hardened person, at least for the time being (ll. 37/38). His dreams have been destroyed and he has returned to harsh reality (l. 28, "None of that happened").

3.1 *In dieser Aufgabe müssen Sie Aspekte der Beziehung zwischen Sal und Louise herausarbeiten, die für viele andere junge Leute mit Migrationshintergrund typisch sind. Den Aufhänger bildet eine kurze Auseinandersetzung mit dem Zitat und seinen Implikationen für das junge Paar, der Schwerpunkt liegt indessen auf vergleichbaren Erkenntnissen, die Sie im Unterricht zum Thema* ethnic minorities *u. a. erworben haben.*

At the beginning of the text, Sal and Louise have their future all planned, just as sure as love is made in heaven. Their love will prove strong enough to bridge the chasm between their families. Their children will grow up in abounding love, without the biased atmosphere they themselves were raised in.
But their picture-book relationship shatters without warning. All of a sudden they must face realities they have so far been able to ignore. Their upbringing has left traces of enmity that they have previously been able to offset, and even deny the existence of.
Sal and Louise are not alone. Throughout the world, relationships between men and women of varied ethnicities produce offspring caught between two disparate worlds. There is no one set pattern of how immigrants raise their children, as there is no one set pattern as to how such children react to their parents' customs and those of the "new" society they grow up in. Many parents emphasize the importance of fitting into their chosen community and acquiring the best education and language skills possible. At the other end of the scale, however, many immigrant families try to live life as they did in "the old country", fencing themselves in from the outside society they experience as hostile to everything they cherish.
The degree to which immigrants readily accept their new home is influenced greatly by their level of education, the rigidity of their own upbringing and their reasons for emigrating in the first place. While political fugitives might eagerly adopt the values and way of living of their safe haven, immigrants whose sole motive rested on financial necessity often attempt to reproduce their old home on foreign terrain, particularly when they cannot relate to religious practices in the new environment.

All these aspects and many more feed into the socialization of second- and third-generation immigrants. Where educational opportunities and ensuing friendships with peers abound, they generally blend into the society they grow up in, while still holding in high regard numerous ingredients of the culture of their parents and forefathers. On the other hand, when young people are surrounded by perpetual prejudice and animosity on both sides of the cultural fence, often accompanied by substandard job training and poverty, they frequently retreat back to the lifestyle and religion of their parents.
In modern society, ethnic diversity and mixed-race families bear an immense potential to bring a fresh breeze into everyday life, and to be a driving force that can help society grow and prosper. But this potential can only be achieved through understanding and acceptance on the part of all those involved.

3.2 *In dieser Aufgabe müssen Sie die übergeordnete Situation von Sal und Louise überblicken und einige Kernaspekte mit der Situation einer fiktiven multikulturellen Beziehung vergleichen. Es können sich sowohl Ähnlichkeiten als auch Unterschiede ergeben, am besten beides. Im konkreten Fall bietet sich ein generationsübergreifender Vergleich an, zumal Sal und Louise maßgeblich beeinflusst werden durch ihr jeweiliges kulturelles Umfeld.*

I would like to contrast the situation of Sal and Louise and the multicultural context they grow up in with that of George and Ella Khan and their seven children, as depicted in the film "East is East".
It is apparent that both Sal's and Louise's respective backgrounds are a decisive factor in Sal's withdrawal from Louise after the attack. After years of biased babble in their home environments, both young people have adopted mental heirlooms of false pride in their own descent and prejudices towards other ethnic groups. But Louise and Sal have their future worked out, and they seem to be above the daily banter full of clichés until Sal is mugged by Irish youths and his emotions get the better of him when he remembers that Louise is Irish, too.
In "East is East", George and Ella Khan and their seven children live in a simple working-class community in England. George was born and raised in Pakistan, but has moved to England in hopes of better fortunes, where he has fallen in love with Ella. The film begins twenty-five years later, when their eldest son flees before the final ceremony of a marriage arranged by his father.
The viewer soon learns the crux of the story. George, in all of his complexities, is not able to cope with his own identity. He has married a Caucasian and enjoys all the amenities of liberal England, but he has decided that his own children should revert back to the life and customs of Pakistanis, although they have never truly been part of the Pakistani community. They do not speak Urdu, and most of them participate spiritedly in local Christian parades and have romantic ties of varying intensity and quality to their young English peers. George attempts to rule his family with a patriarchal iron fist, eventually even hitting his wife for the first time ever. Yet Ella, who

has supported her husband in every imaginable way all those long years and still defends him towards their children, proves to be their only hope of salvation.
In the end, all is well and the future is as bright as can be expected. George has learned to accept what he cannot change and respects the desires of his children to be more British than Pakistani. His wife still loves him and stands beside him, and he is still revered by his children, albeit hardly as a model for the way they want to shape their own destinies.
In coming back to Sal and Louise, the reader might well hope that the young couple find a way to mend their strife and continue their mutual path into adulthood; that they learn and profit from the discord and the resulting healing process, just as George matures as a father and husband when confronted with inevitabilities which others consider both normal and desirable. If all goes well for Sal and Louise, they might well play a mitigating role for their own parents similar to the one George's children play in his progressive mellowing.

3.3 *In dieser Aufgabe stellen Sie Ihre Fähigkeit unter Beweis, den richtigen Ton zu treffen. Sie schreiben einen* informal letter *(Format beachten!), in dem Sie als erwachsene Bezugsperson einem Jugendlichen unaufgefordert einen wohlgemeinten Rat geben. Sie sind Sal und Louise gleichermaßen zugetan. Ihre Worte müssen Empathie zeigen, und Sie müssen sich sowohl auf die Geschehnisse beziehen (Textbezug) als auch eine Perspektive für die Zukunft aufzeigen (außertextlicher Bezug). Ansonsten gibt es zahlreiche mögliche Antworten. So können von Sals Verhalten enttäuscht sein oder sich verständnisvoll zeigen, Sie können sich als Mediator anbieten und vieles mehr.*

Mr. McCourt, Roosevelt High School
13525 Rochester Blvd.
Brooklyn, NY 11215

May 23, 2010

Dear Sal,

I guess you know why I'm writing. A few days have passed now since your encounter in Prospect Park, and it's about time we talked about the incident and the way it led you to treat Louise in class.
I realize that you are in a lot of pain. I expect your bruises are just about gone, but there are lots of other ways to hurt. Right now, that three-minute attack is likely all you can think about. It would be a shame, though, if you let your hate for that gang get such a grip on you that you give up your relationship with Louise and the goals you've been working towards for these last two years.
Having both you and Louise in my class has been an experience I will cherish for the rest of my life. The two of you – as individuals and together – were role models for the whole class. You're open-minded, industrious, full of sound ideas, and about the best friend anyone could have. Don't throw all your ideals out the window because of some idiotic footnote in your personal history.

Look at it this way: Both you and Louise come from fine families, but those families come from different traditions. And there are lots of other boys your age who come from such backgrounds – Italian, Irish, Polish, you name it. And thousands of teenagers are out there trying to cope with growing up in between two cultures, that of their parents and that of their chosen home. Sal, those boys were not representative of the Irish. They were just a bunch of juveniles. They could just as well have been Italian, or whatever. Louise still loves you and is patiently waiting to tell you that herself. Together, you could dispel the prejudices surrounding so many young people in your situation.
I hope we can get together and talk this over from eye to eye sometime soon. Just give me a call.

Your friend,

"Teach"

Abiturprüfung Berlin/Brandenburg 2010
Englisch Grundkurs – Aufgabe 2

Themenschwerpunkte: *Personal relations in their social context; The challenge of globalisation*

Text A (excerpt from a newspaper article)

"I squatted my repossessed home"

My mum moved around a lot when I was little, and my education and sense of self suffered.

I've always wanted a stable, solid base for my family, and 30 years ago I bought one.

It was a mill keeper's cottage surrounded by sprawling woodland. When we found it, we wanted to spend the rest of our lives there. It was falling down and we had to live in a caravan as the house took shape – we knocked it down and built it from the ground up.

Meanwhile the family business, a talent scouting agency and production company, went from strength to strength. At one point, I was a millionaire. But a few years ago, I encountered some financial difficulties, so I renegotiated my mortgage repayments. It would have been fine in a stable economy, but my lender became a victim of the credit crisis, the period of leniency ended, and we fell into arrears.

We received our first repossession warning last summer. The eviction notice arrived in August, giving us just 10 days to pack our things and leave. Rather than wait for a bailiff to come crashing up our drive, I delivered the key to him myself. For the next few months we slept on friends' couches, moving on before we became a burden. I felt like a fugitive, a criminal, as if I didn't belong.

The shame of having let down my family was unbearable. My sons are old enough to look after themselves, but I'd always imagined leaving them the house when I died. Now, I had nothing.

Without the home, I couldn't work, and considered myself finished. I'm a big man, but I cried every day. At one point I contemplated suicide. There's a high-speed rail link that runs through the village, and I ended up perched on a bridge over the track. As I sat there thinking of Kim and the kids, I thought, "This isn't the way to do it."

The house had not been sold. Our creditors needed to sell the place for far more than its ever-decreasing value, so it wasn't worth their while. I visited one day, stood outside and peered in at the empty rooms. Our ducks, which I'd once fed daily, came running across the lawn. I broke down right there, my head resting against the window.

It was then I remembered the spare key we kept under a rock in the garden, in case of emergencies. Scarcely daring to hope, I went to look, and there it was. Astonishingly, the lock hadn't been changed. So I asked Kim and the boys how they felt about moving back in, as squatters. They said, "OK." There was no discussion, it was that simple.

We were back in time for Christmas. Kim got our services reconnected on the first day – because we're pensioners, we couldn't be deprived of water or heat. We had a Christmas tree, and Kim hummed carols as she put up tinsel. After nearly 30 years there, I don't think we realised how much of our sense of self had been tied up with our home. Back in my own bedroom, I slept properly for the first time in months.

The second eviction letter arrived at the end of January, giving us a weekend's notice. [...] *(547 words)*

Source: Armstrong, Terry. "I squatted my repossessed home." The Guardian Weekend, 28 February 2009, 10

Annotations

heading: to squat: to live in a building without the owner's permission

heading: to repossess: to take back property from sb who still owes money for it and is not able to pay

l. 5 sprawling: spreading in an untidy/chaotic way

l. 10 strength: *here:* success

l. 11 to renegotiate: to try to reach a new agreement

l. 11 mortgage: a sum of money borrowed from a bank in order to buy a house, which is to be paid back over a particular number of years

l. 12 lender: person giving money to another person

l. 13 leniency: lacking strictness

l. 13 to fall into arrears: to be late in paying money that you owe

l. 14 eviction notice: a formal letter or statement saying that you must leave your house at the end of a particular period of time

l. 24 rail link: a railroad connection between two places

l. 25 Kim: Terry Armstrong's wife

l. 37 services: e. g. water, electricity and gas provided by a company

l. 38 deprived: to be without sth because it has been taken away

Text B (graph)

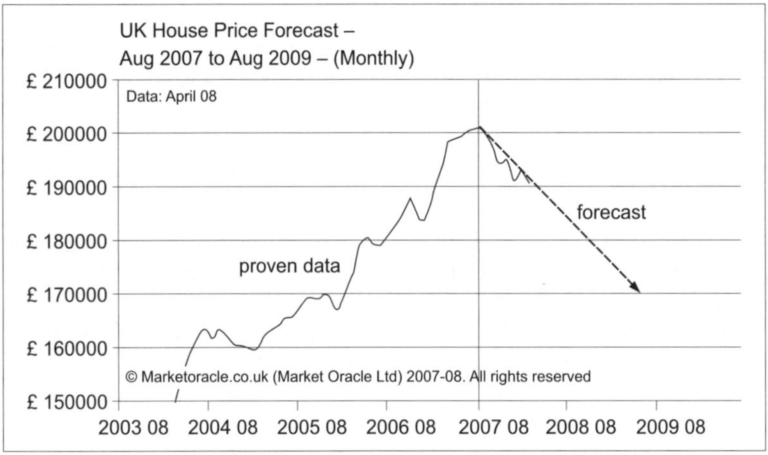

Tasks

1 Outline what Terry Armstrong experiences after buying his house. (Text A) (30 %)

2 Describe the graph (Text B) and explain how it relates to the information given in Text A. (30 %)

3 Choose <u>one</u> of the following tasks.

3.1 Referring to Armstrong's situation, discuss the challenges and chances of globalisation for people striving for success. (40 %)

OR

3.2 Comment on the way Terry Armstrong copes with a very difficult situation and compare his attitude with that of another person in real life or a character from literature or film. (40 %)

OR

3.3 Write a letter to the editor voicing your opinion on Armstrong's squatting his own home.
Address the letter to:
The Guardian
Kings Place
90 York Way
London, N1 9GU (40 %)

Lösungsvorschläge

1. *Diese Aufgabe zielt auf eine gelenkte Zusammenfassung. Der Text ist in diesem Fall nicht-fiktional, aber er zeigt viele Emotionen aus einer für die ganze Familie äußerst schwierigen Zeit. Man muss hier die Inhalte kurz und prägnant wiedergeben und die beschriebenen Gefühle ansatzweise transportieren, ohne eigenes Mitgefühl zu zeigen und den Text zu interpretieren oder auszuschmücken. Wie üblich soll diese Zusammenfassung im Präsens sein.*

   In the text "I squatted my repossessed home", which appeared in *The Guardian Weekend* of 28 February 2009, the author Terry Armstrong tells of his roller-coaster experiences after financial woes lead to serious readjustments in his life.
   Some 30 years before writing the text, Mr Armstrong purchases a house, where he and his family spend decades in apparent contentment. But after years of considerable financial success, they encounter unnamed financial difficulties, so that the author loses his business and falls behind with his mortgage payments. Unfortunately, this occurs at a time when his lending bank is itself feeling the squeeze of the global financial crisis and has to react.
   The bank eventually has the family evicted. For some time, they move around from friends' house to friends' house, taking pains not to overstay their welcome. Mr Armstrong feels great shame at his inability to support his family and even considers suicide as a possible remedy for his woes. In his state of misery, he can hardly think of working and is constantly in tears.
   One day, he discovers that the bank has been unable to sell his home, due to the ensuing real estate crisis. He and his family move back into his former home illegally and squat there for a delightful Christmas season, before eventually being thrown out again.

2. *Diese Aufgabe überprüft die Fähigkeit zur differenzierten Wiedergabe statistischer Daten mit dem fachgerechten englischen Vokabular. Zusätzlich ist eine inhaltliche Brücke zu dem Text von Terry Armstrong herzustellen. Diese besteht im raschen Verfall der Hauspreise und dessen Folgen für Tausende von Haushalten im United Kingdom.*

   The chart presented depicts the development of house prices in the UK from August 2003 to August 2007, when the chart was first published, as well as the predicted development of house prices in the UK up to August 2009.
   The vertical axis of the line graph refers to house prices in English pounds. The range of house prices listed goes from 150,000 £ to 210,000 £, in increments of 10,000 £ per line.
   The horizontal axis refers to the time factor in the price development. According to the subcaption of the chart, measurements were taken monthly, but the marks in the bottom line of the chart indicate only the month of August of the respective year.

The chart positions of all other months would have to be inserted, as would the actual house prices for any given month.
The vertical line slightly to the right of the middle of the graph indicates the point in time at which the graph was published. To its left, the irregular line illustrates that the development of house prices generally increased from August 2003 to August 2007, whereas the falling line to the right signifies that prices were expected to decrease sharply in the following two years by about 30,000 £, beginning abruptly at the time the graph was released and with no foreseeable bottoming out.
There is a marked correlation between the graph and Terry Armstrong's text. Armstrong's predicament resembles the situation of innumerable other families within the UK whose real estate prices plummeted due to the economic crisis which became evident around the middle of 2007. That was precisely the time when the banking, real estate and general financial crisis became the focus of public attention. It is impossible to recall here the numerous interlaced factors involved, but the overall effect was that an international financial recession set in, covering stock markets, job perspectives and, case in point, a vast reduction in the housing prices in the USA, Great Britain and other countries. Thousands upon thousands of homes that could have been re-financed under normal circumstances were foreclosed at short notice, putting a myriad of families on the street, leaving them to their improvisational talents and the mercy of kin and friends, exemplified aptly in Armstrong's account of his own personal dilemma.

3.1 *Diese Aufgabe ist etwas missverständlich formuliert. Man muss sich vergegenwärtigen, dass im heutigen Gebrauch das Wort* challenge *häufig als Euphemismus verwendet wird. Mit anderen Worten: Die Herausforderungen* (challenges)*, die zu beschreiben sind, beinhalten z. B. Dinge wie verbreitete Armut, Arbeitslosigkeit, die es zu überwinden gilt.*

It is quite apparent that Mr Armstrong's situation is, to a large extent, a direct result of globalisation, or more precisely of one piece of that gigantic puzzle. He is virtually homeless due in part to the international financial crisis beginning roughly in 2007, the insolvency of numerous banks and the resulting international collapse of real estate prices. Of course, some of his own personal business decisions likely worsened his plight, but the inevitability of his fall and his subsequent dependence on the mercy of friends and relatives were dictated by mechanisms he had no control over.
There is a proverb that goes something like, "One person's bliss is another's misery." Indeed, the many faces and facets of globalisation can be looked at from many different angles and at many different levels. And each and every person (or company, or government) looks at globalisation in terms of what it gives him, or takes away from him, or both. Falling mobile phone rates in Germany somehow go hand in hand with the outsourcing of mobile phone production to a newly industrializing nation, and an everyday dinner might include ingredients from half a dozen different countries and cultures, often ignoring produce grown around the corner. We look on such

phenomena as part of our modern lifestyle and take it for granted, at least as long as we are on the upside of life, and until something happens that turns the tables on us.
In countless instances, losing one's job or home often leads to personal frustration and loss of self-esteem, which in turn often destroys family structures and prompts reliance on welfare. On the other hand, many people rebound and grow personally out of such setbacks. And with a generous portion of good luck, they can well get back on track and cope with their adversities.
Some of the typical formulas that can counteract negative aspects of globalisation at a personal level include continued education, international work experience, learning foreign languages and fine-tuning one's abilities to interact with various kinds of people. Mobility and flexibility are today's catchwords when it comes to finding jobs, but is one's job everyone's highest priority? What happens to other goals in life, and how does all this affect friends and loved ones? In the case of Mr Armstrong, it is family and friends who help him cope with the challenges that global economic developments have presented him with.

3.2 *Zumeist greift man bei der Lösung von Abitur-Aufgaben auf Quellen aus dem Unterricht zurück. Häufig aber fällt einem unter dem Zeitdruck der Prüfung keine passende Geschichte o. a. ein, die zu dem vorgelegten Text passt. Die vorliegende Aufgabe ist gut geeignet zur Einbeziehung einer Person oder einer Geschichte, die man ggf. auch aus persönlicher Beschäftigung oder Erfahrung außerhalb des Unterrichts kennt.*

Mr Armstrong's living conditions at the time of writing are deplorable, to say the least. He has lost his business, his home and much of his morale and feeling of self-worth. He has no means of supporting himself and cannot buy a new house.
And yet – the way he expresses himself, the way he faces his fate, the way he is able to rouse the energy to radiate with warm Christmas spirit to his family even in the bleakest of personal winters – are these not symptomatic of a strong personality with a will to make the best out of every downturn? Is his story not inspiring to others who might be struggling to cope with fates of comparable severity?
Forrest Gump, the title figure of the famous motion picture, is a person of similar capabilities to encourage those whose paths he crosses to grow beyond their limitations. Regardless of where he goes, whom he meets or what hardship he experiences, nothing seems to discourage him. Every test he is put to seems to fulfill a purpose, to propel him to the next adventurous stage of life. And all along his way, he instills purpose and meaning into the lives of those he meets, be it Lieutenant Dan, his beloved Jenny or the countless admirers who join him in his ultimately pointless cross-country run.
Admittedly, all comparisons between Mr Armstrong and Forrest Gump do remain superficial, as one is a real-life person with a heavy burden on his shoulders, while the other is a character in a movie, whose fate can be manipulated every step of the way to fit the necessities of a good story. It is the prerogative of scriptwriters to turn an utter imbecile into an obscure kind of role model. And so it is that simple-minded

Forrest Gump becomes the epitome of the child in every one of us, while a seeming horde of guardian angels ensures that nothing can harm him.
Perhaps this is the point at which Mr Armstrong and Forrest Gump merge, and where a lesson can be learned. We must strive to keep our balance in every adversity and to look for the lesson in every tribulation. Perhaps we can even become a hero to someone else.

3.3 *Hier sollen Sie einen* formal letter *schreiben. Dies bedingt zum einen eine äußere Form, bei der es bestimmte Konventionen gibt, und man strebt ein gehobenes Sprachniveau an. Ferner soll der Inhalt einen Bezug zum Text von Terry Armstrong herstellen und argumentativ dazu Stellung nehmen.*
Im Allgemeinen sollen Leserbriefe relativ kurz und treffend sein, nicht zuletzt weil dies die Wahrscheinlichkeit ihres Abdrucks in der Zeitung erhöht. In dieser Aufgabe wird eine prägnante Textproduktion erwartet, die einige Argumente zu Themen wie globalisation, legal vs. illegal action, responsibilities of banks or politicians *usw. einschließt.*

Hans Mueller
Berliner Strasse 50
D 13579 Berlin
Germany

The Guardian
Kings Place
90 York Way
London, N1 9GU
England

6 March 2009

I squatted my repossessed home, 28 February 2009

Sir,

Allow me to introduce myself as a legal adviser for a local bank. In this capacity, I have often had to deal with cases like the one in the above-mentioned article.
Mr Armstrong's narrative is the personal record of a tragedy, a tragedy that has unfortunately become a widespread woe throughout our nation in the past few years and will likely continue to fester for some time to come. As such, Mr Armstrong's account was an interesting read, a real "tear-jerker", as media professionals might call it: personal fate coupled with a hint of humour and a decided portion of optimism, with an open end that lets us wonder how the story will continue.
This having been said, the bottom line of the matter is that Mr Armstrong's decision to secretly move back into the house is unequivocally illegal and altogether inacceptable. Mr Armstrong is not a modern-day Robin Hood fighting against tyrants and his squatting is in no way laudable.
Looking at the other side of the coin, we must indeed admit that Mr Armstrong is a practical and responsible realist. Not for a second does he blame the bank officers, bailiffs etc. for foreclosing his house. They were merely doing their jobs in a responsible fashion. Mr Armstrong acknowledges that his lending bank was itself feeling the crunch of the global money crisis. And had the bank chosen not to foreclose his

and many other properties, the bank itself might well have folded, which would have brought on a far greater disaster and involved considerably more families.
In the end, Mr Armstrong's and similar fates are regrettable, but the banks have no other recourse, at least not at the local level. At a higher level, it is high time to call on the government to introduce legislation that would prevent the type of immorally speculative activities which induced the global state of emergency in the first place.

Yours faithfully,

Hans Mueller

Abiturprüfung Berlin/Brandenburg 2010
Englisch Leistungskurs – Aufgabe 1

Themenschwerpunkte: *Ethnic diversity; The challenge of globalisation; Personal relations in their social context*

Text A (excerpt from an autobiography)

Maximum City: Bombay – Lost and Found

Note: *The author, Suketu Mehta, was born in Calcutta and raised in Bombay where he lived until his family moved to New York in 1977.*

[…] Each person's life is dominated by a central event, which shapes and distorts everything that comes after it and, in retrospect, everything that came before. For me, it was going to live in America at the age of fourteen. It's a difficult age at which to change countries. You haven't quite finished growing up where you were and you're never well in your skin in the one you're moving to. I had absolutely no idea about the country America; I had never been there. I was certainly not of a later generation of my cousins, such as Sameer, who at the age of sixteen stepped into JFK Airport fresh off the plane from Bombay wearing a Mets baseball cap and with half an American accent already in place. I travelled, in twenty-four hours, between childhood and adulthood, between innocence and knowledge, between predestination and chaos. Everything that has happened since, every minute and monstrous act – the way I use a fork, the way I make love, my choice of a profession and a wife – has been shaped by that central event, that fulcrum of time. […]

When I moved to New York, I missed Bombay like an organ of my body. I thought that when I left Bombay I had escaped from the worst school in the world. I was wrong. The all-boy Catholic school I went to in Queens was worse. It was in a working-class white enclave that was steadily being encroached upon by immigrants from darker countries. I was one of the first minorities to enroll, a representative of all they were trying to hold out against. Soon after I got there, a boy with curly red hair and freckles came up to my lunch table and announced, "Lincoln should never have freed the slaves." The teachers called me a pagan. My school yearbook photograph shows me looking at the camera with the caption, "It's so strong I can even skip a day," referring to an advertising slogan for a brand of antiperspirant. This was how the school saw me: as a stinking heathen, emitting the foul odours of my native cooking. On the day I graduated, I walked outside the barbed-wire topped gates, put my lips to the pavement, and kissed the ground in gratitude. […]

That was the true period of my exile, when I was restrained by forces greater than myself from going back. It was different from nostalgia, which is a simple desire to evade the linearity of time. I made, in the back of my school notebook, a calendar beginning early in the spring. I had been told by my father, or so I thought, that he would send me to Bombay in the summer of my junior year. Each day I crossed off the previous one and counted the remaining days like a jail sentence. I was happy towards evening because it was one less day in America and one more towards my liberation. Then, in the last week before the summer holidays, my father told me he couldn't send me to India. He'd send me the next year, after I graduated. I was lost.

I existed in New York, but I lived in India, taking little memory trains. The fields at dusk. Birds flying home overhead [...].

My father once, in New York, exasperated by my relentless demands to be sent back to finish high school in Bombay, shouted at me, "When you were there, you wanted to come here. Now that you're here, you want to go back." It was when I first realized I had a new nationality: citizen of the country of longing. [...] *(632 words)*

Source: Mehta, Suketu. Maximum City: Bombay – Lost and Found. New York: 2004, 6–9; 31

Annotations

l. 1 to distort: to change something so that it is no longer true or accurate or that it becomes strange and difficult to recognize
l. 8 Mets: New York baseball team
l. 10 predestination: belief that people have no control over events because these have already been decided by God
l. 13 fulcrum: point on which something turns, *German:* Wendepunkt
l. 16 Queens: part of New York City
l. 17 to encroach upon: to gradually take something from someone else

Text B (Auszug aus einem Zeitungsartikel)

„Globale Wesen"

Anmerkung: *Pico Iyer wurde als Sohn indischer Eltern in Oxford geboren. Er lebt heute in Japan und schreibt u. a. für Time Magazine.*

Ich weiß nicht mehr, wann mir das erste Mal auffiel, dass exakt so, wie meine Freunde sich an das kleine Dorf in Bayern erinnern, in dem sie aufwuchsen, oder andere sich an entsprechende Stadtteile in Indien oder Kenia, ich mich an den Flughafen erinnere, daran, wie ich versuchte, ein wenig britischer zu werden, wenn ich ins Internat nach England flog oder ein wenig amerikanischer, wenn ich zu meinen Eltern nach Kalifornien unterwegs war. Wenn ich beobachte, wie der Blick einer Freundin weicher wird, wenn sie sich an das Haus ihrer Großmutter erinnert oder wenn ein Gericht ihr den Geschmack ihrer Kindheit zurückruft, dann merke ich, dass es mir genau so ergeht, wenn ich das Rattern einer Abflugtafel in einem Flughafen höre. Das Flugzeug war der Ort, an dem ich ganz ich selbst war – nicht die Geisel der amerikanischen oder der englischen Erwartungen und Gepflogenheiten. Dort oben im Himmel fragte man mich nicht, ob ich Inder oder Nicht-Inder sei. Im Flugzeug fühlte ich mich wirklich zu Hause – also nicht an dem einen oder an dem anderen Ort, sondern dazwischen.

Wie glücklich ich damals war: in meiner Klasse der einzige dunkelhäutige Junge, der einzige mit einem radikal anderen Zuhause. Ich war glücklich, weder dem einen noch dem anderen Dogma zu unterliegen. Ich konnte mir das Gute von England,

Amerika und Indien nehmen, ohne einem der entsprechenden Vorurteile anheim zu fallen. Ich war ein Kind aller Möglichkeiten, ein Geschöpf der Zukunft ebenso sehr wie der Vergangenheit. *(267 Wörter)*

Quelle: Iyer, Pico: Globale Wesen. In: Berliner Zeitung (16. September 2006)

Annotation
Z. 18 anheimfallen: zum Opfer fallen

Tasks

1 Give an account of the author's experiences as depicted in Text A. (20 %)

2 Examine the author's feelings as a young boy in New York, referring to the means used to convey them to the reader. (25 %)

3 Mediation
For an American friend who is working on a paper about "Living between two worlds" outline Pico Iyer's background as well as his experiences and memories (Text B). (20 %)

4 Choose one of the following tasks.

4.1 "When I moved to New York, I missed Bombay like an organ of my body" (Text A, l. 14).
Explain the quotation and discuss whether the experience expressed in this statement is typical of migrants. Take into consideration Text A and Text B as well as your knowledge about challenges and chances of migrants. (35 %)

OR

4.2 Compare Suketu Mehta's experiences with people belonging to the mainstream culture (Text A) to those of a character from an ethnic minority in literature or film. Assess the way both cope. (35 %)

OR

4.3 Suketu Mehta is planning a reading tour to Germany. Your school wants to invite him to read from his book "Maximum City" and to discuss it with him. Write a letter of invitation in which you comment on the excerpt from his work (Text A) and explain why it is relevant to you and your fellow students. Address your letter to:

Suketu Mehta
c/o Vintage Books
1745 Broadway Avenue
New York, NY 10019
USA (35 %)

Lösungsvorschläge

1. *Es wird erwartet, dass Sie die Kernaussage erfassen und die wesentlichen Informationen komprimiert, geordnet und eigenständig darlegen. Dabei sollten der Textsorte entsprechend keine Interpretationen, Wertungen und Redundanzen auftreten.*

The excerpt from an autobiography entitled "Maximum City: Bombay – Lost and Found" by Suketu Mehta, published in New York in 2004, deals with the issue of living in a multi-cultural society. It reflects the autobiographical experiences of young Indian Suketu Mehta when he has to accept moving to New York with his family, which has a tremendous impact on his whole life. Their decision to leave for America comes at a crucial moment for an adolescent boy. In the middle of his development as a young person and with no idea of that huge country, he has to start life in a seemingly strange place. But the wide range of challenges he has to cope with makes him grow up immediately.
Faced with racist remarks at school as well as cruel and discriminatory behavior by other pupils and even teachers, he feels lost and increasingly unhappy. So he maintains his hope of being sent back and of escaping these unpleasant circumstances. Instead, his father demands patience and complains about his son's restlessness expressed by the constant longing to be somewhere else. Thus Suketu realizes that he obviously neither feels fully Indian nor fully American. It is always the place left behind which he is longing for.

2. *Sie sollten Suketus Gefühlszustand klar definieren und anhand der zahlreich verwendeten erzählerischen und stilistischen Mittel (Wortwahl, direkte Rede, Aufzählungen, Beispiele, bildhafte Sprache) nachweisen. Beachten Sie dabei, Inhalt und Wirkung miteinander zu verbinden und stets Textbelege anzufügen. Vermeiden Sie eine bloße Aneinanderreihung von Beispielen.*

When the author arrives in New York, as a young boy, we learn that he not only has to deal with a certain kind of culture clash, but first of all is confronted with a variety of emotional experiences that are shown in many ways.
Moving from India to the USA is described as a tremendous turning point in the life of a boy still coping with adolescence. The author uses words with negative connotations such as "distorts" (l. 1), "chaos" (l. 11), "monstrous act" (l. 11) to convey feelings of loss and alienation in particular. From the beginning he underlines his confusion by constantly repeating, with the help of various examples, how difficult it is to leave for a place he has no idea of (cf. ll. 2–11).
To emphasise his statements he also includes words such as "absolutely" (l. 5), "never" and "certainly" (l. 6). Then he employs an enumeration reflecting several contrasts when he says, "I travelled, in twenty-four hours, between childhood and adulthood, between innocence and knowledge, between predestination and chaos" (ll. 9–11). In this way he points out again how quickly he has been taken away and expected to mature without much or any time at all to take a breath and realize what is going to happen.

The anaphora "When I moved […] when I left …" (ll. 14/15) refers to relevant moments in his life when things change, but do not improve. Thus, the new school is compared to the former one and turns out to be even worse.
To illustrate the boy's feeling of homesickness and yearning we come across the metaphorical expression in line 14 claiming that he "missed Bombay like an organ of [his] body." In a biological sense a person may survive, even if not every organ functions perfectly well. And sometimes that person may succeed without one organ or the other. But there will be a feeling of incompleteness, and the personal and emotional experiences after such a loss may depend on the circumstances.
Suketu is confronted with a great deal of humiliation and discrimination at school, which is depicted in examples showing the classmates' and the teachers' attitude towards him at school. Here he includes direct speech, "Lincoln should never have freed the slaves" (ll. 20/21), and the advertising slogan "It's so strong I can even skip a day" (ll. 22/23) to show how much they detest him (cf. ll. 24/25). Consequently, it comes as no surprise that Suketu has no real chance of becoming familiar with and integrated in his new life. All his thoughts remain occupied with the idea of getting back home. He "counted the remaining days like a jail sentence" (l. 32), which is a simile to show his desperation. He feels imprisoned and treated in a cruel and unfair way. Again strong words with negative connotations are used, e. g. "barbed-wire topped gates" (ll. 25/26) and "exile" (l. 27). With the contrasting expression "one less day in America and one more day towards my liberation" (ll. 33/34) he reveals his strong desire and hope to escape. That he cannot stop thinking about his former life is pointed out by further metaphors like "taking little memory trains" (l. 36) or seeing "[b]irds flying home overhead" (l. 37).
In the end, the author realizes that he is trapped between both worlds when his father loses his temper due to his son's ongoing complaints and says: "When you were there, you wanted to come here. Now that you're here, you want to go back" (ll. 39/40). Again, direct speech is employed to underline the author's emotional state and to add to the authenticity of the story.

3. *Beachten Sie bei der Lösung der Mediationsaufgabe Adressat und Situation und stellen Sie dann relevante inhaltliche Aspekte komprimiert und schlüssig dar.*

Hi Joe,

Hope you're doing fine and making progress with your work on the paper about "Living between two worlds". Fortunately, I succeeded in finding the newspaper article I mentioned when we met recently. As my scanner doesn't work at the moment and to save you time, I have decided to outline the main ideas.
The article is entitled "Global Creatures" and was published in the "Berliner Zeitung", 16 September, 2006. It was written by Pico Iyer, who is a young man of Indian descent and who reflects on certain childhood memories.
One day he discovers that his friends usually recall places where they've grown up, or the smell of favorite dishes, whereas he at first thinks of the airport, himself heading for his boarding school in England or his parents' home in California. Every

time he tries hard to adapt and to become more British or more American, respectively. Whenever he hears the noise of a departure board, it takes him back in time and he finds himself up in the air, where nobody cares where he comes from or where he belongs. In between, and therefore free from American as well as British expectations and habits, he cannot deny a certain feeling of home, of pleasure at just being himself.
As he was the only dark-skinned boy in his class at that time, he remembers how content and happy he felt. Being so utterly different gave him the chance to choose the best from every place: England, America or India, without falling victim to any prejudice.
Finally, he regards himself as a child given every opportunity; a lucky individual whose identity is based on positive experiences in the past, which obviously enables him to look into the future optimistically.
So far about some glimpses of an individual traveler among different worlds. If you have any questions, don't hesitate to ask me or just drop in whenever you can spare some time.

Hope to see you soon.

Daniel

4.1 *Ihr Text sollte eine durchgängig logische Gliederung aufweisen, die entsprechenden Textbezüge (zu A und B) beinhalten, sowie durch außertextliche Sachverhalte sinnvoll ergänzt werden. Dabei illustrieren passende Beispiele eine widerspruchsfreie, differenzierte Diskussion und führen letztendlich zu einer überzeugenden und nachvollziehbaren persönlichen Stellungnahme.*

When people decide to leave their home country, no matter the reasons why this happens, they are always faced with the big challenge of settling and finding their way in an often completely different world. The author calls it a "fulcrum" (l. 13) when everything seems to change and you are not able to take along the things which are most relevant to you.
In the quotation, the author compares Bombay with an organ of his body, which clearly indicates how much Suketu misses the place he has grown up in. He suffers a lot, so that for him the connection to his home town is obviously essential to his survival. Whether the experience as described in the quotation applies to every migrant probably depends on the conditions.
Suketu's relocation takes place when he is in a special phase of his development, described by himself as "a difficult age" (l. 3), not "quite finished growing up" (l. 4). He travels from one world into another within one day with his whole life being influenced and altered.
However, nobody seems to realize the problems he is confronted with, such as the harsh discrimination he experiences when even the teachers at school address him with racist labels like "pagan" (l. 21). So Suketu becomes an outsider who loses himself in his memories (cf. ll. 36/37) and hopes (cf. ll. 30–32) to be sent back one day.

The excerpt leaves open whether this journey will ever happen. In the end it displays a vague idea of being trapped between both worlds.
Perhaps Suketu is too young to cope and not mature enough to take the challenge to finally arrive at home in one of these places. Perhaps he does not get the guidance young people especially need when they are faced with utterly different lifestyles and might not know what to do.
In contrast to that, the newspaper article provides a completely different perspective. Here we meet a young boy of Indian origin, travelling between England and America. He finds his own way to handle the situation. Although he tries hard to adapt to British and American values and expectations, he finally feels most at home in the air, where nobody cares where he comes from or goes to. Here he does not worry, but relies on himself, an Indian boy who has the chance of travelling and thus makes use of the best of everything. Fortunately, he does not feel trapped or disadvantaged; he apparently enjoys the freedom of movement while encountering different cultures.
Whereas Pico Iyer experiences his situation as a rewarding enrichment of his life, Suketu has to struggle with discrimination against him, which is definitely not a constructive way of approaching integration. Worldwide an ever greater number of people move in search of a better life, a movement which is supported by the process of globalization. Consequently, the issue of integration in order to make a multi-cultural society work is becoming increasingly important. The question of whether we will manage to live together, or not, can no longer be ignored.
Apart from the responsibility which lies on the shoulders of the respective governments to work on acceptable legislation, it is up to people themselves to see that mutual understanding and support are required to make integration possible. But as long as immigrants are repeatedly used as scapegoats or targets of discrimination, this process will be hindered.
Positive examples can be found, though. In Berlin, there is the mayor of Neukölln who was awarded for the tremendous efforts he makes with integration projects. And I have heard of young migrant women who support migrant families and help them with difficulties in their daily lives in Germany.
Nobody should demand that migrants forget about their heritage, their culture. They should not be forced to deny their identity. But the moment they decide to settle somewhere else, they should be willing to acquire certain knowledge, learn the language and accept the laws. When I hear that there are an estimated number of 1,000 forced marriages in Germany, which is not allowed under German law, I get really angry and feel sorry for the girls affected.
Leaving your home country can certainly be hurtful and scary. Yet, gaining insight into a new culture, exchanging views, and perceiving the world from different perspectives can be wonderful, too. But no matter what we do, both immigrants' behaviour and measures undertaken by the host society to confront such new situations should never ever curb people's personal rights, abridge their freedom, or violate the principles of humanity.

4.2 *Hier wird ein treffender Vergleich zwischen den Erfahrungen von Suketu Mehta mit denen einer von Ihnen gewählten fiktionalen Gestalt erwartet. Diskutieren Sie das Verhalten beider Charaktere und führen Sie Ihre Gedanken zu einer überzeugenden Schlussfolgerung.*

After young Suketu has been forced to leave India behind to settle in America, he arrives in a white working-class neighbourhood where people feel "steadily being encroached upon by immigrants from darker countries" (ll. 17/18). So it does not take long before he is discriminated against in that "all-boy Catholic school" (l. 16), whereas he had hoped to be able to enjoy much better school days than before (cf. l. 15). Instead, his reality is filled with prejudices and soon he feels absolutely excluded. Here I wonder if he could have done anything to improve his situation. But the excerpt only concentrates on his suffering and the hopes he has for a brighter future.

Manny, the protagonist of the novel "(Un)Arranged Marriage" by Bali Rai, deals with his situation differently. He is also a young boy of Indian descent, belonging to the group of second generation immigrants. It is his father who once came to England for economic reasons, but has never wanted to become integrated and has always kept his own traditions alive even by avoiding contact with British culture as much he can. Contrary to his father, Manny absorbs British culture and its customs. He likes his school, his English friends, and feels attracted by what we call a modern Western lifestyle. It is no surprise that he wants to become integrated into society, although his father and his brothers interfere with him as much as possible. Manny compares himself with a coconut, which means brown on the outside and white on the inside. But he is not really interested in his roots, which might be explained by the fact that he feels closer to his friends and their lives than to the old traditional ways his family dictates. While Suketu "missed Bombay like an organ of [his] body" (l. 14), Manny has no idea of India or his Punjabi family. Only when he is taken to India does he find out about its beauty and learns more about its people. He soon becomes aware of more contrasts and learn about the caste system, the role of the family and the position of women. He feels confirmed in his modern way of thinking and knows that his place should be in Britain rather than in India. Unfortunately, he has no idea that his parents intend to leave him behind to make him accept the arranged marriage they have planned with an Indian girl. In the end, Manny pretends to agree so that he can get back to Britain. With the help of his British friends and his uncle he escapes the marriage, which at the same time means breaking away from his family.

So Manny also feels miserable. At least he is not discriminated against, like Suketu is, but his school performance gets worse because he is constantly occupied with the thought of the planned marriage. He is convinced that he wants to determine his own life, and therefore has to find a solution. To conclude, we can say that both young people are in a tragic situation. While Suketu has to fight racism and is divided about his identity, Manny is confronted with family traditions that are opposed to his own idea of a modern lifestyle. Both of them are young people who want to be themselves, be respected and live where they feel at home. But they are closely

linked to and in a way dependent on the social conditions around them as well as on the families they belong to.
Finally, I would say that multi-cultural societies, wherever they exist, provide a unique opportunity for a rewarding, diverse life together, as long as tolerance and respect can be guaranteed on all sides. Otherwise, this could lead to unrest and conflicts and make it hard to establish a sound basis for a common life in peace and harmony, in which bitter experiences as described above could be prevented.

4.3 *Es wird von Ihnen erwartet, dass Sie die Merkmale eines förmlichen Briefes, der gleichzeitig eine Einladung ist, beachten. Sie sollen sowohl textliche Bezüge als auch außertextliche Argumente einfließen lassen, die einen entsprechenden kommunikativen Effekt bewirken.*

Suketu Mehta
c/o Vintage Books
1745 Broadway Avenue
NEW YORK, NY 10019
USA

Lisa Ledig
Gröperstraße 12
16909 WITTSTOCK
Germany

12 March 2010

Your reading tour to Germany

Dear Mr Mehta,

I am writing to you regarding the reading tour to Germany which you are planning. I am addressing you on behalf of my fellow students. We would appreciate it very much if you were able to include our home town in your journey and visit our school.
But let me introduce myself first so that you may hopefully understand the relevance of our request. I am a student in the 12th grade at a German high school in the federal state of Brandenburg. In our English lessons we were presented an excerpt of your book "Maximum City". It corresponds perfectly with our topics of ethnic diversity, living in a multi-cultural society, coping with its drawbacks, but also seeing its advantages.
We were deeply impressed by the account of that period in your life. It must have been very hard, maybe like a clash of cultures or even a shock to you, when you were forced to change countries without being asked or prepared in any way. So it sounds quite plausible when you say that "you're never well in your skin in the one you're moving to". At least it usually takes time to adapt, and the younger you are, the more support and guidance you might need. Not enough that you had to leave all familiar things behind, you also immediately fell victim to harsh discrimination at school immediately. I mean, considering the fragile age you were at, it seems comprehensible that you suffered a lot. From a distance it is always easier to judge, but we really wonder why you could not find any help or advice in coping with your unhappy situation in a better way. We also were surprised that in the late 70s racism like that existed in Britain.

Our school is middle size, just about 500 students. In the course of time there has been an increasing number of students of Asian or East European descent. Although I claim that most of our young people stand up for equality and values like respect and tolerance, I cannot deny that there is also a certain potential for prejudice. Sometimes I feel irritated when I hear that people mean not to be racist on the one hand, but make racist jokes on the other.

There have even been some racist attacks in our surroundings recently. It is a creeping development that should be stopped long before it can spread further. So you may agree that to instill important values in young people should definitely be part of school education. And whenever you want to convince somebody, it is communication or authentic encounter that works – not theory or dogma. Your visit would provide us with a chance to tackle racism from such an authentic, real-life point of view.

I do not want to finish my letter without mentioning the two migrant youngsters in our course who say that your way of writing has appealed to them in particular. The rest of us are making a lot of effort to integrate them, but still, finding common ground is not always easy. To have the pleasure of meeting you might make a contribution, and who knows, perhaps eventually a difference.

Actually, it should no longer be a question of finding your own place, no matter where, in this globalized world. Isn't the freedom of movement a chance to broaden horizons in a way so that discrimination and stereotypes can be overcome? My classmates and I would be very happy to hear more from your book, your life and your experiences with such challenges. Therefore, we would very much like to welcome you to our school for a discussion of such issues as mobility, integration and mutual respect.

We would be more than pleased if you could find time for us while you are in Germany.

I look forward to hearing from you soon.

Yours sincerely,

Lisa Ledig

Abiturprüfung Berlin/Brandenburg 2010
Englisch Leistungskurs – Aufgabe 2

Themenschwerpunkte: *Urban, suburban and rural lifestyles; Personal relations in their social context; The challenge of globalisation*

Text A (excerpt from an autobiography)

Farm City
By Novella Carpenter

I have a farm on a dead-end street in the ghetto.

My back stairs are dotted with chicken turds. Bales of straw come undone in the parking area next to my apartment. I harvest lettuce in an abandoned lot. I awake in the mornings to the sounds of farm animals mingled with my neighbor's blaring car alarm.

I didn't always call this place a farm. That didn't happen until the spring of 2005, when a very special package was delivered to my apartment and changed everything. I remember standing on my deck, waiting for it. While scanning the horizon for the postal jeep, I checked the health of my bee colony. Honeybees buzzed in and out of the hive, their hind legs loaded down with yellow pollen. I caught a whiff of their honey-making on the breeze, mixed with the exhaust from the nearby freeway. I could see the highway, heavy with traffic, from the deck.

[I noticed that three bees had fallen into a watering can. As their wings sent out desperate ripples along the water, I broke off a twig from a potted star jasmine and offered it to the drowning insects. One bee clambered onto the stick and clung to it as I transported her to the top of the hive. The next bee did the same – she held fast to the twig like a passenger gone overboard, clutching a lifesaver. Safe atop the hive, the two soggy bees opened their wings to the morning sunlight. Once dry and warm, they would be able to fly again. Just to see what would happen, I lifted the final rescuee to the entrance of the hive instead of the top. A guard bee stomped out from the dark recesses of the brood box. There's always one on vigil for disturbances, armed and ready to sting. As the guard bee got closer to the wet one I braced myself for a brutal natural history lesson.

The waterlogged bee started to right herself as she waved a soggy antenna. Another guard bee joined the first, and together they probed the wet bee. She couldn't have smelled of their hive anymore, which is how most bees recognize one another. Nonetheless, the guards began to lick her dry.*]

"Hey! Hey!" a voice yelled.

I peered down to the end of our dead-end street.

[*] *nicht Teil der Prüfung*

A new car, a silver Toyota Corolla, had arrived on 28th Street the night before, probably the victim of a joyride – Corollas are notoriously easy to start without a key. Local teenagers steal them and drive around until they run out of gas. Already the car had lost one wheel. By nightfall, I predicted, it would be stripped completely.

Amid the jumble of abandoned cars and trash and the shiny Toyota Corolla, I made out the figure of the man who was yelling. He waved vigorously. Bobby.

"Morning, sir!" I called and saluted him. He saluted back.

Bobby lived in an immobilized car. He switched on his television, which was mounted on top of one of the other abandoned cars. An orange extension cord snaked from a teak-colored house at the end of the block. The perky noise of Regis and Kathie Lee joined the sound of the nearby traffic and the clattering trundle of the San Francisco Bay Area's subway, BART, which runs aboveground next to the highway.

Just then, a monk came out of the Buddhist monastery across the street from my house and brought Bobby a snack. The monks will feed anyone who is hungry. Next to the fountain in their courtyard there's a giant alabaster statue of a placid-faced lady riding a dragon: Kuan Yin, the goddess of compassion. My bees loved to drink from the lotus-flower-filled fountain. I often watched their golden bodies zoom across 28th Street, at the same height as the power lines, then swoop down behind the temple's red iron gates.

The monk who handed Bobby a container of rice and vegetables was female, dressed in pale purple robes, her head shaved. Bobby took the food and shoved it into a microwave plugged in next to the television set. Nuked his breakfast.

I heard the clattering sound of a shopping cart. A can scrounger. Wearing a giant Chinese wicker hat and rubber gloves and carrying a pair of tongs, she opened our recycling bin and started fishing around for cans. She muttered to herself in Chinese, "Ay-ya."

I watched as Bobby jogged over to her. I had never seen him run before. "Get out of here," he growled. His territory. She shook her head as if to say she didn't understand and continued fishing. Bobby butted her with his belly. "I said get out," he yelled. She scurried away, pulling her cart after her. Bobby watched her retreat.

Then, when she was almost around the corner, as if he felt bad, Bobby put his hands to his mouth and yelled, "I'll see you at the recycling center!" Just a few blocks away, the center paid cash by the pound for metal. Chuckling to himself, Bobby glanced up at me on the deck and flashed me a mostly toothless smile.

This place, this ghetto of Oakland, California, brings out the best and the worst in us.

[Bored of waiting around outside, I headed back inside my apartment. A fly strip dangled from the ceiling, and ripped feed bags piled up near the door. A black velour couch my boyfriend and I found in the street sagged in the corner.

I guess the neighborhood brings out the best and worst in me, too. Sure, my chickens lay eggs – but the flock has spawned an occasional rooster that crowed loudly and often, starting at 4 a.m. Bees do result in honey and wax and better pollination – but they have also stung people from time to time. The garden: verdant cornucopia on one hand, rodent-attracting breeding ground on the other.

I flopped onto the couch and read the chalkboard tally that hung near the door:

4 chickens
30,000 bees [approximately]
59 flies
2 monkeys [me and my boyfriend, Bill]
That tally was about to change.

A long-debunked scientific theory states that "ontogeny recapitulates phylogeny." Basically that means that the order of development in an embryo indicates its evolutionary development — for example, a human embryo first looks like a fish because we evolved from fish. When Bill and I first moved from Seattle to Oakland, I was reminded of that theory, because somehow we ended up re-creating our old life in the exact same order as we had created it in Seattle. The first year in Oakland, we built the garden; the second year, we got the honeybees and then the chickens. In this, our third year of development, it was time to evolve to the next level.*]

Out of the corner of my eye, I watched through the window as the postal jeep turned down our street and pulled to a stop in front of our house. [A man dressed in wool shorts hopped out, holding an air-hole-riddled box in his arms. I bounded downstairs. My neighbor Mr. Nguyen, who lived one floor below me, was sitting outside on the porch, smoke and steam from his morning cigarette and Vietnamese coffee wafting up together in the crisp spring air. In his sixties, Mr. Nguyen dyed his graying hair black, wore button-down dress shirts, and was surprisingly sprightly. He set down his coffee, stubbed out his cigarette, and walked into the street with me to receive the package.*]

The postal worker made me sign an official-looking piece of paper before he would hand me the box. It peeped when I opened it.

It was filled with puff balls. Fuzzy yellow ducklings called out desperately with their orange bills. Long-necked goslings squawked, and fluffy multicolored chicks peeped. Three odd-looking chicks with an unattractive pimple of skin atop their heads gazed up quietly from the box.

The delivery guy shook his head in disbelief. I could tell he had questions. Were we not in the city? Wasn't downtown Oakland only ten blocks away? Who is this insane woman? Is this even legal? *(785 words)*

Source: Carpenter, Novella. Farm City – The Education of an Urban Farmer. New York 2009: 3–6

Annotations

l. 2	turds: a solid piece of waste from an animal's body, excrement
l. 2	bales: a large quantity of straw tied tightly for storing
l. 38	to snake: to move in or have a series of long curves
l. 39	perky: lively and happy
ll. 39/40	Regis and Kathie Lee: "Live with Regis and Kathie Lee" – morning show on TV
l. 40	clattering: making several loud short noises as it hits against another hard object
l. 40	trundle: a truck or carriage on low wheels
l. 44	placid-faced: peaceful face that does not show emotions
l. 51	to nuke: to heat or cook something in the microwave
l. 52	scrounger: someone who gets something he/she wants by asking other people for it instead of providing it or paying for it him-/herself
l. 53	wicker: long thin pieces of wood that are woven together

l. 53 tongs: a metal or plastic object that consists of two connected arms that you push together in order to pick something up
l. 58 to butt: to push or hit someone
l. 99 fuzzy: covered with short soft hairs

Text B (chart)

"Homegrown Hunger Relief in Seattle"

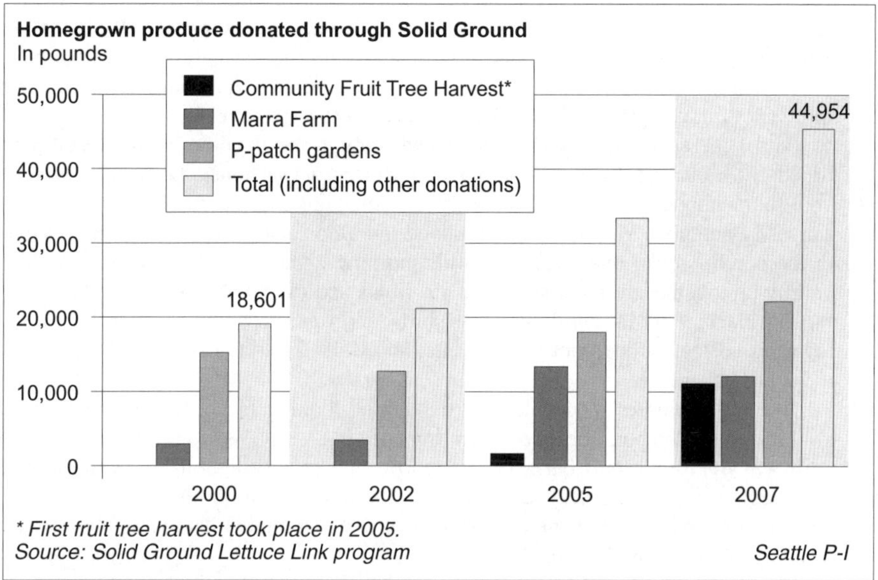

Source: <http://www.seattlepi.com/dayart/20080603/Urban-Farming-0603.gif> [20 September 2009]

Annotations

Solid Ground: organization that organizes fruit harvests for food banks and meal programs in Seattle

Community Fruit Tree Harvest: Seattle organization that motivates homeowners to donate fruit from their trees

Marra Farm: farm that grows organic food in Seattle and donates it through Solid Ground

P-patch gardens: Seattle organization that motivates backyard and community gardeners to donate fruit and vegetables

All the initiatives in the graph use urban land for farming.

Tasks

1 Give an account of how Novella Carpenter and the other people in her neighborhood live in the ghetto. (30 %)

2 Describe the chart (Text B) and explain how it relates to the message of Text A. (30 %)

3 Choose <u>one</u> of the following tasks.

3.1 Explain and comment on Mrs. Carpenter's statement that "[...] this ghetto of Oakland, California, brings out the best and the worst in us" (Text A, ll. 64/65). Refer to Text A and your knowledge about life in urban problem areas. (40 %)

OR

3.2 Discuss whether Mrs. Carpenter's way of coping with the living conditions in a poor urban neighborhood is a suitable approach for meeting the economic and social challenges of life in cities. (40 %)

OR

3.3 Mrs. Carpenter wants to promote urban farming in big cities. Describe the layout of a flyer she might use to request the wealthier residents of her city to raise financial support for this project. Write its text and give convincing reasons for your suggestions. (40 %)

Lösungsvorschläge

1. *Diese Aufgabe verlangt eine kurze Schilderung der Lebensumstände von Mrs Carpenter und ihren Nachbarn. Zeigen Sie, dass Sie die wesentlichen Punkte der Beschreibung verstanden haben, ohne Zitate anzuführen oder bereits zu interpretieren.*

   Novella Carpenter lives in a dead-end street in the ghetto of Oakland. She grows food on an unused plot near her house and raises animals in her backyard. Across from her house is a Buddhist monastery with a beautiful fountain and a statue. Otherwise her area is described as not very appealing, with the everyday sound of car alarms mingling with the constant noise and exhaust fumes from the highway and the subway nearby. Derelict cars that have been stolen by teenagers and then abandoned and stripped of their valuable parts are lined up on the street. One of them serves as a shelter for Bobby, a homeless man who earns a bit of money by fishing for valuable metal in bins so that he can exchange it for cash at the recycling centre. When a Chinese woman, a so-called scrounger, too, intrudes upon his territory, searching for cans in the recycling bin, Bobby drives her away to protect his turf. To run his television and microwave he steals electricity from a nearby house. He gets food from the monks at the monastery, who feed the hungry in the ghetto.

2. *Bei der Analyse einer Statistik sollten Sie zuerst die wichtigsten Fakten nennen, d. h. Überschrift und Thema der Grafik, Quelle der Daten, angezeigte Informationen. Analysieren Sie dann die angegebenen Daten im Detail. Gibt es besonders auffällige Werte? Ist ein allgemeiner Trend zu erkennen? Was lässt sich aus diesen Ergebnissen schließen? Vergessen Sie nicht, die Statistik in Bezug zum Textausschnitt zu setzen. Was ist der gemeinsame Referenzpunkt, wo ergeben sich Unterschiede, welche übergreifende Bedeutung ergibt sich aus den Quellen?*

   The bar chart "Homegrown Hunger Relief in Seattle" shows the amount of homegrown food that is donated by an organization in Seattle called "Solid Ground" to relieve people from hunger. The data provided by the Solid Ground Lettuce Link program includes three organizations, "Community Fruit Tree Harvest", "Marra Farm" and "P-patch gardens", and other initiatives that are not mentioned by name but taken into account for the total sum of donations. The horizontal line shows the donations made by these organizations from 2000 to 2007, whereas the vertical line indicates the amount of donated produce in pounds. The amount of food donated by "Marra Farm" rose significantly from 2000 to 2005, but then decreased again in 2007. "P-patch gardens" started off high in 2000. The figure dropped slightly in 2002 but then rose steadily up to 2007. In all seven years considered in the chart, "P-patch gardens" donated the highest amount of produce. The organization "Community Fruit Tree Harvest" only joined the programme in 2005 with a very small donation, but then raised an amount almost as high as that of "Marra" in 2007. Overall, the figures clearly show a rising trend, as the total sum of donations rose from 18,601 pounds in 2000 to 44,954 in 2007.

The chart relates to the text by Novella Carpenter in that both sources engage with the topic of improving the living conditions of people in disadvantaged city areas. Both Novella Carpenter and the initiatives included in the chart use urban land for growing fruit and vegetables to fight against hunger. While Carpenter portrays her individual way of coping with life in an urban ghetto, the chart provides general statistical data about the same topic. The organizations mentioned here pursue a more community-based approach than Carpenter does in that they try to motivate farmers, homeowners and backyard and community gardeners alike to donate their produce. All in all, the figures show that home-grown food is clearly needed, which indicates that the number of people like Mrs Carpenter will probably be increasing. This might also provide opportunities for farmers using urban land to organize in initiatives or support groups.

3.1 *Versuchen Sie hier, das Zitat treffend zu erläutern, indem Sie erklären, worauf es sich bezieht und in welchem Zusammenhang es im Text vorkommt. Versuchen Sie dann, auch außertextliche Bezüge herzustellen. Sie sollten Ihre Argumente klar strukturieren und am Schluss zu einer überzeugenden Wertung kommen.*

When Novella Carpenter observes Bobby shouting at another scrounger and driving her away, she states that "this ghetto [...] brings out the best and the worst in us." People in the ghetto have to fight for their living, and getting enough money for essentials like food can be very tough. Therefore, social behavior, moral standards and the usual rules of human interaction may easily suffer. Mrs Carpenter points out, though, that ghetto people are not all ruthless criminals.
In the news, reports of inner-city crime, car thefts, drug problems, gang wars and street fights are a daily routine. Poverty gives way to conflicts, it seems, and thus brings out the worst in people. This is described in the text by the way Bobby fights for his turf and even butts the woman with his belly to chase her away (l. 58). Besides, by living in a stolen car he is actually committing a crime, and stealing electricity from his neighbours is morally questionable, too. The same goes for the teenagers who steal the cars in the first place and those who take out all the valuable parts and then leave the cars on some street.
Nevertheless, Mrs Carpenter sees an upside to life in the ghetto. Even though Bobby selfishly drives away a woman who obviously has the same problems and disadvantages as he does, he seems to regret it the minute she runs away. So he says farewell after all and smiles apologetically at Mrs Carpenter, who seems to comprehend Bobby's reaction. It is tough to balance selfishness against the fight for basic needs.
But Bobby does not seem to lose hope. His "home" is a car, he lives on food donations and steals electricity from others, but he is still quite cheerful, and he and Mrs Carpenter treat each other as proper neighbours, greeting each other in the morning with an intimate routine of saluting.
Mrs Carpenter tries to improve her living conditions herself by growing her own food. She is an independent woman who takes action and relies on herself when the situation is desperate. At the same time, though, she is serving her community. The

garden that she plants in an abandoned lot improves the appearance of the neighbourhood and might encourage others to engage actively in food production and the improvement of their desperate circumstances.
On the other hand, there are those who not only wait for help or help themselves only, but who act socially responsible. In the text, it is the monks who show sympathy and compassion for Bobby and feed all those in their area who are worse off. They serve as a positive example of people acting selflessly and taking on social responsibility.
This is a phenomenon most common in situations like the one described in the text. Even though living conditions may be harsh, there are always those who take a stand for the poor and take action against disadvantages. Examples are initiatives like the Solid Ground programme, charity organizations, support and self-help groups, or famous celebrities who commit themselves to charitable projects. Similarly, stories in literature and film often portray the positive ways of life of people who grew up in ghettos under difficult conditions, but made their way in life. These may seem to be unrealistic imaginary stories, but they, too, can serve as models for thousands of people feeling oppressed and disadvantaged.
All these fictional and real examples indicate that Mrs Carpenter has a point when she says that both the best and the worst is brought out by a ghetto like hers in Oakland. There are fights, prejudices, tragedies, but coping with disadvantages also enables experiences of self-reliance, community and strength. Extreme circumstances make people push their limits. If conditions had not been so for Mrs Carpenter, she might never have considered farming, and might have missed the sound of animals in her backyard and the smell and taste of homegrown food. She might never have achieved independene. Of course, you might end up as a criminal, too. There is a thin line between giving your best and behaving your worst when you do not have the same means as everyone else in society.

3.2 *Unabhängig davon, ob Sie Mrs Carpenters Herangehensweise gut oder schlecht finden, sollten Sie anfangs sowohl positive als auch negative Aspekte aufzeigen. Finden Sie dann treffende Argumente, die Ihre Meinung bestätigen und kommen Sie zu einer abschließenden Bewertung. Achten Sie darauf, auch über den Text hinauszugehen und die allgemeine gesellschaftliche Relevanz solcher Projekte zu bewerten.*

The economic and social challenges of life in cities are numerous, as the text by Mrs Carpenter shows. People in her area have to cope with car theft and vandalism by teenagers, pollution and noise from the nearby freeway and subway, homelessness in the case of Bobby, and probably general poverty, as the need for homegrown food and Buddhist charity indicate.
Although Mrs Carpenter lives in a house that even has a backyard and a deck, she seems to face economic difficulties. Establishing her own little farm in the middle of the city is her way of coping with poverty. We learn from the text that she has a hive of bees, grows lettuce, and raises chickens and ducks. This not only provides her with food, but it also adds a valuable and positive aspect to her derelict street. Addi-

tionally, she seems to feel very happy with her plants and animals and the noise and smells they add to the otherwise bleak and unappealing environment.

These factors seem to show that farming is a quite adequate and fulfilling means to cope with urban poverty. The case for farming is not that clear, however. After all, not all people have their own home to grow vegetables and raise animals at in the first place, as for example Bobby. In his case, the rather pressing need for basic hygiene must be solved first, as he lives in a car without sanitation. Even if the basic means were given, laying out a garden in the middle of the city might still be impossible for a lot of people simply due to a lack of space. Last but not least, financial resources are needed to invest in basic equipment, seeds or animals for a start. Even if both financial and spatial requirements are met, one might object that growing vegetables that are exposed to exhaust fumes all day long is not the healthiest idea.

I still think, however, that Mrs Carpenter's way to tackle the challenges of living in urban poverty is a good one. Compared to pre-packed supermarket fruit and vegetables often flown in from the other end of the world, homegrown food like Mrs Carpenter's certainly contains more nutrients and vitamins. Also, as we are dealing with fruit and vegetables fresh from the garden, such produce offers a good and healthy alternative to cheap ready-made meals and fast food that can often be found on the dinner tables of poor families. Growing your own food, in my opinion, raises an awareness of what you are actually eating.

Consequently, farming and gardening would present an even better way of coping with economic difficulties, if more people were involved. It is a shame that Mrs Carpenter started this project all on her own. Urban farming should not only be an individual solution, but act as an incentive for people to join in the fight for a better life. The ideal approach to facing economic and social challenges in urban areas, in my opinion, would be to motivate others to join in, so that the community engages actively in the production of their own food. That way, people could not only see what happens with the things that eventually end up on their plates, but also what is going on with their neighbours and then they could help and support each other in the daily urban struggle.

3.3 *Beachten Sie beim Entwurf Ihres Flyers: Was ist Mrs Carpenters Absicht? Wer ist ihre Zielgruppe? Was sind die Gründe für ihr Vorhaben? Welche Argumente überzeugen den Leser? Sind Inhalt, Struktur und Sprache der Zielgruppe angemessen? Ist das Layout so gestaltet, dass Inhalt und Absicht deutlich werden? Vergessen Sie nicht, dass Sie den Flyer selbst nicht zeichnen, sondern nur beschreiben sollen. Beginnen Sie mit einer kurzen Einleitung zu Absicht und Zielgruppe, schreiben Sie dann den tatsächlichen Text des Flyers (inklusive Überschrift) und erläutern Sie das Layout (Größe, Farbe, Schrift, Bilder …). Begründen Sie Ihre Entscheidungen.*

Mrs Carpenter is convinced that growing your own food can help with both economic and social difficulties in urban problem areas. Therefore she wants to promote urban farming on a bigger scale. Now she is on the lookout for people to support her project financially, which is why her flyer is addressed to wealthier citizens who are asked to donate money. She presents her idea as a communal project and explains its purposes in the flyer, so that she does not appear as the sole beneficiary of the money. To appeal to the readers more personally, Mrs Carpenter first gives a short description of her own experiences with urban farming. Then she presents the reasons why urban farming could be advantageous for everyone involved. This is the text of her flyer:

Heading: Your funds can make our neighbourhood flourish

Subheading: We grow food for people who cannot afford it. We grow food to make our city greener. We grow food to make community grow, too.

Main text: A few years ago, I could not stand all the grey bleakness around my house any longer. So I planted some flowers in my backyard. Some vegetables followed and then some fruit, too. After a while I almost had a proper farm, with a harvest that could provide fresh groceries for me and some of my neighbours throughout the year. The impact was overwhelming. Not only could I grow my own food, I was also surrounded by rich green vegetation in the middle of the city. More and more neighbours came by to help with the harvest, to buy some vegetables or to get tips on gardening and farming. When even some of the youngsters who usually spend their time wrecking things came along, asking how I had managed to convert one of the cars they had abandoned on the street into a flowerbed, I decided it was time to take action. The Urban Gardening Project was born.

We are a collective of privately organized citizens who want to make a difference in the daily struggle against urban poverty. By growing food on abandoned lots, in free city spaces and in backyards and front gardens, we can provide food for hundreds of people who would otherwise go hungry, or who might steal it, who might go begging on the street, who might need government support. By engaging socially disadvantaged people in the process we provide employment and solidarity.

[Printed in bold] But we need your help. Make a donation and support our project!

[Printed in bold] With your help, we can make our urban garden grow even more.

Every dollar is invested in more seeds and more tools to grow food and in jobs for people in need. YOU can help us go further and grow more, YOU can help our neighbourhood flourish!

Bullet points: We feed the hungry. We grow healthy food. We nurture the environment. We generate jobs. We get kids off the street. We make your neighbourhood more secure. We foster a sustainable community. We help your city go green.

Layout: The flyer should be A4 printed in landscape format, but then folded twice so that the orientation of the six parts is in portrait format again. That way, the flyer has a handy format and enough space for information. The front contains the heading and subheading. The first page on the inside describes Mrs Carpenter's personal experience and explains the Urban Gardening Project. The middle page forms the centre of the flyer and contains the appeal for help and the invitation to donate, all printed in boldface to capture the readers' attention. On the right there are the bullet points that explain the project's achievements. Turning the flyer to the back, you see the heading on the far right, forming the front page if the flyer is folded. The left part should contain pictures of green urban space, a basket full of fruit and vegetables, and young people working in a garden. The middle section presents Mrs Carpenter's contact details, including a telephone number and an e-mail address for questions, and the bank details for people interested in making a donation. The last line should be a note, again printed in boldface, indicating that all donations are tax deductible, offering a better incentive for wealthier citizens to give some money.

Abiturprüfung Berlin/Brandenburg 2011
Englisch Grundkurs – Aufgabe 1

Themenschwerpunkte: *Urban, suburban and rural lifestyles; Personal relations in their social context*

Text A (excerpt from an article)

Meeting the neighbors
by Laurie Hertzel

Note: *The following article is a review of Peter Lovenheim's book "In the Neighborhood: The Search for Community on an American Street – One Sleepover at a Time", which was published in 2010.*

Peter Lovenheim lives in a spacious house on a quiet suburban street near Rochester, N. Y. His neighbors are doctors and executives – he knows that much about them, but for years he didn't know much more. The people in his exclusive neighborhood tend to keep to themselves.

When one of the doctors is murdered by her husband, Lovenheim is struck with a deep sadness and a startling sense of guilt. Who on the block had known that Renan Wills was in such a terrible marriage? Who on the block even knew Renan Wills at all? If she had had friends in the neighborhood, might she have had somewhere to run that night? Might her life somehow have been saved?

It is hard not to be charmed by what Lovenheim does next. He decides to get to know his neighbors, and he decides to do so the way children get to know one another: By hanging out. By sleeping over.

"What would it take, I wondered, to penetrate the barriers between us?" he writes. "I thought about childhood sleepovers and the insight I used to get from waking up inside a friend's home."

It is not a perfect solution. Many neighbors turn him down. Some who agree clearly do so out of loneliness – one is a retired doctor whose wife has died; another is a divorced woman with cancer.

What is interesting about this book is his discovery that the absence of community seems to be on everyone's mind; neighbor after neighbor brings it up. "No one cares," says Lou Guzzetta, the retired doctor. "No one wants to be bothered. There are no neighbors in the truest sense of the word. There are no neighbors here."

[Says another neighbor, a hard-charging young woman named Deb, "the thing is, the people on this street, I don't think they want to know you." These busy, driven people reveal lives that are shot through with a sense of isolation.*]

[*] *nicht Teil der Prüfung*

Community space, Lovenheim observes, has migrated from neighborhoods – which often lack parks or other central meeting places – to bookstores, coffee shops, country clubs and the Internet. The resultant void means an abundance of privacy, but no intimacy. "We move in isolation from each other," a neighbor named Bill says. "It's easy to behave [badly] to strangers."

Lovenheim's mission isn't just to get to know his neighbors; it is to try, gently, to bring them together. In some cases, he succeeds. [When Patricia, the radiologist with cancer, needs someone to drive her to the doctor, Lovenheim introduces her to Lou Guzzetta, and a kind of friendship springs up.*]

It is hard to read this book and not think of your own neighborhood, your own street. Who do you know? Everyone? Anyone? No one at all? Dog-walkers, one neighbor observed, usually know the names of each other's dogs, but not the names of each other. [I thought of walking my own dogs down my own St. Paul street and realized sadly that this is often true.*] *(415 words)*

Source: Hertzel, Laurie. Meeting the neighbors. Star Tribune. 24 April 2010 <http://www.startribune.com/entertainment/books/91865584.html?page=2&c=y> [10 May 10]

Annotations
l. 6 startling: surprising or very unusual
l. 13 to penetrate: to get through something
l. 29 void: emptiness
l. 29 abundance: very large quantity of something

Text B (Auszug aus einem Online-Artikel)

Der Nachbar – das unbekannte Wesen

Aktuelle Trendumfrage belegt: Jeder fünfte Deutsche weiß nicht, wer neben ihm wohnt

[…] Berlin, den 8. September 2009 – Die Anonymität unter deutschen Dächern ist groß – das ist das Ergebnis einer aktuellen Trendumfrage von ImmobilienScout24 und der Community www.meinenachbarschaft.de unter 16.279 Teilnehmern. 21 Prozent der Deutschen kennen ihre Nachbarn gar nicht oder haben außer einem „Hallo" im Vorbeigehen noch kein Wort mit ihnen gewechselt. Nur jeder Zweite hält ab und zu Small Talk mit seinen Hausgenossen.

In der Kleinstadt oder auf dem Land herrscht der Befragung zufolge ein etwas engeres Verhältnis unter Nachbarn als in der Großstadt. Während auf dem Land 16 Prozent der Befragten ihre Nachbarn so gut wie nicht kennen, sind es in der Stadt 24 Prozent. 29 Prozent der Kleinstädter geben an, dass sie ein gutes Verhältnis zu ihren Nachbarn pflegen – in der Großstadt sind es nur 19 Prozent. Eine interessante Erkenntnis: Das Nachbarschaftsverhältnis verbessert sich offenbar mit zunehmendem Alter.

Der Nachbarschaftsfrieden ist oft durch Störfaktoren belastet. Die größten sind Lärmbelästigung (für 23 Prozent der Befragten) und zu große Neugierde (18 Prozent). Vor allem auf dem Land und in der Kleinstadt wird offenbar genau geschaut, was nebenan passiert: Hier fühlt sich jeder Fünfte von seinen Nachbarn beobachtet (Vergleich Großstadt: 12 Prozent).

Weitere Ärgernisse sind die Unfreundlichkeit unter Hausbewohnern (14 Prozent) sowie Geruchsbelästigung aus der Nachbarwohnung (10 Prozent). Jeder zehnte Befragte ist von seinen Nachbarskindern genervt. Vor allem die Jüngeren haben für Kinderlärm kein Verständnis. Generell scheint die Toleranzschwelle mit zunehmendem Alter zu steigen. Je älter die Befragten, desto weniger ärgern sie sich über ihre Mitmenschen. […] *(257 Wörter)*

Quelle: Böhm, Andreas. Der Nachbar – das unbekannte Wesen. In: Immobilienscout 24 News vom 8. September 2009 <http://news.immobilienscout24.de/tipps-der-redaktion/der-nachbar-das-unbekannte-wesen,11542.html> [18. August 2010]

Tasks

1 Give an account of how Peter Lovenheim experiences his urban neighborhood. (Text A) (20 %)

2 Examine how the author conveys Lovenheim's concerns about his neighborhood to the readers. Give evidence from Text A. (25 %)

3 For a project on social interaction and problems in urban communities outline the information provided in Text B that is relevant to this issue. (20 %)

4 Choose <u>one</u> of the following tasks:

4.1 Discuss Lovenheim's view on urban neighborhoods. (35 %)

OR

4.2 Using Text A as a starting point, comment on the way a literary or film character experiences isolation in society and how he/she copes with his/her situation. (35 %)

OR

4.3 Including ideas from Text A and Text B, write an article for a brochure for a European campaign promoting volunteer work in neighborhood communities. In your article try to convince young residents to support community life and suggest how they could become active. (35 %)

Lösungsvorschläge

1 *Bei dieser Aufgabe gehen Sie wie bei einer Inhaltsangabe vor. Der Fokus liegt hierbei auf den Erfahrungen des Autors hinsichtlich seiner Nachbarn. Achten Sie darauf, sachlich zu bleiben. Wie bei der Inhaltsangabe dürfen Sie auch hier nicht interpretieren.*

The article tells about Peter Lovenheim's experiences concerning his neighbourhood. At first he is quite ignorant about their way of life, but when a murder happens he begins to wonder if friendships among the neighbours might have prevented the crime. That is why he makes an effort to get to know his neighbours and tries to break the barriers between people by sleeping over at their homes. He notices that many welcome his idea because they are lonely.
He also realizes that everybody is aware of the growing isolation and the lack of community spirit and that community space has shifted from local neighbourhoods to anonymous urban places. Real neighbours do not seem to exist any longer.

2 *Bei dieser Aufgabe sollen Sie die stilistischen Mittel analysieren und dabei darlegen, inwiefern diese die Darstellung der Sorgen Lovenheims unterstützen. Es ist wichtig, dass Sie den Beleg für das entsprechende Mittel mit Zeilenangabe korrekt zitieren.*

The author often describes Lovenheim's attitude towards his neighbourhood by using contrasts. On the one hand, he describes it as "exclusive" (l. 3); he has a "spacious house" (l. 1) and "[h]is neighbours are doctors and executives" (l. 2). On the other hand, he mentions that "for years he didn't know much more" (l. 3). There is a lot of opulence as far as status and wealth go, but considering the depth of human relations these do not run deep at all. In fact, everything seems rather shallow as people living next door to each other hardly know each other. Lovenheim starts to question this anonymity when one of his neighbours is murdered. To describe Lovenheim's shocking experience of virtually being witness to a murder and the beginning of his concerns, the author uses the image of Lovenheim being "struck with a deep sadness and a startling sense of guilt" (ll. 5/6) to illustrate the enormity of the event better.
Another contrast, "abundance of privacy, but no intimacy" (ll. 29/30), shows the gap between opportunity and actual reality, i. e. there is plenty of space to do things aside from other people. However, without relations between each other, intimacy is missing, and comfort, too.
The lack of solidarity and community spirit is stressed by the use of parallel constructions in "No one cares …" (l. 20), "No one wants …" (l. 21), and an example of anaphora can be found in lines 21/22, where the first phrase is repeated to make the message more poignant: "There are no neighbors …. There are no neighbors here."
To point out that isolation is the main problem, some of Lovenheim's neighbours are quoted directly. One of them says, for example, that they "move in isolation from each other" (l. 30). The people Lovenheim gives a voice to support the truth and authenticity of this article. The sense of isolation is stressed even more by the rhetorical

questions in lines 6–9, "Who on the block had known …?", and line 37, "Who do you know? Everyone? Anyone? No one at all?". That way, the author emphasises the anonymity of the environment and at the same time involves the reader in his thoughts about Lovenheim's concerns.

3 *Bei dieser Aufgabe sollten Sie die Informationen aus dem deutschen Text sinngemäß skizzieren – eine wörtliche Übersetzung ist nicht gefordert. Beginnen Sie die Zusammenfassung mit einem einleitenden Satz, in dem Sie alle wichtigen Informationen zum Artikel kurz nennen.*

Neighbours – strange beings

The article by Andreas Böhm, published on *Immobilienscout24.de* in September 2009, provides statistical data about Germans' relationships to their neighbours, which are characterized by a high extent of anonymity, especially in urban areas. People in small cities or in the countryside maintain better relations to their neighbours. Whereas 24 % do not know their neighbours at all in big cities, the figure is only 16 % for the countryside.
The article also enumerates the problems standing in the way of good relations, like noise or nosiness, which are more prominent in smaller towns and rural areas. Every fifth inhabitant feels closely watched by their neighbours there. Other annoying factors in all areas are unfriendliness and smells. In general, tolerance increases with age.

4.1 *Der Arbeitsauftrag* to discuss *ist mit einer Erörterung vergleichbar, in der Pro- und Kontra-Argumente gegeneinander abgewogen werden sollen. Sie können entweder erst alle Pro-Argumente und dann alle Kontra-Argumente nennen, oder immer abwechselnd ein Pro- und ein Kontra-Argument anführen.*
Wichtig ist, dass Sie am Ende ein Fazit ziehen. Entscheiden Sie sich für eine Position und stärken Sie diese mit Argumenten. Für die Gegenposition brauchen Sie nicht so viele Argumente zu nennen wie für die eigene.
Die Einleitung sollte Interesse für Ihre Erörterung wecken. Dies kann durch eine Frage erreicht werden, eine kurze Anekdote oder ein Sprichwort. Ein Zitat aus dem Text kann sich ebenfalls eignen.

"A spacious house on a quiet suburban street" – the description of Peter Lovenheim's home sounds like a dream come true. However, there is too much quiet for Mr Lovenheim. The calm also implies anonymity, which eventually turns into a heavy burden as a neigbour gets killed. Are American neighbourhoods really deteriorating to that extent, or does Mr Lovenheim tend to exaggerate?
Surely, life in a big city can be overwhelming: people have to deal with all sorts of problems. Getting to work is often a struggle, colleagues at work are a challenge that is sometimes difficult to take, let alone work itself. Your home should then meet the requirements of a haven – a secluded place which keeps you away from the troubles of the world. Pensioners, however, and others without the routine of a workday, lack

social contacts, so that they tend to feel lonely. How can the gap be bridged between the different interests?
Lovenheim is certainly right in pointing out the high fluctuation and modernisation in neighbourhoods. The American idea of shopping malls prevents rather than enhances personal contacts within urban culture; American cities hardly have a sidewalk to speak of; all life is centred around the "fast lane"; it looks like everything is done to keep people at bay, to stop them from interacting. Surely, there are plenty of coffee shops fostering interaction, but there is also the deterioration of local downtowns and community centers, as hinted at in the discussion of Lovenheim's book.
Furthermore, with new trends in technology, the internet is becoming increasingly important in today's society, so that the need to interact with people can easily be met by people who are not necessarily your next-door-neighbours. You do not even need a coffee shop to chat with someone online.
All in all, Lovenheim's vision of deteriorating neighbourhoods is quite real. It would indeed look very gloomy if it were not for other developments like multi-ethnic and multi-generational neighbourhoods, which show that there is a certain desire for interaction. Even though independence may go along with the need to shut oneself off, the human being is still not happy with isolation in the long run – we cannot bear complete solitude. Thus, such neighbourhoods as Lovenheim tries to establish just seem the natural course of a development which is nearly overdue, but not too late. Will sleep-overs be the new trend of our age? Hopefully, personal social networks among neighbours will be.

4.2 *Für diese Aufgabe kann als Vergleich ein beliebiger Film- bzw. Literaturcharakter herangezogen werden. In der Schule werden zum Beispiel oft Salingers „Catcher in the Rye" oder Hornbys „About a Boy" behandelt. Im Folgenden wird der Film „Into the Wild" verwendet. Ein weiteres mögliches Beispiel wäre der Film „Nothing Personal".*
Gehen Sie zuerst kurz auf die Situation im vorliegenden Text ein und erläutern Sie dann den Zusammenhang mit dem gewählten Werk. Wird Isolation dort genau gleich dargestellt, oder gehen die Charaktere auf andere Art und Weise mit Ausgrenzung um?

Isolation in society may present a great burden to many people. As we can see in the text at hand, some suffer a great deal from negligence and are very lonely. Not being in touch with your neighbour may indeed have horrible consequences, as described in Lovenheim's account of the murder happening next door. However, one may also feel alone and excluded in different terms. People might also feel isolated from society if they do not share the same values with the people they are surrounded by.
This is the case in the film "Into the Wild", in which the main character despairs with the society he has to deal with. Firstly, there are his parents, who, for the protagonist, have lived a fake life of treachery and betrayal. As far as he can see, they have hardly ever been honest to themselves or to each other. In his eyes, his parents have tried to aspire to ideals they have not been able to reach. Only later does he

find out that his parents were not actually married. However, they pretend to be the perfect couple and the perfect parents. The love they think they are giving to him does not include his interests – it is about them being proud of him. Their love is expressed in assets and consists only of materialistic values. These have no meaning to the protagonist, so that he cannot appreciate their gifts.
The protagonist, formerly called Christopher, now Alexander Supertramp, turns away in disgust. Wherever he looks, he finds everyone focusing on material wealth. Money and prestige are the two pivotal factors the world is revolving around. Alexander increasingly shrinks back from these values, as he sees them as rather destructive and absolutely pointless. Mankind is sacrificing nature's welfare for something that has no value in itself. Moreover, money fosters greed, which then again leads to more destruction.
Finally, he decides to give up all his assets and live in the wild, relying on nature to provide for the essentials. He wants to find out what really matters in life by being all by himself. He realizes that utter solitude is not a way to actual happiness, but solitude gives him the opportunity to find out what is actually necessary for it. Alexander Supertramp seeks complete isolation to find his true self in the wild. At the same time, he leaves everybody behind who cares about him. He neither tells anybody about his plans nor does he inform them about his wellbeing. This kind of isolation is as irresponsible as the one Lovenheim talks about. As we do live in a society, I believe that we are obliged to maintain some relations either way: we cannot go for complete loneliness, and likewise, we should not shut ourselves off from our neighbours.

4.3 *Für den Artikel sollten Sie auf die Gliederung achten. Wählen Sie eine ansprechende Einleitung, geben Sie dem Artikel einen Haupt- sowie Schlussteil. Schreiben Sie in Standardsprache, um sich der Zielgruppe, junger Leute aus der Nachbarschaft, anzupassen.*

"Love Thy Neighbour"

In a world where real communication is increasingly replaced with a virtual one, we need to make an effort to bring people together to communicate in the real world. We are striving for a European community, but fail at the local level. Newspaper articles, magazine features and friends' personal stories show time and again how badly people are affected by the anonymity and the indifference among neighbours. In mixed-race neighbourhoods, xenophobia and racist attacks are problems to be dealt with. People may suffer from severe illnesses, be discriminated against or even killed, and nobody cares. One day you might be the one who is neglected by his or her neighbours and wish there was someone there for you. This is the chance to work towards that goal. If you make a contribution to better neighbourly relations, you will also be the one to profit from those right now.
There are several ways to establish relations to your neighbours. You might want to go to the community centre and start up a new hobby, where you are likely to meet your neighbours. Or how about having a party and inviting all your neighbours to it?

Ask everybody to bring something along and your party will be a great success without any trouble. If you live in a mixed-race neighbourhood, ask people to prepare their favourite dish from home to get to know their food and culture. This might be the beginning of a network enabling you and others to interact successfully on different levels and foster understanding and respect.
Good neighbourhood relations are also about helping each other out. For instance, you may start helping the elderly with their shopping or how to use the computer. Surely, there is a community centre in your vicinity providing computer facilities. If not, you may get involved in an initiative trying to set one up.
Have you thought about babysitting for single parents? Not only will you, thus, enable single parents to go out and meet other people, you also get the chance to gain experience in dealing with kids.
Or why not offer to walk you neighbour's dog if he or she is ill or does not have the time? You would be helping out someone in need, and there is no better way to start up conversations – soon you would be in touch with half the neighbourhood.
In exchange for helping people in need, you would not only get their gratitude but also their friendship. Establishing friendships among neighbours will prove to be the basis of a new solidarity. It is your initiative that will help to stop anonymity and isolation spreading further like some virus. Making it into a joint venture already provides a sense of community since people are sharing an interest; they are setting a positive example as to what neighbourhood relations may look like. Give it a try, and you will make all the difference to your neighbourhood.

Abiturprüfung Berlin/Brandenburg 2011
Englisch Grundkurs – Aufgabe 2

Themenschwerpunkte: *The challenge of globalisation; Personal relations in their social context; Ethnic diversity*

Text (excerpt from a short story)

Interpreter of Maladies
by Jhumpa Lahiri

Note: *Mr. and Mrs. Das are on holiday in their parents' home country with their children. They are planning to visit the Sun Temple. Mr. Kapasi, an Indian guide, is taking them there in his taxi.*

[…] It was a dry, bright Saturday, the mid-July heat tempered by a steady ocean breeze, ideal weather for sightseeing. Ordinarily Mr. Kapasi would not have stopped so soon along the way, but less than five minutes after he'd picked up the family that morning in front of Hotel Sandy Villa, the little girl had complained. The first thing Mr. Kapasi had noticed when he saw Mr. and Mrs. Das, standing with their children under the portico of the hotel, was that they were very young, perhaps not even thirty. In addition to Tina they had two boys, Ronny and Bobby, who appeared very close in age and had teeth covered in a network of flashing silver wires. The family looked Indian but dressed as foreigners did, the children in stiff, brightly colored clothing and caps with translucent visors. Mr. Kapasi was accustomed to foreign tourists; he was assigned to them regularly because he could speak English. […] When he'd introduced himself, Mr. Kapasi had pressed his palms together in greeting, but Mr. Das squeezed hands like an American so that Mr. Kapasi felt it in his elbow. Mrs. Das, for her part, had flexed one side of her mouth, smiling dutifully at Mr. Kapasi, without displaying any interest in him. […]

"You left India as a child?" Mr. Kapasi asked when Mr. Das had settled once again into the passenger seat.

"Oh, Mina and I were both born in America," Mr. Das announced with an air of sudden confidence. "Born and raised. Our parents live here now, in Assansol. They retired. We visit them every couple years." He turned to watch as the little girl ran toward the car, the wide purple bows of her sundress flopping on her narrow brown shoulders. She was holding to her chest a doll with yellow hair that looked as if it had been chopped, as a punitive measure, with a pair of dull scissors.

"This is Tina's first trip to India, isn't it, Tina?"

"I don't have to go to the bathroom anymore," Tina announced.

"Where's Mina?" Mr. Das asked.

Mr. Kapasi found it strange that Mr. Das should refer to his wife by her first name when speaking to the little girl. Tina pointed to where Mrs. Das was purchasing something from one of the shirtless men who worked at the tea stall. Mr. Kapasi heard one of the shirtless men sing a phrase from a popular Hindi love song as Mrs. Das walked back to the car, but she did not appear to understand the words of the song, for she did not express irritation, or embarrassment, or react in any other way to the man's declarations. He observed her. She wore a red-and-white-checkered skirt that stopped above her knees, slip-on shoes with a square wooden heel, and a close-fitting blouse styled like a man's undershirt. The blouse was decorated at chest-level with a calico appliqué in the shape of a strawberry. She was a short woman, with small hands like paws, her frosty pink fingernails painted to match her lips, and was slightly plump in her figure. Her hair, shorn only a little longer than her husband's was parted far to one side. […]

She walked slowly, carrying some puffed rice tossed with peanuts and chilli peppers in a large packet made from newspapers. Mr. Kapasi turned to Mr. Das.

"Where in America do you live?"

"New Brunswick, New Jersey."

"Next to New York?"

"Exactly. I teach middle school there."

"What subject?"

"Science. In fact, every year I take my students on a trip to the Museum of Natural History in New York City. In a way we have a lot in common, you could say, you and I. How long have you been a tour guide, Mr. Kapasi?"

"Five years."

Mrs. Das reached the car. "How long's the trip?" she asked, shutting the door.

"About two and a half hours," Mr. Kapasi replied.

At this Mrs. Das gave an impatient sigh, as if she had been traveling her whole life without pause. She fanned herself with a folded Bombay film magazine written in English.

"I thought that the Sun Temple is only eighteen miles north of Puri," Mr. Das said, tapping on the tour book.

"The roads to Konarak are poor. Actually it is a distance of fifty-two miles," Mr. Kapasi explained. […] *(720 words)*

Source: Lahiri, Jhumpa. Interpreter of Maladies. London, 2000, 43–47

Annotations

l. 6	portico: roof supported by columns
l. 10	translucent visor: part of a cap to protect the eyes and face allowing light to pass through
l. 14	to flex: to move
ll. 18/19	with an air of … confidence*: here:* sounding confident
ll. 19/20	to retire: to stop working due to age
l. 23	punitive measure: punishment
l. 35	calico appliqué: small piece of cloth made of cotton and attached to a larger piece of cloth to make a decoration
l. 53	to fan: to move air in order to feel less hot

Tasks

1 Outline the information on the Das family. (30 %)

2 Examine how the author characterizes the Dases as Western tourists. Give evidence from the text. (30 %)

3 Choose one of the following tasks:

3.1 Starting from Kapasi's observations on the Das family discuss to what extent it is important to hold on to cultural roots in times of globalization. (40 %)

OR

3.2 Compare Mr. Kapasi's observations on the Das family with how another character from literature or film sees one or more characters from a different cultural background. Assess how they deal with the differences they observe. (40 %)

OR

3.3 *Teen Travel* has invited you to their youth conference to contribute a speech discussing the importance of being well prepared for trips to developing countries such as India. Write this speech and use the Dases' behavior as tourists as an example. (40 %)

Lösungsvorschläge

1 *In diesem Auszug aus einer Kurzgeschichte werden viele spezifische Beispiele genannt. Es ist nicht nötig, alle diese Beispiele in einem* outline *zu erwähnen. Geben Sie die grundsätzlichen Informationen über die Struktur der Familie, ihre Herkunft, ihre Situation, ihr Aussehen und ihr Verhalten knapp wieder.*

In the excerpt, we meet the Das family, who are American tourists on holiday in India. The parents are quite young, and have two sons and a daughter. The daughter is the youngest, and the boys are of an age where they are having work done on their teeth. Mr. and Mrs. Das were born to Indian immigrants in America and were raised there. They still live there, and Mr. Das works as a teacher. Their parents have returned to India and are retired. The Dases pay regular visits to India to visit them. This is the first time they have visited since the little girl was born. The family looks Indian, but dresses, speaks and behaves in an American way.

2 *Der Operator* examine *zielt auf eine genauere Analyse des Textes, und zwar im Hinblick darauf, wie der Autor die Familie Das als Touristen aus dem Westen charakterisiert. Konzentrieren Sie sich im Detail auf Aspekte ihres Aussehens und ihres Verhaltens, die sich vom indischen Aussehen und Verhalten unterscheiden, und erwähnen Sie, wie der Autor diese Informationen vermittelt, z. B. im Dialog, als Beschreibung, als Kontrast.*

In the excerpt from the short story, the author characterizes the Dases as Western tourists. Even before Mr. Das says that the family lives in the USA, the author describes various aspects which hint at the fact that the Dases are American. Their children have very Anglo-Saxon names, Tina, Ronny and Bobby, the boys are both obviously having dental work done, their "teeth covered in a network of flashing silver wires" (l. 8), as most American children seem to have, and are dressed as typical American boys in "stiff, brightly colored clothing and caps" (ll. 9/10). The author gives many examples of the contrasts in their appearance. The whole family "looked Indian but dressed as foreigners did" (ll. 8/ 9). Mrs. Das is described in particular detail. She wears a "skirt that stopped above her knees … and a close-fitting blouse styled like a man's undershirt" (ll. 33–35), she has painted her fingernails bright pink like an American woman and her hair is quite short (ll. 37/38).
Apart from their appearance, the author gives examples of how the Dases also behave like Western tourists. The way they greet Mr. Kapasi is very American. First of all, of course, they speak English, and whereas Mr. Kapasi presses his palms together in greeting, as Indians do, Mr. Das "squeezed hands like an American so that Mr. Kapasi felt it in his elbow" (l. 13) and Mrs. Das smiles "dutifully at Mr. Kapasi, without displaying any interest in him" (ll. 14/15). Through direct speech, "Where's Mina?" (l. 26), and the subsequent description of Mr. Kapasi's reaction to the fact that Mr. Das refers to his wife by her first name when he is talking to his daughter, we discover that this is obviously not what Indians do. With regard to Mrs. Das,

either she does not understand Hindi, or she does not react as an Indian woman would do to a man singing a love song to her. Even the Bombay film magazine she is carrying is written in English. Mr. Das has his information about the Sun Temple from his tour book and did not realize that the information was incorrect.
To sum up, apart from their skin colour, which makes them look Indian, all the members of the Das family are Western tourists in everything from appearance to behaviour to language to attitude.

3.1 *Diese Aufgabe fordert, dass Sie diskutieren, inwiefern es wichtig ist, in Zeiten der Globalisierung an seinen kulturellen Wurzeln festzuhalten. Hierbei sollten Sie mit den Betrachtungen Kapasis über die Familie Das beginnen. Wählen Sie die Beobachtungen Kapasis, die zur Aufgabenstellung passen, nennen Sie anschließend Gründe für und gegen das Festhalten an kulturellen Wurzeln in Zeiten der Globalisierung und äußern Sie am Schluss Ihre eigene Meinung.*

In the excerpt, we are told of several of Mr. Kapasi's observations about the Das family with regard to cultural roots. The fact that they look Indian enhances their ignorance of the customs in India and their lack of knowledge of the language, despite their family background. Mr. Das is obviously not familiar with the Indian way of greeting, or chooses to assert the American way, and Mrs. Das does not seem to understand the native language at all, as she shows no reaction to the lyrics of the love song which the man sings to her and displays a complete lack of interest in either him or Mr. Kapasi. The couple does not appear to have held on to their cultural roots in any way, despite the fact that their parents are from India and are now living there again.
The question is to what extent it is important to hold on to cultural roots in times of globalization. There are many advantages of doing so, of course. In times of globalization it is certainly beneficial to have a deep understanding of more than one culture. It is likely to make you more open-minded, so that you are more able and willing to experience other cultures and to be tolerant and supportive of cultural diversity, and the social variety and enriched cultural life this entails. On the home front, if you are living in a foreign country, knowledge of your own culture and an identification with your own cultural roots can give you a sense of identity, of belonging, strengthen family bonds and give you a better understanding of others.
The downside of holding on to your roots can be that it prevents you from adapting to new cultures and your surroundings. If you believe that your own culture is superior, this will lead to a lack of understanding of other cultures and even hostility towards them. Different people are open to different cultures and the values of others to varying degrees. The less open people are, the more likely they are to have unpleasant experiences of other people and cultures.
In my opinion, the ideal is a happy medium. I think it is important to accept your cultural roots as a part of you and to value what you have learned and gained from them, and then to be open to other people and cultures so that your life becomes increasingly enriched.

3.2 *Diese Aufgabe ist zweigeteilt. Zuerst sollen Sie eine Figur aus der Literatur oder aus einem Film wählen, der mit einer oder mehreren Personen mit einem anderen kulturellen Hintergrund in Kontakt kommt und darauf reagiert. Beschreiben Sie zuerst die Beobachtungen Kapasis und vergleichen Sie sie dann mit den Beobachtungen oder der Sicht der Figur aus dem Film/Buch. Für den zweiten Teil der Aufgabe sollen Sie evaluieren, wie die zwei Charaktere mit den Unterschieden, die sie beobachten, umgehen.*

In the excerpt much about the Das family and the cultural differences between India and America is revealed to the reader by Mr. Kapasi. He notices a great deal about them, such as their youth and precise details about their appearance. He observes the cultural differences that become obvious through their appearance and behaviour. Even though they look Indian, they act like Americans. They treat their children differently from the way an Indian would, Mrs. Das does not understand Hindi and they not only lack knowledge about their parents' home country, they also seem completely unaware that there are any differences between the two cultures at all.
Mr. Kapasi could be compared to Omar's father, Ali, in the film "My Beautiful Launderette". Ali also acts as an observer, because he has little contact with white people in England, but obviously knows a lot about them, which we can deduce from the remarks he makes to his son. Ali was once a famous journalist in Pakistan and is now living in London. In contrast to his brother, who is a rich, successful, money-grabbing businessman, Ali is a poor widower living in a seedy flat with his son. His left-wing politics are in stark contrast to the Thatcherite ideals in Britain at that time. He is bitter and disappointed by his experiences with the British culture. Although he mentored Johnny, one of Omar's friends, when he was a child, he was shocked and disgusted to see Johnny and his friends marching in a fascist demonstration against foreigners. When he meets Johnny again years later, he is disapproving of the fact that Johnny has not made anything of himself professionally, but trusts him enough to ask him to influence Omar to go to college and get a good education. Ali is very aware of the differences between the two cultures. He thinks that the British hate the Pakistanis and is frustrated that his son tries so hard to please them. He believes that the only way to deal with the problem is to get an education, to gain knowledge in order to see what is really going on.
However, the two characters, Mr. Kapasi and Ali, deal very differently with what they observe. Mr. Kapasi behaves like a professional guide, in that his observations are silent and are very likely indiscernible to the Das family, and he is probably used to cultural differences as he is so accustomed to foreign tourists. Ali, however, withdraws from the other culture completely. He spends most of his time drunk in bed. He has given up, and chooses not to participate in society at all rather than adjust to his new surroundings. There is one aspect, however, which connects Mr. Kapasi and Ali: they are both observers who leave other people to make the decisions and to take action.

3.3 *Ihre Rede sollte formal sein, mit passender Anrede für ein hauptsächlich junges Publikum in Ihrem Alter (denkbar wäre die gängige Anrede, "Ladies and gentlemen" plus eine kleine Phrase mit "fellow ...", z. B. "fellow students" oder "fellow travellers"). Fangen Sie zuerst mit einer Einführung zum Thema Reisen in Entwicklungsländern und Kulturunterschiede anhand der Beschreibung der Familie Das an, stellen Sie dann Gründe für und gegen eine gute Vorbereitung dar, und ziehen Sie am Schluss Ihr eigenes Fazit. Vergessen Sie aber nicht, Ihre Rede interessant zu machen, damit Sie die Aufmerksamkeit Ihrer Zuhörer gewinnen. Wenn Sie fertig sind, bedanken Sie sich.*

Ladies and gentlemen, fellow travellers,

As someone who has travelled to many parts of the world, I have been invited to talk to you today about how important it is to prepare for trips to developing countries, such as India. "What's the problem?" you might think, "there's nothing for me to prepare – just a couple of vaccinations, my passport, my plane ticket and my beach towel, that's all I need. The language? They all speak English, don't they? The customs – hey, that's no big deal."
Last week I read this short story by Jhumpa Lahiri, called "Interpreter of Maladies". It was about the Das family – they were of Indian descent but had been born and raised in America, and boy, could you tell! OK, they were dressed like Americans – that's no crime – but they behaved like Americans all the time. They showed no interest in the local culture or customs. They spoke English and expected everyone else to as well, did not adapt to the country at all, and seemed to be completely unaware that there were any differences. Their American guide book was inaccurate and so they were completely dependent on the knowledge, understanding and support of their tour guide, who, luckily for them, was very pleasant.
There is more to developing countries than hot weather, beaches and a cheap holiday. The first time you go to a developing country, be prepared for a culture shock. Many people who have travelled to India, for example, talk of the shock of being confronted with the extreme poverty there. Remember that you will be experiencing radically different cultures and traditions, which will be even more marked when you have no or little understanding of the language and culture of the country you have landed in.
Some of you might think there's no point in being well prepared for a trip to a developing country. You might think that's too much like hard work. You're "only" going on a holiday – you want to have a good time, some entertainment, you have no intention of mixing with local people. You think you can do anything you like – all you need is a good, professional tour guide.
Others might think that if you're better prepared for the culture you will be visiting, you have a better chance of an experience that might mean something to you personally. You will understand the culture better, the people, their traditions, you will know how to behave in such a way that it won't cause offence and will induce the local people to be well disposed towards you and treat you well. There might be fewer misunderstandings and you might find it easier to deal with the things that are so very different from what you know. And being able to communicate with local

people means that you have more chance of finding out what the country is really like, rather than it just being a two-dimensional backdrop to your holiday.
Of course, the choice is yours, but I think you get the idea that I think it's good to do your homework before you visit another country. It shows respect for that culture and its people, and that's what makes life a whole lot better for everyone.

Thank you.

Abiturprüfung Berlin/Brandenburg 2011
Englisch Leistungskurs – Aufgabe 1

Themenschwerpunkte: *Ethnic diversity; Urban, suburban and rural lifestyles; The challenge of globalisation; Personal relations in their social context*

Text A (excerpt from a newspaper article)

Mixed blessings
by Katharina Lobeck

Note: *Katharina Lobeck wrote this article after a black teenager, out with his white girlfriend, was murdered in Liverpool.*

[…] I am a German woman, a Londoner by choice like so many people in this city. I am engaged to be married to a Senegalese man, and the mother of his child. For me, news of Saturday's race attack felt like another brutal sign telling me to try my luck elsewhere, another menacing message from (and to) multicultural Britain. Not only because an axe-swinging psychopath committed a race crime, but also because once again, multiculturalism and mixed-race relationships find themselves under investigation as a result.

My partner and I have now spent two years trying to find a way for him to move to London permanently. He still hasn't been able to obtain a long-term visa; the chances are that we might have had a much easier ride in Germany. And yet, I didn't manage to tear myself away from London. (Having spent some time in Bristol and in other communities in the UK, I do believe that the capital's multicultural spirit is unique among British cities.) Despite its dismal living conditions, its extortionate rents, despite its general aggressiveness and its never-fulfilling promise of success, London seemed to be the only place I could imagine living in. The only place where I felt my (at the time single) motherhood to a mixed-race child and my relationship with an African man could pass, not unnoticed, but without being permanently commented upon. It seemed to be the only place where we would not be reduced to being a hideous cliché and, above all, where we would run a relatively low risk of being harassed. I believe that's still the case, even though Saturday's race attack in Liverpool forces Britain to ask itself some questions.

When I considered leaving London with my child, my home nation Germany was an obvious option to consider. Except that it wasn't. In Germany, even a third generation of immigrants is not seen, and often does not see itself, as being German, and the idea of a nonwhite German is still a completely alien one to large parts of the population. There, comments about our "chocolate baby" or "negro doll" have accompanied me and my partner ever since my daughter was born.

[…] Praising London as one of the great multicultural capitals of the world may sound like verbal floss taken from the mayor's campaign book, but it is London reality, even though there remain many contradictions and confrontations involved in having a multitude of ethnic, faith and cultural groups sitting side by side in one sprawling conurbation.

It's when I walk with my daughter through Brixton market that I get the most questioning, and occasionally menacing, stares, mainly from black women. If I'm with my partner, he gets them, from his male peers. On my own, I look like the archetype of the greedy white woman; the one who got off with a black man, ended up with a child – and now look what you got for it. If we're together, he looks like a traitor to the black community. […]

These days, racist judgment comes in carefully crafted news features, in conversations conducted smilingly. It comes in questions about my partner's virility, about the likelihood of his faithfulness and his assumed musical talent, asked after a few too many glasses of wine. Racial bias exists in this society, and it's something that mixed-race couples have to deal with. Enter a mixed-race relationship, and you may find yourself suddenly confronted with previously unknown prejudice prevailing among close friends and family. You may find that the news will never quite sound the same again – suddenly you catch sight of society's hidden, ugly face. Relationships are hard work. Mixed-race relationships perhaps slightly more so, as outside pressures, different cultural expectations, and family discord can all increase the burden couples have to bear. But they are also just relationships, and in London at least, they are part of ordinary city life. […] *(651 words)*

Source: Lobeck, Katharina. "Mixed Blessings" The Guardian, August 2005 <http://www.guardian.co.uk/society/2005/aug/02/britishidentityandsociety.raceintheuk> [09 June 09]

Annotations

l. 13 dismal: miserable
l. 13 extortionate: very expensive
l. 19 to be harassed: to be attacked verbally or physically
l. 29 verbal floss: nice description
l. 48 discord: conflict, disagreement

Text B (Auszug aus einem Interview mit Xavier Naidoo)

Geboren in Mannheim und „froh über Deutschland": Xavier Naidoo

[…] **sueddeutsche.de:** Südafrika, Indien, Irland: Herr Naidoo, Ihre Ahnen kommen aus der ganzen Welt, Sie sehen sich vor allem als Mannheimer Bürger. Wie kam es dazu?

Xavier Naidoo: Meine Familie geht wohl als ein Beispiel gelungener Integration durch. Ich bin ja in Mannheim geboren und in einem Vorort namens Wallstadt aufgewachsen. Meine Mutter hat dafür gesorgt, dass unsere Familie keine Außenseiterrolle spielte. Bei uns lief viel über die Kirche: Meine Eltern sind beide katholische Südafrikaner, meine Mutter engagierte sich im Kirchenchor, mein Vater ging zum Männergesangsverein, dem ich dann mit 14 auch beigetreten bin – und schon war man mittendrin statt nur dabei. (lacht)

sueddeutsche.de: Sie betonen immer wieder, ein Schwarzer zu sein – warum?

Naidoo: Solange es diese Unterteilungen gibt, solange sich Weiße Weiße nennen, nenn ich mich Schwarzer. Schon als Kind habe ich bei Besuchen in Südafrika gemerkt, wie deutlich zwischen Hautfarben unterschieden wird.

sueddeutsche.de: Wurden Sie in Deutschland diskriminiert?

Naidoo: Bis zu einer gewissen Zeit habe ich einiges ertragen müssen. Als Kind war das manchmal schon schlimm. […]

sueddeutsche.de: Haben Sie sich gewehrt?

Naidoo: Später schon, aber erstmal nicht, vieles habe ich geschluckt. Auf dem Heimweg habe ich 'ne Träne verdrückt. Ich hatte da kein Mittel dagegen, bei meiner Mutter wollte ich nicht petzen. Sie hätte sich nur aufgeregt und wäre dann zu den Leuten hin – für mich war das eine sehr unangenehme Vorstellung. […]

sueddeutsche.de: Nach ähnlichen Erfahrungen wenden sich viele Menschen mit Migrationshintergrund von Deutschland ab – bei Ihnen ist das anders: Sie sind Mannheimer Lokalpatriot und singen auf Ihrem neuen Album: „Deutschland ist ein Land der Ehre." Wie entstanden bei Ihnen solch starke Gefühle?

Naidoo: Für mich war die Sprache der Schlüssel. Deutsch begeistert mich: Diese Tiefe, dieser Reichtum, diese Deutlichkeit. Bildlich gesprochen: Ich knie nieder vor dieser Sprache. Sie ist ein Geschenk. Und das dazugehörige Land kann ja nicht so schlecht sein, im Gegenteil: Deutschland ist schön. Ich habe es lieben und schätzen gelernt. […] *(313 Wörter)*

Quelle: <http://www.sueddeutsche.de/politik/xavier-naidoo-im-interwiew-ich-bin-masslos-enttaeuscht-von-merkel-1.38861> [22. Oktober 2009]

Tasks

1 Outline the various attitudes towards mixed-race relationships as shown in Text A. (20 %)

2 State the author's opinion on living in London and analyse the means she uses to convey it. (Text A) (25 %)

3 Mediation
For an international youth project about blacks in Europe, summarise the information about Naidoo's cultural identity, his childhood experiences and his attitude towards Germany. (Text B) (20 %)

4 Choose <u>one</u> of the following tasks:

4.1 "In Germany, even a third generation of immigrants is not seen, and often does not see itself, as being German, …" (Text A, ll. 23/24).
Comment on Lobeck's opinion, referring to different traditions of migration in Germany and at least one English-speaking country. (35 %)

OR

4.2 Discuss to what extent living in an urban area may help mixed-race couples deal with challenges as described in Text A. In your discussion refer to your knowledge about the chances and challenges of urban life. (35 %)

OR

4.3 Write a letter to the editor. Discuss to what extent Katharina Lobeck's experience is typical of challenges migrants face in today's globalised world. Address your letter to:

Readers' editor,
The Guardian
119 Farringdon Road
London EC1 R3ER, UK (35 %)

Lösungsvorschläge

1 *Diese Aufgabe fordert Sie auf, die in Text A erwähnten Einstellungen gegenüber Beziehungen zwischen Paaren unterschiedlicher Herkunft knapp wiederzugeben. Die Autorin beschreibt die Einstellungen aus verschiedenen Großstädten und Ländern und auch aus anderen Kreisen. Nennen Sie diese verschiedenen Orte und Kreise und fassen Sie die dort herrschenden Meinungen zusammen.*

In her article, "Mixed blessings", Katharina Lobeck shows the difficulty and added complexity of mixed-race relationships by mentioning different attitudes towards them. These attitudes vary according to city, country, medium and community. There is hostile racism everywhere in Britain, as shown by the threatening or violent attacks in places like Liverpool, for example, but Lobeck considers London to be more tolerant of mixed-race couples than many other places.
In Germany, for instance, the concept of mixed-race couples is very unusual and is likely to cause comment. There is also a great deal of prejudice in the black community in Britain, which sees a white woman in a mixed-race relationship as insatiable and taking something that is not hers, and the man as being a traitor to his race. Close friends and family also reveal their latent racism and stereotyped attitudes, and subtle racism is shown on the news.

2 *In dieser Aufgabe sind Sie aufgefordert, die Meinung der Autorin von Text A bezüglich des Lebens in London mit Ihren eigenen Worten wiederzugeben und zu analysieren, wie sie diese Meinung darstellt. Gehen Sie durch den Text und stellen Sie fest, welche Stilmittel die Autorin benutzt, um ihre Meinung zu präsentieren. Leiten Sie ein, indem Sie die Meinung der Autorin zum Leben in London darstellen. Unterteilen Sie dann Ihren Text in Absätze, die jeweils einem Stilmittel gewidmet sind, und nennen Sie Beispiele aus dem Text, die diese Stilmittel exemplarisch darstellen.*

The author, Katharina Lobeck, describes living in London in detail, presenting it as a more or less tolerant, multicultural city which, despite racial prejudices and conflicts, is the only place she can imagine living in with her black partner and child.
The author uses various stylistic devices to convey her opinion on living in London. She presents her article in the first-person, so that it is clear to the reader that she is writing from a personal point of view about her personal experiences. In the first two lines, for example, she repeats the words "I am …" to underline the personal nature of the article. She continues by emphasising her deliberate decision to stay in London, writing that she is "a Londoner by choice" (l. 1) and that she "didn't manage to tear [herself] away from London" (ll. 10/11).
The author shows the positive and negative sides of the city. First, she uses negative descriptions to emphasise the downsides of London when she talks about the bad living conditions, the high cost of living, the aggressive attitude of its inhabitants and the dreams it does not fulfil (ll. 13/14). She uses metaphor to insinuate the difficult time they have had living in London: "we might have had a much easier ride in

Germany" (l. 10), and uses alliteration to support the fact that life in London is not plain sailing when she writes that there are "many contradictions and confrontations" involved in London's multicultural make-up (l. 30).
However, Lobeck uses these negative descriptions as a deliberate contrast to underline her desire to live in London rather than in other cities and communities, such as Bristol (ll. 11–13). She also uses repetition to reiterate her praise of London with the phrase "… the only place …" (ll. 15, 18). She uses positive adjectives to describe the city, such as its being "unique among British cities" (ll. 12/13), and describes it as a relative multicultural haven, "one of the great multicultural capitals of the world" (l. 28), a place of more or less tolerant attitudes, where she and her partner would not be regarded as just a cliché and where they would not be as likely to suffer from harassment (ll. 18/19).
She continues to use comparison and contrast when she writes about places such as Germany, which are less tolerant. She describes Germany as being "an obvious option to consider. Except that it wasn't" (l. 23). She stresses this with hyperbole when she describes the idea of nonwhite Germans as being "still a completely alien one to large parts of the population" (ll. 25/26), and gives examples of derogatory language about her mixed-race daughter which she has heard in Germany (l. 26) to highlight the impossibility of their living in that country.
All in all, for Lobeck the positive features of London outweigh the negative, and her reference to her reservations serve to stress the positive sides of the city.

3 *In dieser Aufgabe sollen Sie bestimmte Informationen so zusammenfassen, dass sie für ein internationales Jugendprojekt angemessen sind. Konzentrieren Sie sich dabei auf Informationen zu Naidoos kultureller Identität, seinen Kindheitserlebnissen und seiner Einstellung zu Deutschland.*

Xavier Naidoo is a young, black man who stresses that he will say that he is black as long as people differentiate between the different colours of people's skin. This became very clear to him during his visits to South Africa. He was born and raised in Mannheim, Germany, by Catholic, South African parents. His family integrated successfully in the community because his parents were very involved in the church. Naidoo also joined the church choir as a teenager. He sometimes experienced discrimination as a child, which he found very hard, but he kept this to himself as he did not want his mother's intervention to make it worse. Naidoo has a very positive attitude towards Germany. He adores the language and he loves and values the country.

4.1 *Hier sollen Sie Lobecks Meinung kommentieren, indem Sie sich auf die verschiedenen Traditionen der Einwanderung in Deutschland und mindestens einem englischsprachigen Land beziehen. Es wäre angebracht, das Zitat aus dem Artikel näher zu erläutern, bevor Sie Lobecks Gründe für diese Meinung darstellen. Vergleichen Sie anschließend die Einwanderungstraditionen in Deutschland mit z.B. Großbritannien oder den USA. Führen Sie die positiven und negativen Seiten der Einwanderung auf und stellen Sie am Schluss Ihre eigene Meinung dar.*

In the quote from her article, Katharina Lobeck is referring to the grandchildren of people who immigrated to Germany several decades ago. Although this "third generation" was born in Germany, Lobeck believes that they do not see themselves as being German and they are not generally regarded as being German by other Germans.
Her opinion is understandable when you consider that she and her partner have been confronted with degrading statements about their mixed-race child ever since she was born, and that this lack of acceptance contributes to her preference for London, where she experiences more tolerance towards mixed-race relationships.
The difference in attitude between Germany and Britain can be explained by the history of the two countries with regard to immigration. There has been far less immigration to Germany than to Britain. Germany only recently began to accept permanent immigrants, and therefore there are fewer people of darker skin colour there than in Britain. Britain has a very long tradition of people immigrating from all over the world. After the Second World War particularly, there was a huge surge of immigrants to Britain from her former colonies. Although there has always been racial intolerance in the country towards people of different skin colour, the immigration rate has remained more or less constant, so that there is a far greater number of first-, second- and third-generation immigrants in Britain than in Germany.
One could argue that a large number of immigrants can lead to increased xenophobia and less integration. The more strongly a foreign culture seems to be represented, the more reservations seem to surface in the national population. A simple headscarf worn by an Islamic woman in Germany, for example, is like a red rag to a bull for some people, fuelling their bias, hatred and racism. In addition, people from other races are soon held responsible for high unemployment rates and economic crises. They serve as general scapegoats and hate figures.
On the other hand, one could argue that the greater the number of immigrants in a country, the greater the opportunity for increased open-mindedness towards people who are in some way different from oneself. This leads to better assimilation of immigrants into mainstream culture and to society gaining a multicultural identity. There is more need for institutional support in the form of welfare systems, training programmes and quota systems in public services in order to maintain a social balance. More immigrants are then likely to consider applying for citizenship as they feel part of the country and accepted by her inhabitants. This in turn leads to further opportunities for acceptance and integration. Furthermore, the growing demand for experts in industrialised countries would seem to point to the advantage of immigration in general.
The question is, however, whether people from another country should be forced to adapt completely to their new home country inwardly and outwardly and therefore give up their cultural roots and identity in order to be accepted, or whether it is possible to maintain your identity and be part of a different country at the same time. In my opinion, it is possible to do this. Granted, in Germany, for example, this is probably easier for white people from countries like Britain, the USA and Canada, which tend to be popular among Germans. For someone from Turkey, Iran or Senegal, however, whose skin colour is obviously darker and can therefore immediately act

as a trigger for latent or blatant racism, things might be more difficult. I believe that the solution lies in knowing who you are and liking yourself and therefore being open to others and looking beyond the colour of someone's skin and one's own prejudices to see the human being beneath.

4.2 *Hier sollen Sie diskutieren, inwiefern das Wohnen in einem städtischen Gebiet Paaren unterschiedlicher Herkunft mit Herausforderungen, wie sie in Text A beschrieben sind, helfen kann. Sie sollen sich auf Ihr Wissen bezüglich der Möglichkeiten und Herausforderungen des städtischen Lebens beziehen. Das heißt, dass Sie sich in Ihrer Antwort nicht nur auf die Informationen in Text A beschränken sollen. Erörtern Sie zuerst die Herausforderungen, die Lobeck in ihrem Artikel erwähnt. Stellen Sie dann die Möglichkeiten und Herausforderungen des Lebens in einer Stadt dar, und ziehen Sie am Ende Ihre eigenen Schlüsse.*

In her article, "Mixed Blessings", Katharina Lobeck describes many of the challenges she and her partner face as a mixed-race couple. Apart from the inconvenience of having to obtain permanent visas in order to be able to live together in peace, more frighteningly they face the very real threat of racial violence, and are constantly the potential focus of unwanted attention. They have to put up with people's comments, derogatory names, disapproval and disrespect, and are often confronted with stereotyping, prejudice and harassment. They have to get through the relationship difficulties which everyone in a relationship experiences, but with the added burden of pressure from outside, their own different cultural expectations and family discord. They suffer insecurity despite the multicultural society they live in.
However, Lobeck and her partner have chosen London as their home, and living in an urban area like London may help them to deal with some of the challenges mentioned above. One of the advantages of urban areas is that cultural diversity is more likely there and therefore more cross-cultural encounters are possible. As a result, there is more likelihood of people in mixed-race relationships or families finding other couples or families in the same position. Where there are people from your own ethnic background, you may find understanding and support more easily. In these areas, society is more used to people from different ethnic backgrounds and so there is perhaps more acceptance of minorities.
On the other hand, living in an urban area also brings its challenges. The greater the number of people with ethnic backgrounds, the greater the perceived threat to those with racist tendencies. This can lead to more racially motivated crime. Furthermore, the larger the ethnic population, the more likely it is to lead to ethnic neighbourhoods, which increases the segregation of ethnic groups. This in turn can hamper integration and even reduce people's need and desire for integration, leading to a divided society.
In my opinion, it is important to be sure of your individual identity whether you live in an urban area or a rural one. The surer you are of yourself as a person, the more open you can be to others, and the more likely you are to have a good experience with other people, no matter what ethnic background they are from. You may not be able to change other people's attitudes, but you can change your own.

4.3 *Hier sollen Sie einen Brief an den Redakteur einer renommierten britischen Zeitung schreiben, in dem Sie diskutieren, inwiefern die Erfahrung Katharina Lobecks typisch für die Herausforderungen, mit denen Einwanderer in unserer heutigen globalisierten Welt konfrontiert werden. Was die Struktur des Briefes betrifft, vergessen Sie nicht Absender, Adressat und Datum zu nennen, und finden Sie eine passende Anrede und Schlussformel. Die Sprache sollte förmlich sein. Erörtern Sie zuerst die Herausforderungen, von denen Lobeck schreibt, dann die Herausforderungen, mit denen Einwanderer unserer globalisierten Welt konfrontiert werden, und wägen Sie dann ab inwieweit die Erfahrungen Lobecks typisch oder untypisch sind.*

Reader's editor
The Guardian
119 Farringdon Road
London EC1 R3ER
UK

Susanne Müller
Sonnenstr. 2
10717 Berlin
Germany

June 7, 2011

Sir,

I have just read the article in yesterday's edition entitled "Mixed Blessings", by Katharina Lobeck. I was impressed by Ms Lobeck's description of her life as part of a mixed-race family in Britain and feel that it is relevant for many societies in today's globalised world.

As the coordinator of a local group to help immigrants become integrated in our community here in Berlin, I was particularly interested to read Ms Lobeck's comments on her experience in our country. Her experience of derogatory comments made about her daughter sounds very familiar, I am afraid to say.

Racial stereotyping is apparently as common here as it is in Britain, and all of the immigrants who come to us suffer from racist treatment at some time or another. Although there has always been racism in our society, it seems to me that our new, globalised world has caused even more disruption in this regard. Due to the new markets that have opened up, times of economic crisis, and the gap between the industrialised and developing worlds which has existed for a long time, more people are emigrating and there is now an increased level of cross-cultural exchange in western societies. Unfortunately, the ethnic minorities often meet with a lack of tolerance in their new communities and find little or no emotional support there, which is the very reason why we started our community project five years ago. It is so hard for immigrants who are struggling financially to find their feet in a new society. I have seen with my own eyes that they are less likely to be given access to education, let alone good jobs – most of the people who come to us are either unemployed or have to work for far less than the minimum wage. Not only that, they are often given a bad press in the media, being portrayed as lazy, good-for-nothing criminals, when the truth is that the vast majority of them are ordinary, pleasant people just trying to make a life for themselves. They have to battle with adjustment to the new culture, language, behaviour and customs, and at the same time are aware of the necessity to

integrate in their new surroundings although they sometimes feel this to be too hard of a struggle.
Therefore, I almost completely endorse what Ms Lobeck writes. I can understand that Ms Lobeck and her partner live in fear of racially motivated crime, because they share this with the people in our group. I believe her when she writes that they seem to meet disapproval, unpleasant, derogatory comments, harassment and prejudice wherever they are – although not as much so in London – and do not feel completely safe anywhere, because the immigrants who come to us tell us these sorts of stories every day. The fact that Ms Lobeck's partner is still having difficulty gaining a visa so that they can live together in London permanently seems to be the least of their problems, but one can imagine the inconvenience and heartache of not having a real home together.
However, although Ms Lobeck's experience is typical of the challenges migrants face in today's globalised world to the extent that she is treated as an outsider by some people, there are many aspects that are not typical. For example, mixed-race relationships are still relatively uncommon. This perhaps adds the extra burden of both partners being from different cultures so that they may never feel completely at home together in one culture. Ms Lobeck is also atypical in that she is a journalist, and privileged in that she can choose where to live and can apparently afford to move elsewhere. She is globally mobile and is not dependent on one particular place for work. Her position is in stark contrast to the majority of immigrants whom I come across and who are in a far more powerless situation than Ms Lobeck. Most of them have no job, little money, no status, little chance of improving their lifestyles to any great extent, and are not generally accepted by society. Their experience is more typical of the challenges faced by migrants today than that of Ms Lobeck, I feel.
All in all, however, I wish to emphasise my appreciation for the difficulties faced by all immigrants to a new culture and wish them and Ms Lobeck all the best for the future.

Susanne Müller, Berlin

Abiturprüfung Berlin/Brandenburg 2011
Englisch Leistungskurs – Aufgabe 2

Themenschwerpunkte: *Urban, suburban and rural lifestyles; The challenge of globalisation; Ethnic diversity*

Text A (excerpt from a newspaper article)

Welcome to Lagos: how Nigeria's dirt poor scratch a living in a city teeming with business flair

A TV series exploring daily life in Lagos finds its inhabitants coping in extreme circumstances with startling ingenuity

By Akin Ojumu

It is initially hard to see why Lagos has been called the "megacity of the future", with the potential to become the "Singapore of Africa". There's plenty to think about if the Nigerian city of 16 million tightly packed inhabitants is the ultimate expression of modern urban living. Lagos is growing at such an astonishing rate that by 2015 it is predicted to be the third largest city in the world, behind Mumbai and Tokyo, but it is an unlikely model metropolis.

Although the country has vast oil resources, the city's infrastructure is appalling. Three-quarters of Lagos residents live in slums. The rail network manages one train per week. Despite being the world's sixth biggest oil producer, power cuts are a daily occurrence and a national joke. Lagosians have renamed the National Electric Power Authority (NEPA) as Never Expect Power Always.

When I first visited Nigeria, my parents' homeland, a decade ago, I was unprepared for the reality. It was like landing on another planet. Although the city is a nightmare to navigate, the Lagosians are a breed apart. Millions of quick-witted economic migrants have created a city characterised by personal ingenuity and entrepreneurship. Nothing is wasted, everything is a commodity. "Lagos is not a kind of backward situation but an announcement of the future," the architect Rem Koolhaas has said. "What is now fascinating is how, with some level of self-organisation, there is a strange combination of extreme underdevelopment and development."

Will Anderson, the series producer of *Welcome to Lagos,* a fascinating new three-part documentary, agrees. He believes the way they have addressed the problems of extreme population growth is a lesson for us all, especially now that half the world's population live in cities […]. "If Martians came down to Earth, they would report back that we are a species that lives in cities. And in some degrees the people in Lagos are doing it better than we are in the west," he says.

The series looks at life on the Olusosun rubbish dump, the workplace and home to more than 1,000 scavengers who sift the garbage looking for recyclable material. This is a vibrant, self-policing community […].

It is soon clear that most Lagos residents will do anything to earn a few dollars a day, from back-breaking labour to sharp business deals, because there is no welfare state to provide a safety net.

But among Lagosians, who tend to combine relentless entrepreneurial flair with the belief that God will provide, there is little time for self-pity, a fact reflected in the series. "We did not want the people to come across as victims because that is not how they see themselves," says Anderson. "They are normal people doing what they have to do to survive. They encounter the same obstacles as the rest of us, but it's just that they do so in extreme circumstances." […]

Eric, 28, works as a scavenger on the Olusosun landfill site, the largest dump site in Lagos, and has recorded his first album "Send Them Come".

"They call me Slender, Vocal Slender, that's my music name. Because I'm very lean in the face, and because I'm always singing my songs. I have so many songs I still want to record, good songs that I've written, but no one has heard. Songs about divine love, peace and unity in Nigeria, and others which praise all the girls.

The film crew have made me a website. MySpace. It's not easy to get a website on your own. I know about 200 singers in Ajegunle where I live, but only two or three have websites. Ajegunle is the biggest ghetto in Lagos. It's where all the biggest Nigerian Stars come from, people like Daddy Showkey, Baba Fryo, Mighty Mouse, African China, B'Clean, and Nico Gravity. Every night there's a party going on somewhere, people playing music on the street corners, or setting up sound systems to dance to.

One day I'm going to be more famous than Craig David. Then I'II have enough money to be able to spend all day on my music, instead of working here on the dump. A lot of people who know me, my friends, and my family, they don't know I work in the dump. They believe I just do music. And I want to keep it that way, so I will have respect. It's not that the dump is bad, because the money I get from it keeps my body and soul together, and helps me make my music". […] *(754 words)*

Source: Ojumu, Akin. "Welcome to Lagos: how Nigeria's dirt poor scratch a living in a city teeming with business flair" <http://www.guardian.co.uk/world/2010/apr/04/documentary-film-welcome-to-lagos-nigeria> [20 April 2010]

Annotations

heading	dirt poor: *informal:* extremely poor
sub-heading	ingenuity: ability to invent things or solve problems in clever new ways
l. 14	a breed apart: totally different in action and way of thinking
ll. 15/16	entrepreneurship: quality of being an organiser or promoter of business ventures
l. 23	Martian: sb coming from the planet Mars
l. 27	scavenger: sb that collects food or other things by searching among waste
ll. 38–56	In a second section of the article some of the Lagosians featured in the film are introduced. Eric is one of them.
l. 51	Craig David: British singer who has sold over 30 million records worldwide

Text B (picture and motto from the website of ASAP Africa)

It is better to light a candle than to curse the darkness.

Source: A Self Help Assistance Program; <www.asapafrica.org> [06 October 2010]

Annotations

ASAP Africa: charitable non-profit organisation that assists people in their efforts to improve their own lives e. g. by providing education and agriculture projects

Tasks

1 Summarise the information on Lagos and its inhabitants as provided in Text A. (30 %)

2 Analyse and compare how Text A and Text B convey their messages about ways of coping with poverty. (30 %)

3 Choose one of the following tasks:

3.1 Comment on the differences between how the Lagosians in the TV-series *Welcome to Lagos* see themselves and how people in industrialised countries tend to perceive people in developing countries. Consider ways of establishing a realistic picture of lifestyle and attitudes in developing countries. (40 %)

OR

3.2 Compare Akin Ojumu's first impression of Lagos with that of a character from literature or film who also experiences a big city like "another planet" (Text A, l. 13). Reflect on possible reasons for their feelings and ways of dealing with them. (40 %)

OR

3.3 As a volunteer at *ASAP Africa,* a self-help assistance programme, write an article for an international online magazine about the advantages of self-help assistance. Consider ideas from Text A and Text B as well as your knowledge about opportunities for developing countries in the global world. (40 %)

Lösungsvorschläge

1 *Beachten Sie, dass in der Aufgabenstellung nur nach Informationen zu Lagos und dessen Einwohnern gefragt wird, nicht nach einer Inhaltsangabe des gesamten Textes. Ihre Zusammenfassung sollte möglichst objektiv sein, Details oder Zitate dürfen in der Inhaltsangabe nicht vorkommen.*

The text "Welcome to Lagos", published in *The Guardian* on 20 April 2010 and written by Akin Ojumu, deals with Lagos' fast expansion and the witty and skilful ways its 16 million inhabitants cope with the dismal conditions of the Nigerian megacity.
On the one hand, the metropolis is growing rapidly and can call considerable natural resources its own. On the other, its poor infrastructure belies these facts.
The number of inhabitants is growing daily as well. The author shows through several examples how well the inhabitants are doing and how optimistic they are, even though most of them live in slums and work under terrible conditions.

2 *In dieser Aufgabe sollen Sie anhand von stilistischen Mitteln die Botschaft des Textes darlegen und dann analysieren und vergleichen, wie das Bild sich zu Wegen aus der Armut äußert. Dabei sollen Sie die beiden Texte miteinander vergleichen.*

In the text, the message that Lagosians are rather successful despite their extreme poverty is conveyed with various means. The contrast which is used in the headline, "scratch a living in a city teeming with business flair", gives a vivid first impression of their situation and their survival skills by the metaphorical language that is used.
On the whole the author uses contrasts to emphasise the difference between extreme poverty on the one hand and extreme ingenuity on the other. Whereas the exaggeration "[m]illions of quick-witted economic migrants" (ll. 14/15) shows how many committed Lagosians there are, the seemingly contradictory words "waste" and "commodity" are put together in the sentence "nothing is wasted, everything is a commodity" (l. 16) and point to the author's enthusiasm in the same context. The Lagosians' commitment is also expressed in the contrast "back-breaking labour" and "sharp business deals" (l. 30). On the one hand, the work seems to be unacceptable for anyone to do it; on the other, the Lagosians are not only doing it, but also managing to get by with the money they make from that work. Additionally, the author points to "relentless entrepreneurial flair" (l. 32) and "little time for self-pity" (l. 33). Furthermore, the author quotes a scavenger who is a musician at the same time, which serves as an example of two very contrastive strands of life and demonstrates the extraordinary energy and optimism the Lagosians have in coping with severe conditions. The direct speech gives the author's message more credibility.
Text B features a picture and motto from the website ASAP Africa. In the centre of the picture there is a girl who is sitting at a desk reading, smiling slightly. On the right hand side there is a boy who also has a book in front of him, but looks up into the camera. In the lower half of the picture, these words are printed: "A self-help

assistance program development that works." The organisation's motto "It is better to light a candle than to curse in the darkness" is printed below the picture.
In contrast to Text A, the people shown in the picture are aiming at educating themselves, instead of working as scavengers or the like. The reading girl who is featured in this picture is supposed to be the focus of the message, conveying that if you make an effort to learn, you will be better off. As stated by the text underneath, lighting a candle, instead of cursing the darkness, is the first step, meaning that even in extreme circumstances, you should get active and start helping yourselves, rather than waiting for someone else to fix the problem. This implies that the ASAP Africa programme is not simply helping people, but assisting them in ways to help themselves.
In conclusion, it can be said that both sources point to making an effort and being active as the winning factors enabling people to finally escape poverty. Text A primarily sees the merits in hard work, whereas Text B also points to the importance of education.

3.1 *Der Kommentar ist eine strukturierte Meinungsäußerung. Im Gegensatz zu einer Diskussion brauchen Sie hierbei Argumente nicht gegeneinander abzuwägen. Sie müssen Ihre Stellungnahme jedoch begründen.*

In Western countries people in developing countries are mostly seen as victims of either poverty, government or both: many are unemployed or their jobs cannot sustain a living; the high rate of illiteracy aggravates the situation; AIDS is wide-spread and often medicine which only costs negligible sums in Western countries is unavailable for the very poor; there is no social network to care for them, either; societies are unstable and wars are killing and maiming thousands or taking away the few possessions the population used to have; and the media often paint a disastrous picture of the living conditions there.
The depicted poverty and famine are undisputable facts in many developing countries. These countries are overtaxed with a multitude of problems they cannot solve all by themselves, and industrialised countries often feel a moral obligation to give support where people are starving or suffering from other ills. Yet donations are frequently used for arms or the personal wealth of authorities who lay their hands on the money before it gets to the poor.
However, the text shows that we not only encounter desolation in those countries. In the TV-series discussed, Lagosians are portrayed as optimistic and self-confident, ready to tackle any task at hand. Even though they are facing a multitude of difficulties, they are not discouraged by them, but challenged. The onlooker gets the impression that Lagosians are close to invincible heroes, as they are not deterred by any problem they have to face. Lagos is not a myth or a fairy tale – it does exist in the real world.
Furthermore, there are projects sponsored by western countries that go beyond mere donations and help people to deal with the actual problems on site. Organisations like MISERIOR, PLAN or the German Technology Organisation make serious at-

tempts at trying to help people in developing countries to become self-sufficient. These are just a few examples among many, but such organisations and the change they make should be included in media broadcasts.
Overall, the media should make an effort to broadcast more balanced programmes, including stories like the one about Lagos, to obtain a more realistic picture. In these programmes the focus should not be mainly on wars and famine but also on functioning self-help programmes like ASAP and individual success stories as seen in the article. If people in industrialised countries see that their money is put to good use and that people in developing countries are not just waiting for someone to get them out of their misery but working hard for a better life, people's willingness to donate money will be enhanced. Some measures have already been taken in this direction. Some posters in the city do show people in developing countries with small enterprises. This is a step towards the right direction.

3.2 *Der Vergleich kann mit einem beliebigen Charakter eines Films bzw. eines Buches vorgenommen werden. Es geht hier lediglich um Großstadterfahrungen, die herangezogen werden sollen. Diese müssen sich nicht in den Erfahrungen von Ojumu widerspiegeln, sondern können sich auch gänzlich von diesen unterscheiden.*
Im Folgenden wird auf „Brave New World" eingegangen. Zwei weitere Beispiele wären die Bücher „Moon Palace" von Paul Auster und „Tortilla Curtain" von T.C. Boyle.

At first, Akin Ojumu is rather appalled by the state of the city and the living conditions in Lagos. He fails to understand how anybody might be able to manage to survive under these extreme circumstances. He seems to have grown up in an industrialised country, and his preconceptions of the city are characterized by prejudices and clichés. Yet when he arrives in Lagos, quite ignorant to what reality there might look like, his expectations are not met. There are some negative connotations, like the desolate infrastructure, for example, but in general he is surprised by the incredible ingenuity with which people there deal with life.
Looking at a new TV series about Lagosians, Ojumu realizes that Lagos is, in fact, a model for future city life. His summary of the TV series' reports and interviews then creates a portrait of the city and its poor that buzzes with optimism. Even though Ojumu feels like he is on another planet at first, he soon realizes that the Lagosians strive for similar things as people from industrialized countries: survival, success and independence. Life in Lagos is not so different after all; only the basic conditions are harsher.
A character who cannot get over his first shock of being thrown into a city that feels like another world is John (the Savage) in Aldous Huxley's dystopian novel "Brave New World". John grows up in a reservation, isolated from The World State, and has never set foot into a bigger city. When Bernard and Lenina, two members of The World State society, take him to London with them, John is appalled by the senselessness of city life. He was not conditioned the way that children in The World State are and, therefore, lacks basic social skills and what is considered to be com-

mon sense. His social background is shaped by the fact that he lived with his mother (a concept completely alien to people in The World State), Native American myths and religion and an extensive reading of Shakespeare (whose works are forbidden in The World State). Consequently, John is shocked by the way the state controls people's lives, their soma-induced dreams and their individuality and independence, which are practically non-existent. Their common concepts are a mystery to him. He does not understand why people should opt for promiscuity instead of real love, for example, and does not comprehend their fascination with inventions like soma and "feely" cinema. John remains an outsider and his behaviour is constantly frowned upon.

Additionally, he does not try to adapt to his new surroundings at all. In contrast to Ojumu, who deals with the shock of being thrown onto another planet by gathering information from experts and the media in order to gain an insight, John flees and sets up camp in a lighthouse to set himself apart from the world around him. He does not want to gain new perspectives to his world view and stays true to his beliefs and convictions. Unlike Ojumu, for whom Lagos seems to have been a source of inspiration, John is not able to cope with life in London. In the end, he commits suicide.

3.3 *In diesem Artikel sollen Sie so schreiben, als wären Sie als Freiwilliger für die ASAP in Afrika tätig, d. h., Sie müssen sich vorstellen, wie Ihre Arbeit dort aussehen könnte. Gleichzeitig sollen Sie darüber informieren, welche Möglichkeiten solche Selbsthilfeprogramme bieten. Beziehen Sie sich dabei auf beide Texte.*

Go light a candle

In a world where one part of the population is getting increasingly richer and the other one poorer, we need to address the issue of enabling the poorest to survive by themselves without having to count on help from the industrialised countries.

We have seen for decades that the donation of money alone does not suffice to foster independence. This measure has mainly had the opposite effect: it has made people dependent and passive and allowed many to make profit from the money intended to help the starving population. There is a vital need to continue to donate money, but we do need to change the ways in how we are "helping".

In ASAP we are convinced that assistance to self-help is the key to improving living conditions in Africa: we are helping people to help themselves. That means we provide education, agricultural programmes and other means of assistance to lead them to independence. "It is better to light a candle than to curse the darkness" is the motto we act on, and, therefore, our goal is to motivate people to get active themselves, instead of waiting for others – that is, the industrialised countries – to do the work for them.

A new TV series about life in Lagos shows how this approach is carried out in real life. The Lagosians portrayed in it are a model for everyone who has to survive in severe circumstances. Numerous examples of people who become active, instead of wallowing in self-pity, show that it pays off to work hard, but also to get creative and to strive for a better life. Parts of this series are broadcast in our ASAP information meetings to show participants of our programme that it is worth engaging in a programme that not only gives out money, but requires work and commitment, too. People have to see the fruits of their labour; they need to see that it pays to make an effort.

However, these people also need others to guide them on their way; to give them the right kind of support. The proverbial candle that lights the darkness can only shine if there is somebody to provide the candle. For the developing countries, this means that the governments have to secure a minimum standard of education so that the inhabitants can become self-sufficient. Surely, the industrialised countries can and ought to secure help in different ways as well. For one, they can offer loans to support local self-help assistance projects like ASAP; secondly, they can help in the medicine sector by financing research and education projects so that fatal illnesses like AIDS do not spread any further; the introduction to modern media like the Internet also opens up new opportunities: the developing countries can get information about other programmes, sell their products more profitably and create networks worldwide.

You, too, can assist people on their way to self-sustainability and a better life. When looking for a way to help by donating money or working as a volunteer, make sure that you do the right thing: find an organisation that is engaged in self-help projects aiming for improving the opportunities for people in developing countries in the long run. You know the saying: if you give somebody a fish, they will survive a day; if you teach them how to fish, they will make a living.

Ihre Meinung ist uns wichtig!

Ihre Anregungen sind uns immer willkommen. Bitte informieren Sie uns mit diesem Schein über Ihre Verbesserungsvorschläge!

Titel-Nr.	Seite	Vorschlag

Bitte hier abtrennen

Bitte hier abtrennen

Zutreffendes bitte ankreuzen!

Die Absenderin/der Absender ist:

- ☐ Lehrer/in in den Klassenstufen: ____
- ☐ Fachbetreuer/in
  Fächer: ____
- ☐ Seminarlehrer/in
  Fächer: ____
- ☐ Regierungsfachberater/in
  Fächer: ____
- ☐ Oberstufenbetreuer/in
- ☐ Schulleiter/in
- ☐ Referendar/in, Termin 2. Staatsexamen: ____
- ☐ Leiter/in Lehrerbibliothek
- ☐ Leiter/in Schülerbibliothek
- ☐ Sekretariat
- ☐ Eltern
- ☐ Schüler/in, Klasse: ____
- ☐ Sonstiges: ____

Unterrichtsfächer: **(Bei Lehrkräften!)**

____

STARK Verlag
Postfach 1852
85318 Freising

21-VDN

Bitte ausfüllen und im frankierten Umschlag an uns einsenden. Für Fensterkuverts geeignet.

Kennen Sie Ihre Kundennummer?
Bitte hier eintragen.

Absender (Bitte in Druckbuchstaben!)

Name/Vorname

Straße/Nr.

PLZ/Ort/Ortsteil

Telefon privat

Geburtsjahr

E-Mail

Schule/Schulstempel (Bitte immer angeben!)

(Bitte blättern Sie um)

Abitur-Prüfungsaufgaben

Von den Kultusministerien zentral gestellte Abitur-Prüfungsaufgaben, einschließlich des **aktuellen Jahrgangs**. Mit **schülergerechten Lösungen**.

Sachsen

Abiturprüfung Mathematik – LK Sachsen	Best.-Nr. 145000
Abiturprüfung Mathematik – GK Sachsen	Best.-Nr. 145100
Abiturprüfung Deutsch – GK/LK Sachsen	Best.-Nr. 145400
Abiturprüfung Englisch – LK Sachsen	Best.-Nr. 145460
Abiturprüfung Physik – LK Sachsen	Best.-Nr. 145300
Abiturprüfung Chemie – GK/LK Sachsen	Best.-Nr. 145730
Abiturprüfung Biologie – GK Sachsen	Best.-Nr. 145700
Abiturprüfung Geschichte – GK/LK Sachsen	Best.-Nr. 145760

Sachsen-Anhalt

Abiturprüfung Mathematik – LKN Sachsen-Anhalt	Best.-Nr. 155000
Abiturprüfung Mathematik – GKN Sachsen-Anhalt	Best.-Nr. 155100
Abiturprüfung Deutsch – GKN/LKN Sachsen-Anhalt	Best.-Nr. 155400
Abiturprüfung Englisch – GKN/LKN Sachsen-Anhalt	Best.-Nr. 155460
Abiturprüfung Physik – LKN Sachsen-Anhalt	Best.-Nr. 155300
Abiturprüfung Chemie – GKN/LKN Sachsen-Anhalt	Best.-Nr. 155730
Abiturprüfung Biologie – GKN/LKN Sachsen-Anhalt	Best.-Nr. 155700

Thüringen

Abiturprüfung Mathematik – Thüringen	Best.-Nr. 165100
Abiturprüfung Deutsch – Thüringen	Best.-Nr. 165400
Abiturprüfung Englisch – gA/eA Thüringen mit Audio-Dateien zum Downloaden	Best.-Nr. 165460
Abiturprüfung Physik – gA/eA Thüringen	Best.-Nr. 165300
Abiturprüfung Biologie – gA/eA Thüringen	Best.-Nr. 165700
Abiturprüfung Geschichte – eA Thüringen	Best.-Nr. 165760

Mecklenburg-Vorpommern

Abiturprüfung Mathematik Mecklenburg-Vorpommern	Best.-Nr. 135000
Abiturprüfung Deutsch Mecklenburg-Vorpommern	Best.-Nr. 135410
Abiturprüfung Englisch mit Audio-Dateien zum Downloaden – Mecklenburg-Vorpommern	Best.-Nr. 135460
Abiturprüfung Biologie Mecklenburg-Vorpommern	Best.-Nr. 135700

Berlin/Brandenburg

Abiturprüfung Mathematik mit CD-ROM – LK Berlin/Brandenburg	Best.-Nr. 125000
Abiturprüfung Mathematik mit CD-ROM – GK Berlin/Brandenburg	Best.-Nr. 125100
Abiturprüfung Deutsch Berlin/Brandenburg	Best.-Nr. 125400
Abiturprüfung Englisch Berlin/Brandenburg	Best.-Nr. 125460
Abiturprüfung Biologie – GK/LK Berlin/Brandenburg	Best.-Nr. 125700

Studi-Kompass

Wie geht es nach dem Abitur weiter?

Die Reihe **Studi-Kompass** gibt Antworten auf Fragen zum Studium:

- ➜ Detaillierte Informationen zu jeder Hochschule – und Hochschulstadt – in Deutschland sowie alle wichtigen Adressen und Ansprechpartner
- ➜ Zahlreiche Berufsbilder, mögliche Tätigkeitsfelder und Arbeitsmarktprognosen für Absolventen
- ➜ Online-SelfAssessment zur Unterstützung der Schülerinnen und Schüler bei der persönlichen Studienentscheidung

Leitfaden zum Online-SelfAssessment inkl. Aktivierungscode	Best.-Nr. 20000
Aktivierungscode zum Online-SelfAssessment	Best.-Nr. 20000C
Rechtswissenschaften, Ausgabe Nord	Best.-Nr. 20085A
Rechtswissenschaften, Ausgabe Süd	Best.-Nr. 20085B
Sprach- und Literaturwissenschaften	Best.-Nr. 20040
Kulturwissenschaften	Best.-Nr. 20076
Politik- und Sozialwissenschaften	Best.-Nr. 20020
Medien, Ethnologie und Journalistik	Best.-Nr. 20080

Ab März 2012 erhältlich:

Wirtschaftswissenschaften und Wirtschaftsingenieurwesen	Best.-Nr. 20088
Biologie, Chemie, Pharmazie	Best.-Nr. 20073
Ingenieurwissenschaften	Best.-Nr. 20010
Psychologie und Pädagogik	Best.-Nr. 20094
Mathematik und Physik	Best.-Nr. 20030

Natürlich führen wir noch mehr Titel für alle Fächer und Stufen: Alle Informationen unter www.stark-verlag.de

Bestellungen bitte direkt an:

STARK Verlagsgesellschaft mbH & Co. KG · Postfach 1852 · 85318 Freising
Tel. 0180 3 179000* · Fax 0180 3 179001* · www.stark-verlag.de · info@stark-verlag.de
*9 Cent pro Min. aus dem deutschen Festnetz, Mobilfunk bis 42 Cent pro Min.
Aus dem Mobilfunknetz wählen Sie die Festnetznummer: 08167 9573-0

Lernen • Wissen • Zukunft
STARK

21-VDN